POSITIVE POLLUTIONS AND CULTURAL TOXINS

POSITIVE POLLUTIONS AND CULTURAL TOXINS WASTE AND CONTAMINATION IN CONTEMPORARY U.S. ETHNIC LITERATURES JOHN BLAIR GAMBER

University of Nebraska Press | Lincoln and London

Some materials from the introduction reprinted from *Survivance: Narratives of Native Voices*, edited by Gerald Vizenor by permission of the University of Nebraska Press. © 2008 by the Board of Regents of the University of Nebraska. A version of chapter 5 originally appeared in PMLA 122, no. 1 (January 2007): 179–93.

Library of Congress Cataloging-in-Publication Data

Gamber, John Blair.
Positive pollutions and cultural toxins: waste and contamination in contemporary U.S. ethnic literatures / John Blair Gamber.
p. cm.—(Postwestern Horizons series)
Includes bibliographical references and index.
ISBN 978-0-8032-3046-0 (cloth: alk. paper)
1. American fiction—21st century—History and criticism.
2. American fiction—Minority authors—History and criticism.
3. Pollution in literature.
I. Title
PS374.P625G36 2012
810.9'3556—dc23   2012009223

Set in Scala by Kim Essman.
Designed by Ashley Muehlbauer.

CONTENTS

ACKNOWLEDGMENTS

The completion of this manuscript has not been an individual effort or accomplishment. There are a number of people whom I must acknowledge for their assistance and support and without whom this would not have been possible. I want to specifically thank and acknowledge:

My friends and colleagues at University of California, Santa Barbara, whose good humor and comradeship made my experiences infinitely better than they would have been without them. You know who you are.

My friends from the College of William and Mary: Elizabeth Barnes, Jack Martin, Colleen Kennedy, Anne Charity Hudley, Phillip Merritt, Will Hausman, Sarah Stafford, and Greg Hancock, for dealing me in. I don't know what I would have done without your kindness and warm welcome. I miss you all.

My sister Jennifer Rockwell, to whom I owe my life.

My brother Michael Petersen, for always being there.

My dissertation committee cochairs Professor Stephanie LeMenager, for her tireless effort and amazing responsiveness and support, and Professor Carl Gutiérrez-Jones, for all his help throughout my career, guiding this project from its inception to its completion; my committee members Professor Cheryll Glotfelty, whose insightful analysis and attention to detail has been invaluable, and Professor Shirley Geok-lin Lim, for her exceptional and unflagging professional guidance and mentorship.

And finally Mr. E. Friend, for his unwavering assistance during the composition of this piece.

I have presented versions of these chapters at conferences around the United States, Canada, and Taiwan. I am deeply appreciative of the feedback I have received at those gatherings. I would also like to acknowledge the William and Mary Faculty Summer Research Grant.

Any errors, oversights, or omissions are mine alone.

POSITIVE POLLUTIONS AND CULTURAL TOXINS

INTRODUCTION

Go against nature,
It's part of nature, too.
LOVE AND ROCKETS, "No New Tale to Tell"

I love trash!
OSCAR THE GROUCH

Positive Pollutions and Cultural Toxins begins with the simple assumption that people are natural. I'm not the first person to suggest such a thing, as the Love and Rockets quote I use here as an epigraph indicates; but I hope this book will push some people's ideas about what is and is not, what can or cannot be considered "natural" in some new directions. Plants and trees are natural, of course. The flowers and the birds are natural. Apes and dolphins. Maggots. Viruses. People. Cities are natural. And traffic. And garbage. So are sewage and toxic waste. Human beings (*Homo sapiens*) are a biological species of the earth. We have evolved within a matrix (or rather, within infinite matrices) of forces, coevolved with innumerable (or at least innumerated) species, and continue to exist within biological, geological, physical, and ecological systems. Like other species, we are socialized. Like many other species, we construct dwellings for ourselves. Like some other species, we use tools. We are born, we breathe, we eat, we expel, we die. We're animals. We're natural. Moreover, as I hope to demonstrate, the impulse to distinguish humans from other life on the planet is dangerous to all life. As Cary Wolfe demonstrates, "Debates in the humanities and social sciences between well-intentioned critics of racism, (hetero)sexism, classism, and all other -isms that are the stock-in-trade of cultural studies almost always remain locked within an unexamined framework of *speciesism*" (1). *Positive Pollutions and Cultural Toxins* works to rearticulate this unexamined framework within comparative ethnic literary studies in particular.

Since Carolyn Merchant's *The Death of Nature*, a number of critics and theorists have described the end, destruction, or elimination of nature as a nonhuman collectivity or a human construct.[1] Merchant points to the 1600s in Europe as the period during which "Western culture became increasingly mechanized" and "the female earth and virgin earth spirit were subdued by the machine" (2). She seeks to identify "the developments that resulted in the death of nature as a living being and the accelerating exploitation of both human and natural resources in the name of culture and progress" during the scientific revolution (xxi–xxii). For Merchant, the death of nature marks a break in especially European conceptions of the other-than-human as a living, indispensable, feminine force. In separating these vitalities from the "real world" of science and mechanisms, European societies came to devalue the other-than-human and the feminine, marking both as things to be conquered (or that had already been conquered).[2] By contrast, Bill McKibbin's *The End of Nature* confronts humanity's growth into a global force on everything on the planet. In his updated introduction to this critically important text, he writes, "We are no longer able to think of ourselves as a species tossed about by larger forces—now we *are* those larger forces. Hurricanes and thunderstorms and tornadoes become not acts of God but acts of man. That is what I meant by the 'end of nature'" (xviii).[3]

Positive Pollutions and Cultural Toxins is not meant to signal the death of nature but rather its expansion. Each of the novels it studies challenges the distinction of the natural from the human by illustrating the permeable and permeated and the interrelated and interconnected realities of all species and ecologies. This text attempts to show that there is nothing, truly nothing, that is not natural (or that is unnatural). Some will argue that in expanding nature to encompass everything, I am in fact emptying it of significance, and there may be some merit to such an argument. However, because the word-concept nature continues to circulate so freely and abundantly, it behooves us to understand what we think we mean when we wield the term and in what ways our concepts of the natural fail upon further review. Wolfe points out that many popular as well as scholarly venues "have made standard fare out of one study after another convincingly demonstrating that the traditionally distinctive marks of the human (first it was possession of a soul, then 'reason,' then tool use, then tool *making*, then language, then the production of linguistic *novelty*, and so on) flourish quite reliably beyond the species barrier" (2). Human exceptionalism, the notion that we as a species are utterly or essentially different from all other life on the planet, has been proven false time and time again.

My approach strives toward an ecosystemic understanding of interrelationality, informed by Barry Commoner's first law of ecology: "Everything is connected to everything else."[4] In short, all species, all creatures, exist in relation to and in the context of others. To consider any in isolation is to misunderstand how life works on this planet. Consider, for example, human flora or microbiota, the microorganisms that live on and in the human body at all times. There are, under normal circumstances, more bacterial cells on and in our bodies than there are human cells (Dethlefsen et al.). We are literally crawling and swimming with nonhuman life, hundreds if not thousands of species of it. Moreover, the bacteria in our digestive tracts (the vast majority of our nonhuman cells)[5] allow us to process food, the nutrients from which we would be unable to absorb without them. It is not merely that we are what we eat; we are also the other beings that allow us to absorb what we eat. And they are us.

The old adage has it that no man is an island. Gendered coding notwithstanding, this has traditionally been taken to mean that people are always connected to other people. Ecology tells us that people (like all other species) are always connected to other species. The story of human flora tells us that we are actually *composed* of other currently living creatures. Human life cannot be understood outside our physical connections to other life. These connections can sometimes be defined as cooperative, sometimes as symbiotic, sometimes as confrontational or predatory. The fact that some of these connections are agonistic does not make them any less connections. In other words, I am not arguing that we exist in a global cooperative, merely a community in which we have certain responsibilities. We are members of complex interrelationalities that cross species lines. We are, whether we want to be or not, deeply and inexorably bound to these complex liquid communities that exist between people as they exist within all ecosystems. Moreover, as we are in fact comprised of multiple other species, the distinction between the human and nature is further confounded.

At this point, the term "nature" has been fairly well documented as a problematic signifier. Indeed, several other ecocritics have questioned the value of this term. For example, in "Cultivating the American Garden," Frederick Turner challenges the assertion that humans and the nonhuman are made of different stuff. He writes, "Nature, according to science, is as much 'in here' as it is 'out there'" (42). Gary Snyder moves to include religious thought to Turner's evocation of science. In "The Etiquette of Freedom," he writes, "Science and some sorts of mysticism rightly propose that *everything* is natural" (8). Indeed, it is difficult for any philosophy that acknowledges humans as biological entities to figure humans (or by extrapolation, human creations) as not natural. One wonders how our creations are any less natural than a bird's nest, a beaver's dam, or a crow's crafting a tool to reach food.

I theorize pollution and waste within these novels as representative of a need to recognize human communities in a broad sense. That is, the authors I examine use waste to show our connections to the physical world in which we live. In this respect, I am deeply indebted, as are so many ecocritics, to Aldo Leopold's construction of community in his oft-quoted concept of the land ethic. In his foundational text, *Sand County Almanac*, Leopold asserts, "The land ethic simply enlarges the boundaries of the community to include soils, waters, plants, and animals; or collectively: the land" (239). He continues, "In short, a land ethic changes the role of Homo sapiens from conqueror of the land-community to plain member and citizen of it" (240). Leopold's straightforward but nonetheless powerful assertion moves from a hierarchical relationship between humans and the other-than-human to a recognition of ecological community (although his term "citizenship" denotes a particular kind of community that is somewhat more specific than my conception). Building off of this idea and ideal of community, I identify a common theme in this study's urban-set novels—authored by Octavia Butler, Alejandro Morales, Louise Erdrich (Ojibwa), Karen Tei Yamashita, and Gerald Vizenor (Anishinaabe). In each of these works, the reclamation of waste objects and waste spaces serves as a necessary parallel to the reclamation of cast-off individuals and communities. In reasserting the importance of marginalized groups, these authors draw on parallels to the nonhuman—to other animals, plants, and landscapes that have been cast as waste or wastelands, beyond reclamation or outside human (or preferred human) habitation.[6] These authors proceed to query pollution from a standpoint of miscegenation discourse to show that the tropes of purity, upon which both of these concepts (pollution and miscegenation) rely, fail in the face of the liquidity and permeability of human selves. The need for the recognition of this liquidity and permeability is the central conclusion of *Positive Pollutions and Cultural Toxins*.

Rather than pollution, I prefer an emphasis on toxicity.[7] In this regard I am indebted, of course, to Lawrence Buell, who describes toxic discourse as a new focus of environmentalism that moves away from traditions of nature writing and preservation toward one of environmental justice, dealing with toxifying practices and events such as "Love Canal, Three Mile Island, Bhopal, Chernobyl, and the Exxon Valdez" (642), though he traces the dawn of contemporary toxic discourse to the 1962 release of Rachel Carson's *Silent Spring*. His essay, apart from being an excellent source detailing the "anatomy and genealogy" of environmental justice and the pastoral, "challenges traditional understandings of what counts as an environmentalist movement or ethos" (639) in order to underscore "the point that environmentalism must make concerns for human and social health more central and salient than it traditionally has if it is to thrive, perhaps even to survive" (639–40). Buell calls for a move, one he later identifies as second wave ecocriticism, away from the bucolic nature of Thoreau and Muir and toward the concerns of contemporary marginalized communities.[8]

Building on Buell's ideas, I devote attention to toxicity rather than pollution or contamination for a variety of reasons.[9] My primary aim is to challenge the seeming divide between first and second wave ecocriticism, to show that any constructions that divide the human from the nonhuman cannot stand. To that end, I focus on the root meanings behind terms that have come to foreground much of environmentalist and ecocritical discourse. I eschew terms like "pollute" or "contaminate" because both imply former states of purity, moments during which spaces and places (and in other discourses, bodies, cultures, religions, and languages) were untouched, inviolate, untrammeled, or unadulterated. To pollute is, "to make morally impure; to violate the purity or sanctity of; to profane or desecrate; to render ceremonially unclean (*obs.*). Now also: to corrupt, sully" (OED). To contaminate: "to render impure by contact or mixture; to corrupt, defile, pollute, sully, taint, infect" (OED). Both of these verbs (and their corresponding nominal forms, pollution and contamination) imply that the afflicted was once pure and is now impure. Contamination's focus on touching connotes dirty human hands groping at some previously untouched wholesomeness. Both indicate a separation between the human or the human made and everything else, a binary that I assert proves indefensible.

On the other hand, toxicity means simply "the degree to which a substance is poisonous." If we follow the chain of signification one step further we learn that poisonous denotes, "causing or capable of causing death or illness if taken into the body." Looking at toxicity, to me, speaks to the point at which a given ecosystem and the other ecosystems downwind and downstream (which eventually, of course, are all ecosystems), become biologically unlivable for the species within them.[10] Nonetheless, the concept of toxicity should be wielded carefully within environmental studies. Ecocritic David Garrard cites chemist William H. Baarschers as "highly critical of environmentalist 'hysteria' surrounding the presence in the environment of chemicals far below levels of observable toxicity" (11). Baarschers, in his book *Eco-facts and Eco-fiction*, calls for a pragmatic environmental discourse, one that abandons impossible ideals of zero-level contamination for realizable goals of minimized toxicity. It would be hard to find a space that does not contain some toxins, whether biological waste, "persistent organic pollutants" (POPs), or what have you. That does not necessarily make them unlivable or even threats to the life within them. Still, herein lies the danger of Baarschers's argument: at what level can we unequivocally assert that a space has become toxic? His definitions follow a scientific method, one of repeatability and certainty. One problem with such an approach when dealing with toxicity is that by the time we have reached a level of certainty as to cause and effect, a number of those toxified bodies have perished or become moribund. Another problem arises from the difficulty of tracing a single cause to toxic effects, when we might better understand a cumulative effect from a number of toxic agents.[11]

Several critics work to address this problematic of either proving causal relationships between toxic exposure and its effects or recognizing strong correlations between them. David Naguib Pellow demonstrates, "Ecological risks are deeply embedded in society and are ubiquitous and extremely harmful, yet frequently difficult to measure" (24). Similarly, Lois Gibbs expands, "The obstacles facing modern environmental health investigators are . . . complex. First, there is the lack of scientific understanding of the body's interaction with chemicals; second, there is the lack of studies that provide clear evidence linking cause and effect in humans, for most of the chemicals in use; and third, there is the enormous financial interest of multibillion-dollar corporations that want to avoid identifying any link between their chemicals and products and adverse health effects." (ix)[12] In short, the cards are stacked in many ways against the victims of toxification—both by the sluggishness of scientific proof and the economic and political structures that favor business interests over bodily health (especially of the communities frequently targeted for toxic exposure). Julie Sze, in her reading of Yamashita's *Tropic of Orange*, asserts that her "goal is to posit the emergence of an environmental justice framework that is not constrained to a particular method or discipline or the paralyzing need to statistically 'prove' environmental racism" (30). Rather than restrict ourselves to the slow-to-develop and difficult-to-prove scientific method, we can recognize the veracity of *narratives* of environmental justice.

I offer the term *positive pollutions* to represent a multitude of transgressive mixings that might be historically coded as negative, but which are demonstrated to be anything but. The positive pollutions within this book take numerous forms, overturning ideals of cultural, linguistic, ecological, racial, ethnic, sexual, and religious purities in favor of embracing liquid mixtures and ideals of broad communities and responsibilities. Rather than assuming an impossible preexisting purity, these liquid conceptions understand the value—indeed the imperative—of understanding that we represent a single but dynamic collectivity. They are not dangerous; or if they are, they are only dangerous to those ideologies that seek to segregate, to contain, in the hopes of physically, socially, politically, and economically marginalizing. In utilizing the term "positive pollutions," I seek to invert the seemingly inherently negative appellation of the verb "pollute" rather than to uphold pollution as a particularly useful trope. Rather, each of the novels I study here reclaims bodies and spaces that have been seen, crafted, racialized, gendered, and sexualized as polluted and/or polluting. However, this is not to say that all muddying of boundaries, let alone toxification, is positive. Indeed, we can think of countless examples of what are currently deemed ecological pollution that I would absolutely assert are negative, destructive, unjust, or just plain wrong. Moreover, these unjust interpenetrations or seepings need not reach the full scale of toxicity. My notions of community suppose an attempt to minimize our destructive impact on the rest of the biosphere. The danger with this ideal, of course, comes in determining what, exactly, "destructive impact" means. I hope to be suggestive here rather than prescriptive, and I recognize the precautionary principle as one helpful model. This principle asserts, "When an activity raises threats of harm to human health or the environment, precautionary measures should be taken even if some cause and effect relationships are not fully established scientifically. In this context the proponent of an activity, rather than the public, should bear the burden of proof. The process of applying the precautionary principle must be open, informed and democratic and must include potentially affected parties. It must also involve an examination of the full range of alternatives, including no action" (Science and Environmental Health Network). Rather than potential victims of toxicity shouldering the burden of proof, we can focus our environmental governance and ethics on ensuring responsible activity.

Along with analysis of ecological or material toxicity, I propose that we think of racism and other oppressive forces as what I term *cultural toxins*. Rather than miscegenation's ideal of a pure body politic—or (as just one example) recent, thinly veiled racism decrying mostly Latina/o immigrants for culturally and linguistically polluting U.S. culture—cultural toxicity refers to a society becoming literally unlivable for its inhabitants. The continuing violent threats of racism, misogyny, and homophobia are examples of cultural toxicity within the United States (though certainly not exclusively) today. Histories of ethnic cleansing and genocide represent cultural toxicity taken to an extreme (albeit a predictable one). Any number of colonialisms, racist wars, or wars justified in racialized terms fit the bill as well, as does environmental racism. Indeed, many of the aforementioned ideologies of purity throughout history create toxic environments for marginalized communities. Throughout this book, I examine textual representations challenging such quests for purity under the rubric of cultural toxins.

While I am challenging the theoretical utility of ideas like pollution or, say, wilderness spaces, I am not suggesting that these rhetorical tropes should be eliminated, particularly as they relate to our political or activist discourse. Within the current cultural moment that gives at least lip service to green living, environmentalism has tremendous opportunities to make political gains, inroads, and allies. These are fundamentally important material concerns and ought not to be hamstrung by an allegiance to theoretically sound terminology. Nonetheless, I think it behooves those of us within ecocriticism and environmental studies to be self-aware that such terms are being wielded tactically and that we disallow a certain level of discourse with their use. It could be argued that this tactical wielding of "pollution" as a term is tantamount to hypocrisy. I find such absolutism (another version of purity) in terms of political struggles somewhat curious, even dangerous, as I am quite certain that organizations and individuals responsible for toxifying our ecosystems are not nearly as concerned or burdened with a morality of absolute truth. In short, I recognize politics and theoretical/critical work as deeply intertwined and informing one another, but as existing within rhetorical traditions that differ in the immediacy of their ends.

Likewise, as the reader has no doubt noticed, I make use of the term "liquid" throughout this text. I choose the term "liquid" rather than "fluid" because of the latter's etymological connection to *flow* (French *fluide*, Latin *fluid-us*, *fluĕre* to flow), which seems to me to connote directionality. I use *liquidity* instead to refer to "a material substance in that condition (familiar as the normal condition of water, oil, alcohol, etc.) in which its particles move freely over each other (so that its masses have no determinate shape)" (OED). Liquids pass over and through one another, blending and separating depending on their properties *and* their temporary conditions (temperature, for example). Their motion is difficult to predict, often vectorless; but within the course of their motions, they invariably take on properties they did not possess before. As Stephen Hong Sohn explains, "As the state of matter between solid and gas, the liquid inhabits an interesting state of dynamic equilibrium that at once cannot be fully grasped, but yet has a texture and a 'feeling'."[13] I imagine this liquidity representing the permeability of everything. All bodies, cultures, and processes are not only permeable, but permeated, affected by the other bodies, cultures, and processes that flow or seep on, over, by, and through them. Such liquidity challenges claims of purity as not only theoretically but practically difficult to defend. Such a lack, or rather absence, of purity need not be lamented or maligned, however. Instead, the fact that even the most solid matter maintains a liquid quality reinforces the interconnection and community that I advocate here.[14]

Much of the hegemonic discourse surrounding the United States' idealistic and nostalgic views of itself imagines rural and small-town (later suburban) clean living.[15] A recent GOP vice presidential candidate, in 2008, called small towns "the real America" and "pro-American areas of this great nation." The implication, of course, is that cities are both not really America (by which I suspect was meant the United States) and anti-American. The discursive tradition out of which such comments grow draws a distinction between the dirty, dystopic urban and the pristine, utopian natural.[16] Cities are often portrayed as places to be fled, metropolitan wildernesses that offer nothing more than the maladies of overcrowding, poverty, crime, and pollution. More often than not, these areas are coded as black/brown and white, respectively (though representations of rurality in texts by authors of color as ideal, idyllic, or, at least, preferable to urbanity certainly complicate—or troublingly participate in—such a generalization). The texts I examine dismantle the human/nature dichotomy, detailing and imagining African American, Chicana/o, Native American, and Asian American urban communities in which humans are recognized very much as natural, corporeal, and material systems.[17] Moreover, these novels utilize the physical signs of human corporeality like garbage and sewage to refigure cities as natural. All the texts I examine overtly address environmentalist issues (particularly toxic air and aquifers as well as waste dumping and containment). However, each text also demonstrates the parallels between hierarchical views of cultures and those of nature/culture and/or humans/other species. Each novel shows urban spaces as indecipherable or inseparable from the other-than-human or the natural—though they do this to varying degrees and with varying levels of consistency.

It is not a coincidence that urban centers (which, as Andrew Light points out, have come to be seen as the new, built wilderness that ought to be fled for the safety of the ruralized suburb) are also generally the most racially diverse spaces in the United States. Eric Avila notes that Ronald Reagan rose to power in California, and eventually in the United States as a whole, by pandering to and bolstering suburban white voters' fears of people of color in the cities (91). Similarly, James Kyung-Jin Lee states, "Nowhere does the shattering of multiculturalism's dream become more apparent than in U.S. cities during the 'belle epoque' of the Reagan era" (xiv). He notes that under the twelve years of the Reagan and Bush administrations, "Cities and their residents suffered economic, political, and cultural hemorrhage so great that it constituted nothing less than a great urban crisis of terminal proportions" (xiv). These antiurban ideologies are among the fundamental tenets of neoconservativism. It has sown and continues to cater to white fears of people of color in the cities. Unfortunately, middle-class environmentalism has tended to parallel this antiurbanism. While the suburbs embody material white flight, it is not a stretch to aver that environmentalism is a form of political white flight. Rather than confront the ecological injustices of the cities, many environmentalists are happy to write off urban spaces and their denizens (human and nonhuman alike) as beyond help. All too often, environmentalism's arm of cultural criticism, ecocriticism, becomes a similar form of academic white flight.[18]

In her classic investigation of purity and pollution, Mary Douglas notes that creating differences such as within/without, male/female, and clean/dirty allows a semblance of order on life but that this binary-constructing compulsion disappears in great religions. While contemporary readers are troubled by Douglas's universalizing claims as well as her distinction between primitive and great religions, her more basic premise—the source of her lasting contributions to cultural studies—certainly holds true. She notes, for example, "These danger-beliefs are as much threats which one man uses to coerce another as dangers which he himself fears to incur by his own lapses from righteousness" (3). Distinctions between the pure and the polluted serve an administrative purpose, governing behavior. But Douglas shows that they do more; she continues, "Ideas about separating, purifying, demarcating and punishing transgressions have as their main function to impose system on an inherently untidy experience. It is only by exaggerating the difference between within and without, above and below, male and female, with and against, that a semblance of order is created" (4). People utilize these binary distinctions (*exaggerating* them) to make sense of a world that is messy, vague, and murky. Throughout this work, I strive to question the us/them binary that becomes buttressed by notions of purity and pollution and constructed along species, racial, ethnic, and cultural lines. While these binaries mark an attempt to define where and how we can close our ranks, they limit our abilities to create, maintain, and recognize our broad, but very real, lived material communities. Nonetheless, minoritized communities (like all human communities) will sometimes circle the wagons in terms of identity. I am not attempting to elide cultural differences or striving for a color-blind society. Rather, I find it generally positive to understand the permeability of self and culture to recognize rather than deny or condemn ethnic adaptation. Instead of static ideas and ideals of cultural conservatism, we can understand that cultural changes need not threaten, reduce, or water down ethnic, racial, or national identifications. The novels I study throughout this text present communities comprised, as communities always are, of multiple ebbing and flowing liquid identities, interpenetrated culturally as well as spatially and temporally. Indeed, these texts move to show that racial differentiation need not serve as the sole criterion used to mark ethnic belonging. Nor do I intend in any way to downplay the material importance of racial categorizations (and the physical threats that arise from the cultural toxin of racism). People continue to be read and coded racially, especially by phenotype.

The tendency to create divisions between humans and the rest of the world very closely parallels the divisions between groups of people. Some ecologically minded critics and scholars have marked this correlation. Pellow, for example, asserts, "The basic functions of industrialized societies (primarily in the global North) involve the production of both intense ecological harm and extensive social hierarchies (primarily by race, class, gender, and nation)" (5). Jeffrey Myers similarly argues, "The ethnocentric outlook that constructed 'whiteness' over and against the alterity of other racial categories is the same perspective that constructed the anthropocentric paradigm at the root of environmental destruction" (5). Eric Katz focuses on "imperialism—and all that it represents concerning power, force, and domination—as a model or metaphor for understanding the human relationship with nature" (164). Finally, Jake Kosek demonstrates, "Discourses of purity placed diluted racial subjects and degraded landscapes into the same 'grid of intelligibility,' wherein understanding of and fears surrounding race at the turn of the twentieth century became the raw substance out of which wilderness as an idea and a landscape was forged" (129). Each of these scholars understands the direct relationship, whether causal or otherwise, between racialized and anthropocentric hierarchies as well as the social and ecological dangers and cruelties they lead to.

I place my examination of waste as part and parcel of this challenging of the pure and the polluted. I argue that, although we tend to think of garbage as inherently offensive: toxic, smelly, dangerous, and useless, in short, abject, these conventional judgments place a negative value on a simple byproduct of existence; all animals produce waste. I refigure waste and garbage by showing how these urban-set novels illustrate that we cannot partition ourselves from the waste we produce. This inclusive worldview emphasizes communal responsibility in regard to the things and the people we cast off and refigures waste and pollution as tropes with potentially positive attributes: cast-off places, objects, and people can be regenerative sites of community building.

In studying these recent texts, *Positive Pollutions and Cultural Toxins* intends to help continue ecocriticism's and environmentalism's evolutions. One of its goals is to maintain and foster discourses of environmental justice and studies of environmental racism. Civil rights activist Benjamin Chavis describes the connection between environmental and racialized social issues: "Racial discrimination is the deliberate targeting of communities of color for toxic waste disposal and the siting of polluting industries. It is racial discrimination in the official sanctioning of the life-threatening presence of poisons and pollutants in communities of color. And it is racial discrimination in the history of excluding people of color from the mainstream environmental groups, decision making boards, commissions, and regulatory bodies" (3). Environmental justice responds to the fact that, as Jace Weaver notes, "Those involved in the environmental movement are overwhelmingly White" ("Introduction" xv). Similarly, Joni Adamson, a central figure in the literary study of environmental justice, describes its goal: "to redress the disproportionate incidence of environmental contamination in communities of the poor and/or communities of color, to secure for those affected the right to live unthreatened by the risks posed by environmental degradation and contamination, and to afford equal access to natural resources that sustain life and culture" (4).

Two events are most commonly cited as the dawn of the environmental justice movement: protests surrounding Love Canal in upstate New York (1978) and the Warren County PCB Landfill in North Carolina (1982).[19] Local residents in Love Canal pointed to higher-than-normal rates of birth defects, miscarriages, and congenital diseases stemming from toxic waste seeping into their aquifer. Warren County residents charged federal, state, and local governments with choosing their area for dumping because they housed a rural, predominantly African American community. Another oft-cited example of this type of waste targeting is nuclear mining, testing, and dumping on American Indian lands in the desert southwest.[20]

While a number of ecocritics have complicated the division between humans and the nonhuman, ecocriticism itself fails to give sufficient attention to narratives of cities. A few texts have begun to correct this oversight, however. Collections like Terrell F. Dixon's *City Wilds: Essays and Stories about Urban Nature* and Michael Bennett and David W. Teague's *The Nature of Cities: Ecocriticism and Urban Environments* are two examples. Bennett and Teague lament, "Ecocriticism has come to be associated with a body of work devoted to nature writing, American pastoralism, and literary ecology" (3). Likewise, Dixon points out that "Even as interest in environmental literature has grown over the last four decades, urban nature has figured most often as an intriguing, if mostly marginal oxymoron" (xi). Both of these texts address ecocriticism's myopia in terms of urban spaces. Moreover, basic understandings of interconnection should imply the importance of cities to a global, local, regional, and bioregional understanding of space and place. As McGranahan et al. note, "The fact that cities have large ecological 'footprints' makes them more, not less, important" to ecologically minded studies (8). Nonetheless, Dixon's focus remains on the natural as something distinct from the human, something that interacts all the time with humans but that is still separate. According to this point of view, there may be nature in cities, but the cities themselves are not natural. My interest is not in showing that there are nonhuman elements in cities; of course there are. Trees, plants, birds, insects, rodents, all these live in cities; many have evolved in tandem with human beings in centralized, high-density urban settings. Along with that coevolution is the simple fact that we are natural. So are the things we make.

If ecocriticism "itself has been slow to survey the terrain of urban environments," as Bennett and Teague assert, it was, in its earliest stages, equally slow in surveying work from authors of diverse ethnic and cultural backgrounds (3). Myers lays out a road map of the development of ecocriticism along these lines in *Converging Stories: Race, Ecology, and Environmental Justice in American Literature* (6–7). He points out that the bulk of ecocriticism dealing overtly with issues of race have focused on American Indian writers and, to a lesser degree, African American authors. Until quite recently, and largely after the inception of this project, very little work had been done with Asian American– or Latina/o– authored texts, despite the fact that a number of them serve as excellent subjects. However, in recent years this dearth of diversity has undergone a rapid and welcome change. Lawrence Buell and Ursula K. Heise represent two of the very impressive scholars to address issues of race and ethnicity in ecocriticism. Other sources include Alison Deming and Lauret Savoy's *The Colors of Nature: Culture, Identity, and the Natural World* (2002), Joni Adamson's *American Indian Literature, Environmental Justice, and Ecocriticism: The Middle Place* (2001), Lee Schweninger's *Listening to the Land: Native American Literary Responses to Landscape* (2008), Tom Lynch's *Xerophilia: Ecocritical Explorations in Southwestern Literature* (2008), Lindsey Claire Smith's *Indians, Environment, and Identity on the Borders of American Literature: From Faulkner and Morrison to Walker and Silko* (2008), Paul Outka's *Race and Nature from*

Transcendentalism to the Harlem Renaissance (2008), and Ian Finseth's *Shades of Green: Visions of Nature in the Literature of American Slavery, 1770–1860* (2009). The publication dates of these texts illustrate just how contemporary these changes to the field are. And these represent only the book-length texts devoted to this socially engaged ecocriticism.[21]

CRITICAL AND THEORETICAL ANTECEDENTS

Throughout this text, I draw on urban cultural studies texts including those by Eric Avila, Edward Soja, James Kyung-Jin Lee, Mike Davis, Raúl Villa, and Josh Sides.[22] However, the single most influential scholar to my studies of modern urban life is Michel de Certeau, especially his text *The Practice of Everyday Life*. Certeau's work reexamines urban identity, which is so often painted as a form of victimization at the hands of urban administrators, in order to show the individual and communal power that denizens of cities actually possess. Certeau specifically examines issues of waste and pollution as they relate to abnormality, deviance, and illness. Because his work is so influential to my own, I dedicate some time to my explication of his thesis and the terms he employs.[23] Certeau challenges administrative panoptic mandates and serves as a corrective for overly deterministic notions of ideological indoctrination—emphasizing instead the agency, tactical navigation, and adaptability of marginalized and disenfranchised individuals and communities. His work illuminates cultural and personal evolutions, emphasizing survival rather than what Gerald Vizenor calls "victimry," the adopting and internalization of the role of victim by marginalized populations.

My correlation between marginalized communities and images of pollution parallels Certeau, who argues that planners and administrators of cities seek to codify the lives of the people who live in the city with the aim of maximizing order and that "rational organization must thus repress all the physical, mental and political *pollutions* that would compromise it" (94, emphasis mine). The city's agency—or the agency of those who attempt to control, organize, and plan the city—seeks to override the agency of the inhabitants of that city as an operational concept. Rather, "Everyday life invents itself by *poaching* in countless ways on the property of others" (xii, emphasis original). Poaching, a legal term, refers to human ownership of the nonhuman (both in terms of land and the species on that land); the crime combines trespassing with illegally taking game. Poaching represents an encroachment on the rights of a wealthy, empowered, or administrative body by someone looking to fulfill the most basic of animal needs (the need for food). More broadly for Certeau, poaching implies a tactical agency that works outside the rules but is most efficient when it avoids detection (rather than direct confrontation).[24] Certeau continues with his trope of poachers qua pollution: "There is a rejection of everything that is not capable of being dealt with [via differentiation and redistribution] and so constitutes the 'waste products' of a functionalist administration (abnormality, deviance, illness, death, etc.)" (94). Pollution and waste products within this mode are defined simply as those people and things that do not fit the mold of the organizationalist urban planners.

Certeau offers the idea of the *tactic* as a counternarrative to administrative attempts to control. He argues that despite the best efforts of the administrators, "the city is left prey to contradictory movements that counter-balance and combine themselves outside the reach of panoptic power" (95). He continues describing a tactic as "a calculus which cannot count on a 'proper' (a spatial or institutional localization), nor thus on a borderline distinguishing the other as a visible totality. The place of a tactic belongs to the other. A tactic insinuates itself into the other's place" (xix). Moreover, for Certeau, "The 'proper' is a victory of space over time. On the contrary, because it does not have a place, a tactic depends on time—it is always on the watch for opportunities that must be seized 'on the wing.' Whatever it wins, it does not keep" (xix). Ultimately, essentialism rests on the proper, on the strategic, and on the place. Fixed essentialisms (as Douglas notes) come from places of power and attempt to control existence by naming and describing something (and the borders, boundaries, and frontiers delimiting that something from everything else).

Throughout *Positive Pollutions and Cultural Toxins*, I draw on Certeau's terminology clarifying the differences between strategy and tactic and between space and place. He writes, "I shall make a distinction between space (*espace*) and place (*lieu*) that delimits a field. A place (*lieu*) is the order (of whatever kind) in accord with which elements are distributed in relationships of coexistence. It thus excludes the possibility of two things being in the same location (*place*). The law of the 'proper' rules in the place. . . . A *space* exists when one takes into consideration vectors of direction, velocities, and time variables. Thus space is composed of intersections of mobile elements" (117). Place equates to structure, stasis, strategy, and a conceived but unlived, unlivable theory and panoptic mandate. On the other hand, space corresponds to movement, intersection, subversion, tactic, and, in short, the real way that humans experience and shape the shifting locations in which they live. Place is the illusion of solidity; space is the recognition of liquidity. We must, furthermore, relate the movement and interrelationality of tactical and space-based existence to the tenets of ecology, which likewise recognize the fundamental truth that living bodies never exist in isolation or stasis—whether that stasis is spatial or temporal. We would do better to understand bodies and spaces as processes rather than as distinct entities. These are liquid mixtures of elements, always on their ways toward becoming something else. Moreover, the concepts of time and space are foundational for one another: spaces are always in flux, shaped by our presence and motion, and always in motion themselves.[25] The novels I examine throughout this project all reflect Certeau's notions of the urban dweller as tactical agent and administrative pollutant while connecting humanity to the rest of the biosphere.[26]

Certainly, these narratives of polluted urban spaces and bodies have not materialized ex nihilo in the contemporary moment. Tales of environmental apocalypse bloomed in the 1960s; Rachel Carson's *Silent Spring* and Paul Ehrlich's *The Population Bomb* are two examples of what Mike Davis calls texts of ecocatastrophe (318). Davis asserts, "Like the inevitability of nuclear war, the biological unsustainability of the giant city is now firmly lodged in contemporary doom consciousness" (318). He continues, "It is not surprising, then, that the climax of the postwar boom in the mid-1960s saw the parallel emergence of fictional and non-fictional accounts of imminent ecological collapse, frequently in tandem with Malthusian fears about too many poor people of color" (318). Fears of the urban center, and the imaginative death drive of cities, stem in no small part from classist and racist fears. Avila adds other social elements, including fears of excessive sexuality, as a part of white flight from city cores. He notes that postwar suburbanization, especially in Los Angeles, stemmed from "an emergent sociospatial order that promised a respite from the well-known dangers and inconveniences of the modern city: congestion, crime, pollution, anonymity, promiscuity, and diversity" (xv).[27]

Finally, throughout this project, I build upon foundations from religious studies and Native American studies scholar Jace Weaver (Cherokee), who emphasizes inclusive and permeable communities that encompass our physical environments and the animals therein. Weaver's concept of communitism in particular has influenced my approach tremendously. This neologism is "formed by a combination of the words 'community' and 'activism'" (*That the People Might Live* xiii). He continues, "Literature is communitist to the extent that it has a proactive commitment to Native community, including what I term the 'wider community' of Creation itself" (xiii). Although Weaver's approach is one of Native American studies—and later, American Indian nationalism— we can apply it more broadly. Because Native American communities are members of a global (or perhaps more expansively, cosmic) community, encompassed in the wider community of creation itself, communitism stretches to cover that wider community. It is not exclusively Indian. The community of communitism is comprised of all humanity as a part of everything, including all elements of the other-than-human. In this recognition of broad communities, we are charged with recognizing the self in the other, to come to terms with the fact that destructive acts are not only cast outward but also always inward.[28] I argue that literary and ethnic studies need to continue to build toward examining these relational identities formed by and with our ecological communities.

ORGANIZATION OF THE BOOK

Positive Pollutions and Cultural Toxins explores the conjunction of, and the frictions between, studies of twentieth-century U.S. ethnic literatures, urban studies, and ecocriticism and works to refigure the above portrayals of urban spaces. I have selected the novels I study here for a few reasons. First, each of these texts places itself in the broader conversations of contemporary literary studies. Butler's novels represent the neo–slave narrative, which, under the umbrella of African diasporic texts, occupies a central position within African American literary studies; Morales's text grapples with the controlling ideologies of Chicana/o studies, the pervasiveness (and masculinist tendencies) of Chicano nationalism in the face of a postnationalist impulse throughout much of ethnic and postcolonial studies; similarly, Erdrich's and Vizenor's novels tackle issues of tribal nationalism, the single most hotly debated issue in Native American studies today, along with the ever-present tensions around mixed-blood and urban Indian identities; Yamashita's text embodies the transnationalism that has come to dominate conversations within but also far beyond Asian American studies. Of course, my approach of dividing the chapters according to racialized categories has the danger of upholding the divisions between these communities. That upholding is not my intention. However, I also realize that ignoring or eliding the communities on which these texts focus is not a preferable option.

Instead, each of these texts understands that the racialized community represented within its pages can never properly be understood in isolation. Every one of these novels represents its primary community as part of a larger, multiethnic one, and in this sense these texts prefigure a growing element within ethnic studies fields as they move beyond the isolating nationalisms that have bound them in order to recognize broad communities (which herein are both interspecies and interethnic). While these novels are all concerned with how we act locally, they are nonetheless all thinking globally, working in transnational frameworks that more accurately represent the world as it is than do many other accounts. Each text, while U.S. in its origin, nonetheless understands the nation as a permeated space—one which generates certain toxic hierarchies while asserting its purity only to contravert that purity in terms of movements of bodies (of many species) and commodities (including those same bodies).

These chapters serve as connected essays demonstrating the wielding of the themes I identify and theorize throughout this introduction. I have not attempted to organize them as a progressive linearity, an approach that would counter the liquid permeations I privilege. All these texts, I argue, ultimately embrace cities as natural outgrowths of human collective behaviors and as spaces of healing and reclamation. At the same time, they draw attention to the cultural and ecological toxins faced by urban minoritized enclaves. Rather than fleeing these sites, however, or giving up on them as lost causes, the texts suggest methods by which human societies can recognize our communal responsibilities within cityscapes in order to prevent and reverse ecological destruction.

My first chapter, "'Failing Economies and Tortured Ecologies,'" examines the toxic dystopic vision of Los Angeles within Butler's *Parable of the Sower* (1993) and its sequel *Parable of the Talents* (1998). *Parable of the Sower* offers an optimistic pastoral conclusion for its multiethnic cast of characters. But the failure of *Parable of the Sower*'s pastoral dream in *Parable of the Talents* shows that flight from urban blight, whether couched in terms of suburban segregation or more recent nonwhite middle-class departures from city centers, is short-sighted and doomed to failure. Instead, these novels illustrate the impossibility of fencing oneself off from socioecological ills. I place my reading alongside recent scholarship examining Southern California's history of racialized suburban exclusion and isolation, especially as pertain to African American bodies and communities, to reinforce this assertion.

In chapter 2, "Toxic Metropolis," I investigate the roles of toxicity and positive pollution in Morales's *The Rag Doll Plagues* (1992) and argue that this novel's theme of the *pepenador* (or rummager) exemplifies a recognition that humanity cannot be differentiated from the waste it produces.[29] This text shows how urban communities especially reclaim cast-off objects and individuals to show their inherent value. In so doing, Morales figures a community between humans and other animals within a Mexica religious framework that has gone unexamined by critics. Interethnic communities also abound in this novel as people of diverse descents commingle to create an idealized hybrid within the occasionally toxic cityscapes of Mexico City and Los Angeles. These urban spaces themselves, furthermore, require attention that has not been undertaken by critics of this novel. To that end, I include the environmental histories—especially in terms of their parallels—of these two cities, looking at how they became among the most toxic regions in the Western Hemisphere.

Chapter 3, "Ridding the World of Waste," illustrates that, in *The Antelope Wife* (1998), Louise Erdrich (Ojibwe) creates a recurrent theme of garbage in an urban Native community (portrayed as a broad and diverse spectrum of mixed-blood identities), which is built on top of that garbage. I argue that Erdrich's ambivalent portrayal of garbage reflects issues of environmental justice that Native people across the continent continually face, such as legal and illegal dumping on tribal land. Erdrich's pairing of mixed-bloods with trash reclamation counters the ever-present but historically and theoretically flawed suppositions of and calls for Native racial and cultural purity. This novel examines relocation, set in a locus the Bureau of Indian Affairs Relocation Program, Minneapolis, Minnesota. This program, which operated from the 1950s through the 1970s, fostered Native people to move from rural and tribal lands to urban centers in order to encourage assimilation and industrial vocational training. Revolving around a discourse of balance, Erdrich's text vilifies selfishness from an Ojibwa perspective by invoking the image of the *Windigo*, a monster of greed that can overcome people who lose their connections and sense of responsibility to their communities.

In chapter 4, "'An Eerie Liquid Elasticity,'" I discuss Yamashita's *Tropic of Orange* (1997) to show the novel's understanding of human identities, cultures, language, and space as always in flux. Yamashita wields Southern California's seismic activity, location along the Pacific Rim and Ring of Fire, shared border with (and perhaps more importantly, historical location *in*) Mexico, and role as global center as a site for recognizing fluid natures of a humanity that cannot properly understand itself within any manner of static construction. The text refuses monoracial, monocultural, and anthropocentric worldviews and instead privileges an understanding of multiethnic communities and individuals as sites of regeneration and hope, while also understanding human connections to our ecological communities. Furthermore, along with the insistence within the text that space and place are truly fluid, the reader also encounters a recognition that time (as bound to space in time and space) cannot properly be understood as linear (let alone as a progressive march) but rather is experienced as a singularity in which past, present, and future constantly ebb and flow, rise and submerge, and exist simultaneously.

Finally, in chapter 5, "'Outcasts and Dreamers in the Cities,'" I discuss Vizenor's *Dead Voices: Natural Agonies in the New World* (1992) to show the ways that people can come to form profound relationships to place even in sites of (in this case Native American) displacement and relocation. I argue that this text reflects a complete formation of an urban community in its reclamation of landfills and sewers as integral and religiously significant spaces that must not be ignored. The community within this novel is not only interethnic and interracial but also interspecies, as human ties to physical place and to plant and animal species are reinforced. I engage again with the history of the Relocation Program particularly in terms of Oakland as a marginalized space and in terms of stereotypes of urban Indians as isolated, lost, and degraded.

In short, my work examines what happens when we imagine our communities—or more to the point, *recognize* our communities—as being not just intrahuman but across species and even kingdom lines (in the Linnaean sense of the term). The novels I study illustrate and imagine these communities of liquidity and motion, of interpenetrations and interactions. I argue that they advocate broad understandings of community and the recognition that we are all responsible for what happens within those communities. Similarly, we are responsible for what we dump, what we excrete, what we leach into our ecosystems and, by extension and dispersion or diffusion, into the connected, local, and distant ecosystems of our planet. We might expect such environmentally engaged texts to ignore or vilify urban life and communities, but they do not. Instead, they reclaim urban spaces as natural and naturalized sites where interactions between the deeply and broadly interconnected human and nonhuman are the norm. Moreover, they emphasize the similarities between human behavior and that of other species. Finally, in taking back the urban wilderness as a vital locus for marginalized communities, they challenge mainstream environmentalism's and ecocriticism's existent if lessening white flight impulses. Cities become sites, not of total disaster, but of hope. The city and its inhabitants are not doomed; instead, they are, we are, the future.

1

"FAILING ECONOMIES AND TORTURED ECOLOGIES" OCTAVIA BUTLER'S *PARABLE OF THE SOWER* AND *PARABLE OF THE TALENTS*

I think people who traveled to extrasolar worlds would be on their own—far from politicians and business people, failing economies and tortured ecologies

OCTAVIA BUTLER, *Parable of the Sower*

We can't never have peace till you . . . clean up this mess you made, till you . . . clean up this dirt you dropped

TUPAC SHAKUR, "Never B Peace"

This chapter studies the dystopian, near-future SF worlds of Octavia Butler's novels *Parable of the Sower* (1993) and its sequel *Parable of the Talents* (1998).[1] In the epigraphs above, Butler and Shakur each assert the impossibility of social improvements within the framework of a United States enamored with the cultural toxins of its status quo. While Shakur insists that peace can only come about through repairing a society that has been made a mess, Butler's narrator calls for a literal flight from the ills of this world. Indeed, both draw attention to the relationship between social and environmental inequities, as Shakur alludes to political injustices as a form of detritus (a "mess" and "dirt"). In order to underscore Butler's protagonist's desire for escape, I examine the correlation between flight from urban social and ecological blights and toxicity in both of her texts of the diptych and the failure of that flight to create any lasting, positive change for the novels' characters. *Sower's* protagonist idealizes a kind of pastoral illusion, while her flight from south to north, mirroring historical moves by African American individuals and communities seeking freedom and opportunity, nonetheless inverts the rural (or pastoral) to urban shift made within those migrations. She seeks the refuge of rural spaces far from the urban center of Los Angeles. I argue that while *Sower* appears to have a utopian conclusion, *Talents* irrefutably shows it to be dystopian—a failure of misguided idealism. Specifically, the implicit critique of antiurbanism and flight that comprise the pastoral impulse and aesthetic we see in *Sower* becomes explicit in *Talents*. The primary failure of this impulse comes in the protagonist's inability to recognize her role within a wide-reaching community or her fundamental connection to local and distant structures of power, oppression, and marginalization.[2] She sees Los Angeles as a polluted space (which in itself is far from uncommon), but she fails to recognize any positivity in that pollution. Instead, LA's urban spaces, and eventually all urban spaces, occupy an abject and toxic position within her worldview.

This chapter addresses the interminglings of the ecological and social within these novels, paying particular attention to images of contamination and to the tensions between community and isolation as well as flight and mobility that go hand in hand with fears of physical, social, cultural, racial, and biological contamination. Within this analysis, I show the connections between white flight and ghetto flight in Los Angeles in particular to show the critique this diptych levels at those who would ignore social or environmental problems by attempting to flee, deny, deflect, or disassociate from them either literally or psychologically. Ultimately, the novels privilege a conception of community that moves beyond the limiting, place-based pastoral, to embrace a much more shifting, adaptive, even subversive set of social relations that counter the pastoral impulses held by their own protagonist.

Sower begins in 2024 and follows the narrator-protagonist, Lauren Oya Olamina. The novel's setting at its outset is in "Robledo—20 miles from Los Angeles, and, . . . once a rich, green, unwalled little city" (*Sower* 9). The Olamina family's multiethnic neighborhood in Robledo (comprised of African Americans, Latinos, Asian Americans, and European Americans), once unwalled, is now a walled cul-de-sac; its denizens hope to protect the block from the dangers of the ever-encroaching city.[3] However, the wall is eventually breeched by marauding hordes of painted drug addicts who burn the houses to the ground. Lauren joins the thousands flocking northward to escape the Southland in hopes of reaching the promised lands of Oregon, Washington, British Columbia, and Alaska, all made more climatically welcoming due to global climate change as Southern California has grown drier and hotter. Throughout the novel, Lauren proselytizes her newly created (or discovered) religion—Earthseed, whose primary tenets include the idea that "God is change" and that God can be shaped by human action.[4] As such, Lauren does not so much advocate change as an ethereal ideal as recognize the inevitability and need for it, especially for those of marginalized positionalities. She eventually meets Taylor Franklin Bankole, a doctor who owns land in Northern California, with whom she falls in love. The pair walks, along with eleven other people, to his property and establishes a settlement, Acorn, based to some degree on the teachings of *Earthseed: The Books of the Living* as written by Lauren.

Sower's ending is ambiguous, and the reader is left to wonder whether Acorn will succeed or fail. However, *Talents* quickly clears up this confusion, as a band of Christian Crusaders invades the camp, enslaving its residents shortly after the birth of Lauren and Bankole's daughter, Larkin Beryl Ife Olamina Bankole (171).[5] Lauren's cohort lives in captivity for seventeen months, until a freak accident (discussed below) precipitates their freedom. *Talents* goes on to tell the story of Earthseed's rise to prominence and Lauren's quest to find her daughter, taken by the Crusaders. *Talents* also differs from *Sower* in its employment of multiple narrators, including Bankole and Larkin, both through their own writings. Both *Sower* and *Talents* utilize first person narration; and although *Talents*'s narrations and narrators also work in dialogue or conversation with one another, both works do so with other formative texts, especially from African American literature.[6] These novels act, within this broader literary discourse, as what Henry Louis Gates Jr. calls "talking books," blurring boundaries between texts. Butler's use of first person narratives, furthermore, riffs off of traditions from African American autobiographies and slave narratives (and both of these texts can be considered within the genre of neo–slave narratives), particularly with her inclusion of the themes of liberation, bondage, freed subjectivity, and especially the ability and right to write.[7]

In *Talents* we learn that the period from 2015–30 is called "the Pox," short for apocalypse (8). *Sower* lasts from 2024 until 2027, while *Talents* covers 2032 until 2090; exactly sixty-six years (to the day) span between the beginning of the first and the end of the second, although Larkin's narrative begins after Olamina's death, which concludes the novel's narrative. The five intervening years between texts seem to mark a period of relative stability, as Acorn exists mostly unencumbered and undeterred.

This chapter examining polluted spaces and the juncture of ecological and social issues in these novels is not the first study to do so. Some scholars have looked at one environmentalist angle or another in Butler's work. However, those critical texts that most fully make use of ecologically minded criticism to examine Butler's parable texts focus mainly on the first of the diptych, *Sower*, and not on the second, *Talents*. This is not to say that critics ignore the second text. Most of the articles simply were written before *Talents*'s release. I argue throughout this chapter that the second novel serves largely as a corrective to the first. That is, many of the inconsistencies in Lauren's philosophy in *Sower* become tacitly or overtly questioned in *Talents*. These inconsistencies include her vacillating views on the viability of isolation, her reliance on or condemnation of static dogma, and her wavering ecological sensibilities. As such, and because Butler originally conceived of the two novels as one, I argue that any reading of *Sower* that could but fails to take into account the action of *Talents* is necessarily incomplete.

ACORN, ISOLATION, COMMUNITY, HYPEREMPATHY

I begin my analysis in this chapter with an examination of the novels' tension between community and isolation, a theme with socioecological implications. This tension, time and time again within *Sower* in particular, is emblematized by the community's wall. Very early in the novel, Lauren notes, "The neighborhood wall is a massive, looming presence nearby. I see it as a crouching animal, perhaps about to spring, more threatening than protective" (*Sower* 5). Indeed, within these works, when read together, the wall *is* a threat. It cordons off, or rather gives the illusion of cordoning off, this community that would like to see itself in isolation. That isolation is untenable, of course, as Lauren knows. She comments, "God, I hate this place. I mean, I love it. It's home. These are my people. But I hate it. It's like an island surrounded by sharks—except sharks don't bother you unless you go in the water" (*Sower* 44). Lauren recognizes and mourns the impossibility of her community's survival, the fact that the sharks will most certainly devour them at some point. In this passage, Lauren wields for the first time her recurrent image of predators lurking nearby. Of course, this image of the surrounded, civilized, walled town predates Lauren's vocalization and U.S. preoccupations with toxic cities. Colonial discourses abound with examples of the fear of the white enclave constantly under threat of siege by savages lurking just beyond the gates. Captivity narratives in which British or American colonists are seized by Native Americans and dragged out into the wilderness, particularly Mary Rowlandson's wildly popular *A Narrative of the Captivity and Restoration of Mrs. Mary Rowlandson* (1682), are perhaps the most obvious example in U.S. literature. We must also recall Barbary captivity narratives in which white sailors and civilians, especially in coastal towns, are captured by North African pirates and sold into bondage.[8] However, Butler's texts invert the racial connotations of these narratives, as the racially diverse Robledo community protects itself from a racially ambiguous enemy (as we will see shortly). Indeed, in this case the savages may well be white and hold more security and power than their victims. Butler challenges images of urban decay and, especially, violence spreading from the urban core, read as predominantly black ghettos, as well as images of the dangers to white suburbanites at the hands of savage people of color. At the same time, however, Lauren adopts the separatist ethic of suburbanites throughout the latter half of the twentieth century.

The suburban dwellers of Robledo look upon the city as a blight. Lauren notes, "According to my father, the big city is a carcass covered with too many maggots. I think he's right" (*Sower* 8). Later in the novel, she wonders at her brother's desire to spend more time in the city, stating, "He's always wanted to go to LA. Any sane person would be thankful for the twenty miles that separate us from that oozing sore" (*Sower* 96). The city serves as a site of abjection for the suburbanites of Robledo. It is a carcass or an oozing sore; both are images of rot and of either recent or imminent death.

Eric Avila, in *Popular Culture in the Age of White Flight*, notes that the image of LA as a rotten city has traditionally arisen largely from fears of racial contagion. He contends a simultaneity between an increasing African American presence in the City of Angels and white flight as evidenced in film noir. As Los Angeles became an increasingly black city (during and immediately following World War II), filmic representations of the city moved from sites of "individual opportunity and the summit of social progress" to "erotic portrait[s] of an urban wasteland" (Avila 71). The rise of suburbanization correlated to specifically white flight, not so much because only whites desired to leave the inner or central city for the new, explosively growing and popular suburbs, but because only they were allowed to do so, due to specific legal strictures. He further notes, "Federal agencies such as the HOLC [Home Owners' Loan Corporation] deployed certain terms that betrayed a perception of racial minority groups as a kind of urban pathogen, threatening white neighborhoods with the prospect of 'contamination'" (Avila 97).[9] Meanwhile, in his fascinating historical study *L.A. City Limits: African American Los Angeles from the Great Depression to the Present*, Josh Sides notes that when African Americans moved in to certain predominantly white neighborhoods, neighbors would put signs on their homes urging, "Black Cancer here. Don't let it spread!" (105). These images of people of color as pollutants are certainly not confined to the post–World War II era, but their presence in the material history of Los Angeles offers a critical lens for reading the portrayals of contagion and the impulse toward isolation and quarantine by the characters in Butler's novels.

Several critics of Butler's novels draw on the work of Mike Davis to discuss the increasing walling off of suburban spaces, especially his chapter "Fortress L.A." in *City of Quartz* (also referenced in *Tropic of Orange*). Davis notes that in Los Angeles, "the defense of luxury lifestyles is translated into a proliferation of new repressions in space and movement, undergirded by the ubiquitous 'armed response'" (223).[10] In alluding to "Fortress L.A." Jerry Phillips notes, "Privatopia, the walled or gated community, is, at bottom, a fantasy of escape, that one can be in the world without having to live through the sharp contradictions that the world presents" (302).[11] Indeed, this fantasy of escape seems to lie at the heart of the post–World War II evacuation of urban centers for the suburbs as well as the walling off of the Robledo neighborhood. However, the fantasies of flight from the urban core are only that. Along those lines, Madhu Dubey notes of *Sower*, "The Robledo neighborhood cannot be sustained because its relative financial and social stability is structurally interconnected to the extreme instability of the poor and the pyromaniacs who throng outside" its walls (6). Financial and social isolation are myths that the people of Robledo concoct—as many others have before and since them—to protect themselves. Just as the wall is an illusion of security, social and ecological isolation are illusions. People are inexorably linked, bound together in matrices of responsibility.

Los Angeles's history speaks to this perceived need for and imagined possibility of racial containment, especially in the period after the Second World War. Sides notes, "Postwar economic development and worker responses forced, in the minds of both Blacks and whites, the notion of clearly defined black spaces and white spaces that would ultimately exacerbate racial distance and tension in Southern California" (88). He continues, "The multiethnic neighborhoods in which blacks had lived before World War II often became solidly black neighborhoods, while Mexicans, Asians, and Jews experienced varying degrees of acceptance in formerly white neighborhoods" (Sides 96). James Kyung-Jin Lee notes that "many within these communities experience[d] a wholly new kind of racial and urban misery," during which "a new kind of 'American Apartheid' took shape" (xv). This American apartheid invoked increasing de facto segregation as de jure segregation abated. In short, this period saw the beginning of true racial segregation in Los Angeles neighborhoods. Racial covenants and restrictions were wielded to allow access to the suburbs by nonblacks, while the city center and especially areas of South Central Los Angeles became almost exclusively African American. Certainly, it is not a huge leap to associate the symbolic and legal walls of racially exclusive suburban housing laws with those physical ones surrounding the suburban Robledo neighborhood. Likewise, Dubey examines the suburban sentimentalities within *Sower*, averring, "The entire action of the novel reveals the impossibility of maintaining 'village' ideals of bounded community rooted in a stable locale. In this sense, even as it presents the complete collapse of actual cities, the novel insists on an urban understanding of place as the inescapable basis for constructive alternative images of social order" (7). I take the phrase "urban understanding of place" to mean something along the lines of Certeau's conception of the urban dweller and her/his relationships to place and community in terms of contradictory movements, tactics, and space. The static *place* must be reconceptualized as the liquid *space*, despite the legalistic regulations that define cities or the walls that attempt to cordon off the neighborhood.

The aforementioned racially ambiguous enemy to the static suburban enclave comes in the form of "Paints. They shave off all their hair—even their eyebrows—and they paint their skin green or blue or red or yellow. They eat fire and kill rich people" (*Sower* 98). Lauren continues, calling them "bald people with painted heads, faces, and hands. Red faces; blue faces; green faces; screaming mouths; avid, crazy eyes, glittering in the firelight" (*Sower* 137). Critics have yet to comment on the appearance of these pyro addicts, except to note that they are terrifying. However, one must recognize that Butler, in painting these characters, deracinates them. Pyro addicts are literally *colored*; but in covering their skin and shaving their hair, it becomes impossible for the novel's readers (and possibly characters) to code them racially by phenotype. Likewise, the reader's inability to identify the invading hordes by race plays into Butler's move of showing an interracial community, one which cannot vilify a single racial or ethnic construction for its destruction. Lauren's brother Keith further notes the classed connotation involved with these paints: "They said their whole deal was to help the poor by killing off the rich and letting the poor take their stuff. . . . The crazy thing was, a lot of the paint kids really were rich" (*Sower* 99). The paints' invasion of Robledo, rather than a liberation by the masses, becomes an act of hierarchical (top-down) violence. The working-to-middle-class, multiracial, and pastoral community is toppled, one suspects, by other suburbanites from upper-middle-class, pastoral, and more strongly (if temporarily) defended enclaves.

The pastoral nature of the neighborhood is of special importance when read alongside the pastoral tradition generally and in African American literature and criticism specifically. The Olaminas' neighborhood sustains itself in large part through a series of gardens and small-scale livestock (e.g. rabbit) husbandry, and this integration of farming and residence situates it within a pastoral tradition. Dubey, building off Hazel Carby's study of folk practices in Zora Neale Hurston's work, offers an extended reading of Butler's parable novels, stating, "Although [Toni Morrison, Alice Walker, Gloria Naylor, and others] have published city novels, criticism on these novelists has tended to privilege those selected texts and textual elements that help consolidate a black feminine literary tradition derived from southern folk culture" (Dubey 1).[12] Many literary critics seem reluctant to offer positive readings of urban spaces in African American literature (or as I argue in my introduction, in much of U.S. literature), opting instead to code rural spaces as the exclusive sites of positive communal and individual existence—especially in narratives by women. She continues, the "rhetoric of contemporary urban crisis . . . magnetized around the notorious term 'underclass,' tends to frame the issue of urban crisis essentially as a crisis in black culture and community" (1). While the other texts I examine throughout my work might contend that urban crises effect any number of racialized communities in the United States (and across the Americas), there are also numerous examples of the ways that "urban" has come to mean "black" and that, correspondingly, "urban crisis" has come to mean "poor, black, urban crisis" (with poor and black often also crafted as redundant). This emphasis on rural folk community, as I will show in subsequent chapters, is present in Chicana/o and American Indian literary traditions as well. Moreover, as I have discussed in my introduction, the kind of mystical pastoral invoked within each of these traditions is deeply nostalgic and problematic. This privileging of a folk community and aesthetic renders it difficult to discuss urban communities as organic, or even as remotely positive (Dubey 2).

Although the Robledo neighborhood embraces its wall and firmly emplaced pastoralism, Lauren simultaneously longs to flee the ever-urbanizing suburb. Furthermore, although she denies others access to her land, she hopes to access others' lands; specifically, Lauren hopes to flee northward to Oregon, Washington, or Canada. She is certainly not alone in this flight impulse, and her father explains to her, "People get shot every day trying to sneak into Canada. Nobody wants California trash" (*Sower* 73). Butler inverts contemporary immigration patterns as U.S. citizens—and particularly Californians, so often reactionary toward out-group immigration—become the illegals striving for a better life across a distant border (we see a similar querying of illegal status in *Tropic of Orange* and *The Rag Doll Plagues*). Moreover, Lauren's position is inverted; she transforms from the figure who fears outsiders crossing her Robledo community's boundaries into one who would cross those of her neighbors to the north. Finally, we note how the poor are seen as "trash," a contaminant and waste product without value. As with the protagonists of all the novels I examine, those speaking in the first person become associated with the trash, are cast off. But, of course, the California trash of this novel is no more disregardable than the paints outside Robledo's walls. By casting her protagonist in the role of waste object, by focusing the entire diptych on this abject character, Butler implies the impossibility of disregarding such marginalized populations.[13]

Butler continues her theme of connection (contrasting containment and isolation) by crafting a peculiar medical condition for Lauren, one which serves to emphasize her liquid identity. She suffers from hyperempathy, "what the doctors call an 'organic delusional syndrome'" (*Sower* 10). If Lauren witnesses the pain of another person (and to a lesser degree, another animal), she thinks she feels that pain.[14] It is nearly impossible for Lauren to pretend she is not connected to the world around her. Jim Miller notes, "By turning profound compassion into an illness, Butler defamiliarizes our current indifference toward each other" (357). The novel marks empathy as a curiosity in order to show the reader how indifference feels to many of us. Lauren herself, after witnessing one of the many acts of incredible brutality that occur within these novels, explains, "It's beyond me how one human being could do that to another. If hyperempathy syndrome were a more common complaint, people couldn't do such things. . . . A biological conscience is better than no conscience at all" (*Sower* 102). Lauren is forced into a kind of morality that is certainly impractical given the time and society in which she lives. We see the limitations of her morality as a biologically determined delusion. However, this is not to say that Lauren's affliction should be seen as anything else. Butler has commented in interviews, for example, "I have been really annoyed with people who claim Lauren is a telepath, who insist that she has this power. What she has is a rather crippling delusion" (Potts 335). Indeed, while hyperempathy could serve as a biological conscience, that is not to say it would be the preferred conscience within these novels—it is merely better than nothing. For Lauren, particularly within the dystopian worlds of these novels, hyperempathy is an enormous hindrance. She is often overwhelmed by her condition when she protects herself or her community from attacks. Along these lines, Miller asserts, "Butler offers us the aporetic ideal of reciprocity, but warns us that there are those who might kill us for embracing it. Butler's hope is a post-utopian one, tempered by the lessons of the past" (357). The lessons of the past to which Miller alludes include those learned from the resistance to the continuing work toward racial and gender equality. These movements work to overcome the cultural toxins that unfortunately remain entrenched in contemporary society—threats to social, ecological, and bodily health that cannot be wished away. Members of marginalized groups can strive, Butler implies, for morality and empathy, but those who willingly marginalize them will only use these moral and ethical practices as an opportunity to continue their oppression.

TREES AND SEEDS

Just as Butler unites Lauren to those around her via her hyperempathy, she extends kinship between humans and plants throughout these novels; the oak is perhaps the most obvious example, as both of Lauren's communities' names (Robledo, Spanish for "oaken," and Acorn) derive from that tree. Butler crafts the oak as a source of sustenance as a nod to Californian indigeneity as well as endemic sustainability. Butler's characters make a point of discussing their consumption of acorn bread— that is, bread made from acorn flour. Lauren's father notes, "Most of the people in this country don't eat acorns, you know. They have no tradition of eating them, they don't know how to prepare them" (Sower 56). While most people in the United States today do not eat acorns, they were the predominant foodstuff of most precontact indigenous California peoples. The oak is an indigenous, if highly cultivated, tree, shaped by centuries of Native agriculture. Spanish missionary Father Crespi noted of California in 1769, "This whole country . . . is covered [with] oaks, as high and of as great girth as can be found in the finest parks of Europe" (Bolton 195). Though, what appeared to Spanish missionaries as the work of God was, in truth, a shaped and shaping, evolving set of species. Nor do I think this examination of the image of the oak and acorn is a mere aside or coincidence. This specific indigenous plant alludes to sustainable and noninvasive species as a contrast to tortured ecologies—the toxic conditions of the Pox. While this invoking of indigenous lifeways may show a tendency toward viewing Native people as inherently environmentalist and the precontact state of North America as virgin, it more strongly asserts that humans can live within ecosystems, shaping and being shaped by ecosystems, without inducing the kind of toxic landscape that parts of California—and LA in particular—become in these texts.[15]

These strong and often-long-lived hardwood trees serve as a suitably ironic image for Lauren's cause in many ways. First, the oak is the national tree of the United States, selected as such because of its prevalence and strength. Being a rigid hardwood tree, it serves a symbolic purpose (to Aesop, for example) as the tree that breaks because it cannot bend. Robledo, the oaken place, is overrun because it cannot mold its ideology to the changing events around it. The acorn, while symbolizing the potential of new life, is a replication of the oak. The acorn will turn, in time, into the oak, making the place where it is planted a new oaken place, a new Robledo. The oak is also rich in biblical significance. In Genesis, Jacob buries the idols of foreign gods beneath an oak (*Bible*, Gen. 35:4). This purging of other gods is complete when they are laid to rest beneath the strong tree. At Acorn, the dead are buried under oak saplings, that their bodies might fertilize new life. Nor is this the only biblical example of people and things being buried beneath oak trees. Likewise, Joshua erects a stone beneath an oak to "be therefore a witness unto you, lest ye deny your God" (Josh. 24:27). In both of these examples, the oak serves as the site of embracing a new conception of God while forsaking older household gods. Similarly, *Sower*'s second chapter begins, "At least three years ago, my father's God stopped being my God" (6). Lauren's rebuke of her father's religion and God (her father is a Baptist minister) and her formation of a new faith parallel these biblical religious evolutions.[16]

The acorn, as well as seeds in general, becomes a controlling metaphor for Lauren's life and the lives of her followers. She describes the day that she discovers the name of the religion she outlines, recalling,

"Today I found the name, found it while I was weeding the back garden and thinking about the way plants seed themselves, windborne, animalborne, waterborne, far from their parent plants. They have no ability at all to travel great distances under their own power, and yet, they do travel. Even they don't have to just sit in one place and wait to be wiped out" (*Sower* 68–69). Likewise, Lauren sutures her worldview and religion to plant images at other times. The very title of the first of these novels refers to the Christian allegory of a farmer sowing seeds.[17] But unlike the passive reception of seeds by various welcoming and foreboding soils in the biblical parable of the sower, Lauren's seeds refuse to wait idly to be destroyed. In short, Earthseed, and much of the parable novels, speaks to survival and perseverance. The movement of these seeds, "windborne, animalborne, waterborne," serves as exemplar of the tactical mobility that Lauren advocates in her followers, and in fellow survivors more generally. We will see this emphasis on tactical survival as this chapter progresses. Lauren's choice of seed metaphor, however, privileges a passivity to movements—being carried by external if interrelated forces—that Lauren elsewhere disavows as a survivable methodology.

Various other tree species also mark a sense of home and place within this novel. As Lauren's group moves northward, she notes that persimmon, avocado, and citrus trees grow in Mendocino County because of the warming climate, which makes it like a slice of Southern California. She observes, "Old-timers among our neighbors complain about the loss of their fog, rain, and cool temperatures. We don't mind, those of us from southern California. To us it's as though we've come to a somewhat gentler version of the homes we were forced to leave. Here, there is still water, space, not too much debilitating heat, and some peace. Here, one can still have orchards and groves" (*Sower* 59).[18]

Lauren's notion here is one of place in a Certeauian sense, a landscape that adheres to human mandates. Her narrative downplays the effects of climate change, as she carries with her from Los Angeles a mental image of what a space's climate ought to be. She is pleased that Mendocino's climate is molding to that of LA, despite the fact that such changes wreak tremendous havoc with the former's ecosystems. The changes here can hardly be understood as positive pollutions of the landscape. That is, Lauren lacks a bioregional understanding of place by not recognizing that one bioregion should not be like a different one; and she *naturalizes* the ecologically toxic aspects of global warming. By contrast, within two pages of Lauren's ecological misunderstandings, Bankole laments, "Our coast redwood trees are dying. . . . Sequoia sempervirens is the botanical name for the tallest of all trees, but many are evergreens no longer. Little by little from the tops down, they are turning brown and dying" (*Sower* 61). Bankole contrasts Lauren's selfish and shortsighted worldview, mourning the dying trees as he draws on the irony of the sempervirens (or evergreen) genus.[19] We have found a way to alter the climate to the point of killing the giant and otherwise exceptionally long-lived redwoods, trees with life spans of up to two thousand years. Butler, then, draws on charismatic megaflora, a twist on the charismatic megafauna wielded by environmentalist movements (particularly the giant panda as the symbol of the World Wildlife Foundation). The invasive species Lauren celebrates above serve as arboreal examples of the California trash mentioned earlier. Although she is pushed out of Southern California, she glorifies the destruction and expulsion of indigenous species of Northern California. Lauren's approach further marks her as a flawed savior figure. Although she guides her faith with ecological metaphors, she lacks an ecosystemic worldview or understanding. Rather than recognizing the rights of endemic species and their evolutionary relationships to one another, she longs for them merely to comfort her.

FLIGHT VS. MOBILITY

Lauren decides that community can only be constructed via a literal departure from old or traditional methods of group formation. Acorn, Lauren's promised land, is the product of the flight from Southern California, the polluted site of the abject urban Other. Lauren, however, fails to contemplate the striking similarities between Acorn's attempts to separate itself from the surrounding world and the ways that Robledo tried to accomplish the same goal. However, Butler clearly addresses the impossibility of Acorn's success or survival in *Talents* with its destruction. She shows that although Lauren pretends she can distance herself enough from the urban decay of Los Angeles to protect herself and her new faith, such an attempt is doomed to failure. After denigrating the vertical wall around Robledo, Lauren, in effect, attempts to create a horizontal wall of the seven hundred miles between Acorn and Robledo. She fails to understand that the impulse of withdrawing to Mendocino is the same as her parents' impulse of withdrawing to the suburbs. Larkin, Lauren's daughter, picks up on this irony directly, challenging her mother's ideology and faith as little more than an extension of the failed philosophies of previous generations that led to the unlivable condition of Los Angeles and to the inevitable failure of walled communities like Robledo. She declares, "If there are sins in Earthseed, shortsightedness, lack of forethought, is the worst of them. . . . As an adolescent, [Lauren] saw her father's error when he could not see it—his dependence on walls and guns, religious faith, and a hope that the good old days would return. Yet what more than that did she have? If her good days were to be in the future on some extrasolar world, that only made them more pathetically unreal" (*Talents* 138). Larkin expressly states the irony underlying (and undercutting) the optimism in *Sower*. While the reader might hope Acorn will succeed, s/he knows it cannot. Moreover, Larkin points out that Lauren's strategies for survival include nostalgia, religious faith, guns, and distance from lower-class hordes. In short, she relies on some of the core elements of neoconservative suburban discourse, as popularized by Ronald Reagan in particular (a thread of analysis to which I will return shortly).

In the end, Lauren recognizes the error of her early attempts at establishing an Earthseed community that resists mobility in favor of the pastoral grounding in a specific place—the farm at Acorn. She realizes, "I must build . . . not a physical community this time. I guess I understand at last how easy it is to destroy such a community. I need to create something wide-reaching and harder to kill. That's why I must teach teachers" (*Talents* 297). Similarly, Larkin notes, "Gathering families had not worked. She had to gather single people, or at least independent people—people who would learn from her, then scatter to preach and teach as, in effect, her disciples" (*Talents* 355). Lauren understands, finally, that a place-based ideological framework cannot stand. Instead, she fosters a space-based system that recognizes liquid interrelationality rather than an untenable isolationism. Her approach becomes viral, or as Certeau describes urban tactics, "microbe-like," a seemingly organic ripple effect. To that end, Lauren pens:

> Consider: Whether you're a human being, an insect, a microbe, or a stone, this verse is true.

> All that you touch,
> You Change.
> All that you Change,
> Changes you.
> The only lasting truth
> Is Change. (*Sower* 70)

Lauren recognizes a feedback loop among all things, which in turn alter and are altered by their ecologies. In light of this focus on change, any system that relies on static place—rather than on space, with all its flux, permeability, and liquidity—is doomed. Planting seeds in single locations, as in some agriculture models, will not suffice. She must spread the seed of her message to the winds, accepting the liquid change of chaos—letting go of attempts to control. The parent plant must relinquish dominion for the seeds to spread and survive.

In the end, Lauren takes another approach to spreading her Earthseed community, though (frustratingly) this one also embraces directed flight from a troubled place. She avers, "We can, we must, scatter the Earth's living essence—human, plant, and animal—to extrasolar worlds" (*Talents* 46). Lauren's idealized extrasolar flight begs a number of fundamental ecological and social questions. One wonders, for example, what will happen to the ecosystems of the worlds to which Earthseed's adherents travel and what will happen to the ecosystems of this one. Because species and their spaces are interrelated, it is not enough to take a few of each into space. Without the microscopic species within the soil, for example, in various relationalities, symbiotic and otherwise, individual plant species will suffer or perish. Moreover, this ideology portends a host of other questions. We wonder if Earthseeders will transport diseases. If so, which ones, and which others will be excluded? The diseases are life-forms that have coevolved on this planet with all the other species. Very few people would be qualified to make ecologically minded decisions about which should go and which should stay. Furthermore, the reader recognizes that moving people and animals to a new planet is not likely to improve social and ecological relationships. People will remain the ignorant, frightened creatures we have proven to be on Earth when we move to other worlds. And since these novels take place in times of great turmoil, as seemingly inevitable human reactions *to* turmoil, it is reasonable to assume that in settling somewhere else out in space, amid the turmoil of that transition, people will be particularly prone to the kinds of apocalyptic impulses they engage in during the Pox. The extrasolar colonization that Lauren advocates is bound to fail just as Acorn failed.

Lauren's predestined failures become obvious in the tone set by the second novel's opening line. *Talents* begins in Larkin's voice as she laments, "They'll make a God of her. I think that would please her" (1). Whereas *Sower* focuses on Lauren as a savior figure, *Talents*, from its very inception, calls the wisdom and accuracy of such a deification into question. After all, if she truly were a god, she wouldn't need to be made into one. Kimberly Ruffin avers, "With this narrative multiplication, the novel embodies the kind of critical literacies Lauren's Earthseed ministry champions" (8). This is the fundamental correction accomplished by the second novel, and Ruffin offers an excellent tool by which to look at the multiple narrative voices. *Talents* is both evidence of the naïveté of Olamina's religion and its culmination. Because Earthseed is a religion of inclusion and of ongoing dialogue—with God, with other believers, with nonbelievers—voices of dissent must not be excluded from Earthseed; they must be welcomed. So *Sower* should be seen as an incomplete Earthseed text, specifically because Olamina is its sole narrator. *Talents* fulfills Earthseed's promise while illustrating the ways it has strayed from Olamina's original (and ironically static) ideals.

ADAPTATION, SURVIVALISM, AND THE TRICKSTER

Butler communicates an ideology that emphasizes change and adaptation—personal, communal, and cultural *evolution*—as a mode of survival. *Sower* opens with a verse from *The Books of the Living*, which states:

The only lasting truth
Is Change.
God
Is Change. (*Sower* 3)

Lauren's view of adaptability states that in a changing world, people
must adapt to situations in order to survive. This adaptability goes hand
in hand with what I elsewhere describe as situational ethics, but it also
reflects Certeau's tactical mobility.[20] These situational ethics may involve
activities that in other circumstances would be considered unacceptable,
including violence and scavenging—what Certeau calls *poaching*. Before
her suburban community falls but presaging its collapse, Lauren urges
her neighbors to prepare to defend themselves with violence if necessary.
She argues, "We can get ready. . . . Get focused on arranging to survive
so that we can do more than just get batted around by crazy people, desperate people, thugs, and leaders who don't know what they're doing!"
(*Sower* 48). Butler crafts survival in the form of communal self-reliance.
That is, as Lauren declares, "Nothing is going to save us. If we don't save
ourselves, we're dead" (*Sower* 51). Lauren's worldview challenges ideologies framed in certain liberal discourses but is quite reasonable for
members of marginalized communities confronting the cultural toxins
of race-, gender-, sexual-, and class-driven violence. Moreover, Butler's
protagonist challenges ideologies that advocate peaceful or passive resistance. In their place, she offers a tactic less akin to Martin Luther
King Jr. or Cesar Chavez than to the American Indian Movement, Black
Panthers, or Malcolm X, who famously advised, "Be peaceful, be courte-
ous, obey the law, respect everyone; but if someone puts his hand on
you, send him to the cemetery" (X 12). Later in the novel, Aura Moss,
one of the eventual Acorn settlers, says, "it's the men's job to protect us"
and "women shouldn't have to practice with guns" (*Sower* 78). But Aura's
brand of passive femininity refuses responsibility. In this novel's world,
a woman (or a man) who fails to prepare to use a weapon or a number
of weapons is merely a target, a victim in training. While this passage
could serve to support Second Amendment apologists, I see it mainly as
a statement about the importance of collective self-preservation and survival (Lauren speaks in the first person plural). As Trudier Harris notes,
"In the world that Butler has created, the formula that guides behavior is

simple: be strong or die" (155). Lauren insists that people be able to take care of themselves and their communities. That protection sometimes comes in the form of violence against violence, though it is rarely a revolutionary violence. Again, this violence of self and communal survival challenges the Christian notion of turning the other cheek, which is so foundational to the civil rights movement of the mid-1960s, and offers a new religious philosophy for times that are changing and increasingly violent. Lauren writes in her *Books of the Living*:

All successful life is
Adaptable,
Opportunistic,
Tenacious,
Interconnected, and
Fecund. (*Sower* 111)

Cultural toxicity must be confronted, not with purified, rarified, or ethereal ideologies, but with the muddy situational ethics of survival.

Lauren's approach to dealing with others, her tactical mobility, reaffirms trickster traditions that emphasize shiftiness as survivalism.[21] Like the other authors whose work I examine, Butler emphasizes the importance of the trickster figure. In later chapters, I will address the role of trickster as a foundational story figure across a great many American Indian cultural narratives. But, of course, tricksters are no less central to African American (and African diasporic) traditions. In his 1988 text, *The Signifying Monkey: A Theory of African-American Literary Criticism*, Henry Louis Gates Jr. uses "two signal trickster figures, Esu-Elegbara and the Signifying Monkey" to "allow the black tradition to speak for itself about its nature and various functions, rather than to read it, or analyze it, in terms of literary theories borrowed whole from other traditions, appropriated from without" (340).[22] Winston Napier notes that "verbal tricksterism and resistant signification" have "traditionally been a defensive maneuver in the formation and survival of African American culture" (7). Tricksters offer a mode of survival by which marginalized and disempowered agents can manipulate situations and interactions with empowered agents and institutions that are conceived and maintained to exclude them. Tricksterism is a method by which to subvert power structures in order to game the system. Within the shifting conception of God as change in Earthseed, Lauren contends:

God is Pliable—
Trickster,
Teacher,
Chaos,
Clay.
God exists to be shaped. (*Sower* 22)

In a Nietzschean turn, Butler obliterates the objectivity or absolute, noumenal truth asserted by Christianity's God in favor of a god of comic flexibility and irreverence, a god of *jouissance* embodied by trickster aesthetics.[23] Nietzsche asserts, for example, that we must be on guard against concepts of Kantian pure reason, or knowledge in itself. Instead, we should recognize the multiple perspectives that always color—or in Earthseed's lexicon, *shape*—what we think of as truth or God. He continues, "There is *only* a perspective seeing, *only* a perspective 'knowing'; and the *more* affects we allow to speak about one thing, the *more* eyes, different eyes, we can use to observe one thing, the more complete will our 'concept' of this thing, our 'objectivity,' be" (Nietzsche 3:12, emphasis in original). Butler's creation of a religion based around an unfixed, trickster god further challenges the idea that religion must inherently serve as a methodology of essentialist thinking.

But mere survival, according to these novels, is insufficient. Lauren notes, "It isn't enough for us to just survive, limping along, playing business as usual while things get worse and worse. If that's the shape we give to God, then someday we must become too weak—too poor, too hungry, too sick—to defend ourselves. Then we'll be wiped out" (*Sower* 67). Scraping by while accepting the status quo and hoping the world will improve will ultimately lead to one's own destruction. Butler makes a clear argument for social engagement here. Rather than merely fleeing, running about without a plan, people must shape the world into what they need it to be. This emphasis on positive change is bolstered by the fall of the Robledo community, but it also foreshadows the fall of Acorn in *Talents*. In both instances, people create walls around themselves and hope situations outside their walls will somehow spontaneously improve. In contrast to such passivity, Earthseed advocates "God-shaping," creating a world and overarching power structure that will benefit believers and nonbelievers, humans and other species, even the earth and worlds beyond.

MIXED ETHNICITY, INTERSECTIONALITY

In these texts, Butler creates several multiethnic communities that parallel the interspecies communities the novels privilege; both Robledo and Acorn stand as examples. Fittingly, Lauren preaches:

Embrace diversity.
Unite—
Or be divided,
robbed,
ruled,
killed
By those who see you as prey.
Embrace diversity
Or be destroyed. (*Sower* 176)

Certainly, this call for an embracing of diversity reflects Robledo, but it also speaks to the multiethnic and geographically diverse makeup of Southern California more generally. Avila points out that "the unique social mix of Los Angeles, conditioned by its proximity to Mexico and the Pacific Ocean, provides a fascinating context for understanding how diverse peoples—midwesterners, Jews, Italians, 'Okies' and 'Arkies,' Mexicans, Chinese, Japanese, Native Americans, African Americans—confronted the racial binary that shaped the reality and representation of the postwar urban region" (7). Certainly, this wide-reaching diversity is reflected within the parable novels, challenging a black/white racial binary. Confronting such a dualistic racial paradigm similarly pushes the culturally toxic white supremacy model of U.S. history. We must also note Avila's summoning of Okies and Arkies, those migrating groups who, during the Great Depression, sought a better life in California, as a parallel to the characters in *Sower* in particular.

While Lauren's followers comprise an ethnically diverse crowd, as did her former Robledo community, Butler takes steps to show that this acceptance of difference is still not the norm in the near future of her novels, where the cultural toxin of racism remains firmly entrenched. Zahra, one of the few other survivors from Robledo, notes, "Mixed couples catch hell whether people think they're gay or straight. Harry'll piss off all the blacks and you'll piss off all the whites. Good luck" (*Sower* 153). Butler posits that the toxic fear of racial mixing will continue well into the future. This fear, of course, relies on an inherently flawed notion of racial purity. Butler shows that these fears are particularly problematic for members of already marginalized groups. Miscegenation discourse serves to separate rather than unite. In order to combat these external racial taboos, Lauren decides to travel disguised as a man. She asks if Zahra would be willing to pose as her girlfriend: "We can be a black couple and their white friend. If Harry can get a reasonable tan, maybe we can claim him as a cousin" (*Sower* 153). We note the multiple levels of passing happening in this passage: a woman passes as a man; two heterosexual women pass as a romantic heterosexual couple; and inverting historical hierarchical racial paradigms, a white man hopes to pass as a light-skinned African American.

Despite the emphasis on diversity and inclusion in these texts, Lauren's rhetoric of the hatred or distrust of cities recurs over and over. She notes, "Cities are dangerous" (*Sower* 221–22) and maintains a grudging ambivalence when she reaches Sacramento: "Water and food were cheap there compared to what you could buy along the roadside, of course. Cities were always a relief as far as prices went. But cities were also dangerous. More gangs, more cops, more suspicious, nervous people with guns" (*Sower* 244). Later in *Sower* she asserts, "The more people there are packed together in cities, the more danger there is" (*Sower* 287). Raymond Williams refers to such an urban distrust as "a deeply pessimistic projection of the city itself" that "is by now a convention" (276). He continues, "The problems of the city—from traffic to pollution, from social to psychological effects—are often seen as overwhelming and as, in some views, insoluble" (277). However, this idea that cities are inherently more dangerous than rural locations is proven false in *Talents*. Bankole urges Lauren to move to a nearby small city, Halstead. Lauren refuses, still convinced both that Acorn will survive despite or perhaps because of its isolation and that cities offer less protection. Eventually, Acorn is overrun, Bankole is killed, and Larkin is kidnapped and raised by an abusive Christian Crusader family. Larkin, understandably angry at her mother's rejection of all urban spaces, writes, "Should she have left Acorn and gone to live in Halstead as my father asked? Of course she should have! And if she had, would she, my father, and I have managed to have normal, comfortable lives through Jarret's [Andrew Jarret, the born-again Christian Texan who becomes president in *Talents*] upheavals? I believe we would have" (*Talents* 137). Larkin understands that cities are not necessarily the sites of toxicity that Lauren believes them to be. After all, Lauren's supposedly safe rural environment proves indefensible. Instead of the isolation of rural idealization, Butler's texts emphasize a long-term communal responsibility.

As in many dystopian novels set in or around Los Angeles, *Sower* focuses largely on its moribund freeway system.[24] Lauren notes, "It's against the law in California to walk on the freeways, but the law is archaic. Everyone who walks walks on the freeways sooner or later. Freeways provide the most direct routes between cities and parts of cities" (*Sower* 157).[25] Mike Davis notes that freeways are emblems of suburbanization, which "is like another one of Southern California's natural disasters—recurrent, inexorable" (*Ecology* 91). There is something about the LA freeways themselves that signals damage and yet something about their destruction that seems to signal the end of the world. Los Angeles is associated, by Angelinos and non-Angelinos alike, with freeways. The end of the freeway as a functioning system (to whatever degree) figures the end of LA. But as the introduction of the freeway system began the process of flight from the urban core, freeways are emblems of suburban disassociation. Their end as a method of rapid escape should serve to convey the end of suburban isolation. However, we do not encounter a return to a centralized pedestrian city or the urban flaneur tradition in *Sower*. Instead, flight from the city merely decelerates, while becoming more permanent. And while this flight could be seen as something positive, the great natural or social disaster that eliminates the toxic metropolis, Butler's novels illustrate that worldviews that disregard urban spaces replicate the toxic, segregating impulses of suburbanization and do not improve upon them.

The freeways Butler chooses bear particular importance within the toxic histories of California. She chooses the 118 and the 101 for the flight of her characters from the crumbling and dangerous megalopolis. Lauren explains, "We would take the 118 to the 23 and the 23 to U.S. 101. The 101 would take us up the coast toward Oregon. We became part of a broad river of people walking west on the freeway" (*Sower* 157).[26] Interestingly, they begin their trip on the 118, fittingly the Ronald Reagan Freeway. Ronald Reagan, prior to his presidency, was a major figure in California politics. Avila calls particular attention to the ways that Reagan directly opposed LA's prewar integrationist assumptions in favor of an increasingly segregated and gated city. Moreover, he notes, "In his thirty-year ascent to the White House, Reagan espoused patriarchy, privatization, patriotism, law and order, hard work, and self-help, modeling a new political subjectivity set against the tenets of New Deal liberalism and personifying the values incubated within the spaces wrought by suburbanization, urban renewal, and highway construction" (7).[27] In the passage of Proposition 13 (1978), the "People's Initiative to Limit Property Taxation," property tax increases, a primary method for generating state funds, became locked in at 1 percent per year. With this, "suburban homeowners adopted [an] insular political outlook that disavowed any connection to other urban constituencies" (Avila 232). These tax-cutting or tax-limiting measures and politicians—supported predominantly by white, suburban voters and contributors—uphold the precise notions of personal, communal, economic, and ecological isolation that lead to the crises within the parable texts. That Butler opts to begin this journey of flight from the encroaching city on the Reagan freeway points to a textual awareness of the irony. While *Sower* seems supportive of Lauren's endeavors, subtle moments like this one challenge that support, implying to the reader that Lauren possesses a certain unreliability as a religious, social, and environmentalist leader. The central tension between responsibility and flight or abandonment comes to the fore.[28]

The bulk of *Sower* takes place on U.S. Highway 101, a north–south freeway that spans from Los Angeles, California, to Port Angeles, Washington. Lauren narrates, "Earthseed is being born right here on Highway 101—on that portion of 101 that was once El Camino real, the royal highway of California's Spanish past. Now it's a highway, a river of the poor" (200). El Camino Real marks the path between the California missions established between 1769 and 1823 under the rule of Spain's Charles III and Ferdinand II.[29] Moving, generally, from south to north, Franciscans led by Junípero Serra, as well as Francisco Palou, Juan Crespi, and Fermín Lasuén, established twenty-one missions stretching from San Diego to Sonoma, a distance of over five hundred miles. These missions mark a distinct colonial history within California, one upon which the state relies heavily in terms of its own mythmaking. Like many colonial enterprises, Spain's mission system was justified as religious outreach, an opportunity to save the souls of California's Native peoples. The material, economic, and physical realities were, however, crushing (and in truth largely corresponded to Russian incursions in Northern California). Along with the introduction of diseases to which Native people had no immunity that always accompanied initial European and Native contact, the missionaries brought forced and coerced labor practices and relocation, an often-brutal brand of Catholicism, and the general attempt to eliminate the cultures and lifestyles of Native Californians. Nonetheless, Californians frequently gloss over their own history of slavery, partaking in nostalgic imaginings of their mission history as an innocent proselytizing. This glossing is evident in the naming of this freeway as El Camino Real and, as Avila notes, "in [the] 1950 *California Highways and Public Works* . . . centennial edition, which situated the new freeways within a larger regional history of conquest and settlement. . . . Renderings of conquistadors were placed alongside portraits of high-ranking bureaucrats within the Division of Highways, represented as latter-day incarnations of California's 'founding fathers'" (200). In other words, "the Division of Highways paused to create a usable past for its efforts. That history echoed not only the national rhetoric of manifest destiny, but also the regional myth of the Spanish Fantasy Past, which imparted a romantic gloss to the history of conquest in California" (Avila 201). Raúl Homero Villa calls such glomming on to the usable past of Spanish colonialism "the Spanish romance," which serves to contrast the "Mexican problem" in California and throughout the Southwest (16). In her selection of Highway 101 and her explicit use of the term El Camino Real, Butler alludes to another period of colonization and, apropos of these texts, religiously justified

"Failing Economies and Tortured Ecologies" 49

slavery in the Americas. Moreover, we must recall the massive ecological changes that came after colonization of what would become California. The Spanish attempted to convert the Native Californians not only in terms of religion but also agriculture. The ecosystems shaped by indigenous land practices, especially in terms of fire use, altered quickly as Native populations began to dwindle and Native cultures were profoundly interrupted.

While most critics assert that Robledo is in Los Angeles (despite the novel's clear evidence to the contrary), it seems as though it must in fact be somewhere in the San Fernando Valley (simply "the Valley" in the parlance of Southern California), possibly in the hills north of Northridge.[30] Butler's decision to place Robledo within the Valley means that the community is decidedly not Los Angeles, not the city. The Valley, a sprawling suburbia directly northwest of LA proper, serves as a primary destination for white flight's mobility.[31] In selecting the Valley as the site of her protagonist's multiethnic community, Butler illustrates that the suburban impulse of isolation is not limited to white exurbanites. Moreover, because the desire to isolate themselves from the urban wilderness dominates the collective psyche of Robledo's multiethnic community, the impulse cannot and must not be seen as purely the product or bastion of racism. As such, the decay of the urban core is not a simple coincidence of economic hardship, but a node within a complex causal chain that begins with *philosophical* or *ethical* isolation. In short, the blame for ignoring social and ecological injustice must not fall exclusively on the rich or on the white. The blame, Butler's texts assert, lies with any of us who would ignore those injustices, whether through complacence or flight. The failing economies and tortured ecologies of the Pox, and indeed the Pox itself, are our problem. And if we do not address those problems, the histories of violence, oppression, slavery, torture, catastrophe—histories we so often believe ourselves to be beyond—will return. They will come crashing through whatever gates, fences, and walls we construct.[32]

Butler takes pains to link the ecological and social throughout the parable novels, tying governmental deregulation to environmental issues. The newly elected president in *Sower*, Christopher Charles Morpeth Donner, "hopes to get laws changed, suspend 'overly restrictive' minimum wage, environmental, and worker protection laws for those employers willing to take on homeless employees and provide them with training and adequate room and board" (*Sower* 24). Donner's platform, of course, is reminiscent of contemporary neoconservatives, whose faith in business to regulate itself exists despite overwhelming historical precedents that directly show that faith to be misplaced, particularly in the realm of ecological toxicity. For example, Ronald Reagan's environmental legacy is most widely known for his establishment of James Watt as secretary of the interior and Rita Lavelle and Anne Gorsuch as heads of the Environmental Protection Agency (EPA). These figures are renowned for being among the most hostile toward environmentalist concerns of anyone to have held their positions (although they may have met their matches in George W. Bush's appointees). Lavelle and Gorsuch were each convicted of contempt of Congress during Reagan's first presidential term. That administration also saw the EPA face massive budget cuts and Reagan's 1987 veto of the Clean Water Act. Lauren wonders of Donner's administration, "Will it be legal to poison, mutilate, or infect people—as long as you provide them with food, water, and a space to die?" (*Sower* 24). In short, she wonders, will slavery and utter ecological devastation become relegalized. In showing these two elements as interconnected, Butler's texts illustrate how both rely on the refusal to recognize connection or community; both fail to perceive the most basic rights to exist. Indeed, these two novels narrate the return to the American political and physical landscape of several types of slavery: the wage slavery of Olivar and the religiously motivated incarceration and enslavement of Acorn.

Butler connects the new wage slavery of Olivar with the ecological catastrophe of global climate change—showing that the business-first philosophies, which are responsible for both, have disastrous consequences. Lauren explains, "Sea level keeps rising with the warming climate and there is the occasional earthquake. Olivar's flat, sandy beach is already just a memory" (*Sower* 105). Olivar's ecological and economic fortunes are in disarray. It becomes a company town in the most literal sense: it is not a town built around a single business but a town purchased by a company. This company takes over every aspect of Olivar, providing room and board as well as payment in the form of company scrip to its resident-employees. As Lauren's group moves northward, they encounter escaped workers from farms being run on similar systems. Of course, as employees accumulate debt, they lose the freedom to leave their jobs. Their liberty as human beings disappears as they are bound into debt slavery. Lauren's father declares of the changes in the U.S. economy, "This business sounds half antebellum revival and half science fiction" (*Sower* 109). Still another example comes as Lauren frees her brother Marcus from a slaver before Acorn is overrun.

Butler demonstrates this connection between the ecological and the social quite overtly, especially in *Talents*. Bankole notes, for example, "I have . . . read that the Pox was caused by accidentally coinciding climatic, economic, and sociological crises. It would be more honest to say that the Pox was caused by our own refusal to deal with obvious problems in those areas. We caused the problems: then we sat and watched as they grew into crises" (*Talents* 8). While Lauren's flight from Robledo, a secondary flight from Los Angeles, may have been the only option left for her, that singularity stemmed from a lack of communal responsibility for the decades leading up to the Pox. Bankole continues, understanding the blended nature of ecological and social ills, "I have watched as convenience, profit, and inertia excused greater and more dangerous environmental degradation. I have watched poverty, hunger, and disease become inevitable for more and more people" (*Talents* 8). Bankole's words serve as a warning to the contemporary reader about inactivity; psychological separation, disassociation, and willful ignorance are all cultural toxins that lead directly to climatological, ecological, and social damage.

The Crusaders, certainly guilty of all the sins Bankole laments and emblematic of all that is wrong in Butler's dystopian future, are undone from a lack of ecological understanding. Noticing that the Earthseed believers plant trees, the Crusaders assume they do so because they worship them. Carrying on a long tradition of theocratic rule, they cut down the trees they perceive as the objects of pagan idolatry. They fail to recognize that the trees are planted by the Acorn residents in order to commemorate their dead; for the nutrients and calories their seeds provide; and most importantly in this case, in order to reinforce the hills surrounding their property. California's hills are particularly prone to mudslides if their vegetation is removed. And after a very large storm—the kind quite common along the Northern California coast—the hill gives way and slides over the building that houses the control units of the collars the Christian Crusaders use to enslave Lauren and her neighbors. We might be tempted to read this landslide as a kind of divine intervention, but such a reading goes against the teachings of Earthseed. Instead, Olamina asserts, "The weather, and our 'teachers'' own stupidity has freed us" (*Talents* 254). The Crusaders' deaths and the freedom of their captives stems from the former's inability to recognize that they are smaller than the landscape and from their mistaken assumption that their God would protect them from a torrent of mud. They fail to recognize themselves as part of an ecosystem, a failure that arises from their interpretation of Christian doctrine that holds them as socially and ecologically superior. This failure destroys them.

Similarly, Butler shows the connection between the human and the nonhuman by likening certain human traits to those of other mammals. Commenting on groups of people she sees on the road, she notes, "There were a few young guys around, lean and quick, some filthy, some not dirty at all. . . . Predators. They looked around a lot, stared at people and the people looked away" (*Sower* 158). Butler crafts these young men to resemble other kinds of predators—great cats, packs of dogs. They are lean, all teeth and claws. She continues, "Most predators are opportunists. They prey on old people, lone women or women with young kids, handicapped people. . . . They don't want to get hurt. My father used to call them coyotes" (*Sower* 181). However, not all her human/animal analogies carry the negative connotations one might read into this coyote analogy. Lauren also refers to her own group as "a pack, the three of us and all those other people out there aren't in it. If we're a good pack, and we work together, we have a chance. You can be sure we aren't the only pack out here" (*Sower* 163). These characters must realize that they are animals like any others, engaged in a constant tension between predator and prey. Butler's novels challenge human exceptionalism, asserting instead that people are far more like the rest of the species of the earth than many are comfortable admitting.

However, not all parallels between the human and the nonhuman are so benign; like the other texts I examine, Butler's make use of the marginalization of certain groups through the discourse of detritus and disease. Jarret describes non-Christians in the following terms: "These people . . . these pagans are not only wrong. They're dangerous. They're . . . as contagious as plagues, as poisonous as snakes to the society they infect. They kill us" (*Talents* 88). He continues, rhetorically asking, "What do we do to weeds, to viruses, to parasitic worms, to cancers?" (89). Jarret makes use of the discourse of contamination in particular; the elements he mentions invade what he sees as a healthy cultural and religious body and destroy it. Weeds are unwanted plant species, though what makes a plant a weed is entirely subjective. He wields both contamination and toxicity, all the while spewing the culturally toxic venom of exclusion and violent supremacy. Lauren's brother, Marcus, discusses his life on the streets after Robledo's destruction. A family, the Durans, take him in. He explains, "The Durans and I were squatters. We shared a big, abandoned stucco house with five other families. That meant we were part of the trash that the new mayor, the city council, and the business community wanted to sweep out" (121). As I show throughout this text and as I discuss in greater detail in my introduction, this parallel between garbage and the poor, especially the poor of color, stands as a consistent trope throughout the history of the United States and, indeed, of the Americas broadly speaking. The colonial enterprise rests upon this facile categorization. However, it is not only people who are contaminants; ideas are treated similarly. Lauren notes:

> They've burned our books and our papers.
> They've burned all that they could find of our past. It's all
> ungodly trash, they say. (*Talents* 212)

Ideas serve as cultural pollutants for those espousing the reactionary cultural conservatism and theocracy within this novel.

However, Butler is quick to show how this emphasis on trash, on things and people to be thrown away, contrasts the philosophy of Earthseed. After they become freed from the Christian Crusaders, Lauren muses on the dump that their enslavers have created. She points out, "We had had no dump before. We had a salvage heap and a compost heap. Neither was trash. We could not afford to be wasteful. Our teachers have made trash of our entire community" (*Talents* 255). Butler ties together issues of ecology and economy—or more to the point, she shows how bound together they are. Like those of all the poor communities in the texts I examine, the members of Earthseed make use of the objects that the rich generally simply discard. A salvage heap is a pile of materials that people know, think, or hope will be useful at some point. A compost heap contains organic matter decomposed for use in fertilizing later crops. Making either denotes foresight and a recognition that nothing is truly trash. Nothing is useless. But the discourse of the Crusaders casts this community in the role of waste, as polluting elements that must be isolated, contained, reclaimed (read reeducated), or destroyed.

The ecological engagement in these texts is of particular interest in light of the dearth of critical examination of texts by African American authors that overtly take environmentalist messages as central to their work. Mayer points out one cause of this separation: "The fact that since its emergence in the second half of the nineteenth century American environmentalism has predominantly been a white, middle-class pursuit, preoccupied with notions of wilderness and wildlife preservation, explains the mistrust black people have harbored toward long-established environmentalist organizations" (Mayer, *Restoring the Connection to the Natural World* 2). On the other hand, bell hooks offers another explanation: "The sense of wonder and reverence for life cultivated [in the rural South] was largely lost in the migration to the North" (hooks 51). In her view, the urbanization of African American groups created a distance and indifference toward environmentalism that countered a former agrarian lifestyle that emphasized communal identification with the land. Elsewhere, Mayer asserts that *Sower* "can be read as performing a kind of consciousness-raising with respect to the crucial importance of both basic literacy, the ability to read and write, and environmental literacy, the knowledge about biological and ecological phenomena, for human survival" (Mayer, "Genre and Environmentalism" 192). The interconnection between the social and the ecological, what Mayer calls literacy and I describe as community, comes to play throughout Butler's work and throughout much of the discourse surrounding urban spaces, be they in praise of or in defamation of those spaces.

In discussing the destruction of the working-class and lower-income neighborhood of Bunker Hill in order to create a "business friendly" downtown in Los Angeles, Avila asserts, "Film noir cast Bunker Hill as

Southern California's heart of darkness, a site that harbored crime, fear, and psychosis" (77). Just as Lauren and her family look disparagingly on Los Angeles as a whole, LA's general population easily dismissed Bunker Hill as a site of cultural contagion, a place to be avoided until it crumbled, unable to withstand its own moral and structural decay. To that end, Avila continues, "Only a few years prior to the arrival of bulldozers in Bunker Hill, film noir had already annihilated that space in public consciousness" (78). Perhaps the danger of these narratives of ecological catastrophe is that in imaginatively destroying the cityscape, we invite the real destruction of those spaces, the spaces in which, not at all coincidentally, a large number, if not the majority, are people of color. We protect the homes of the (largely white) middle class by destroying the homes of the people they fear, a fear made evident by their desire to see the city destroyed as well as by their refusal to live therein. Butler's decision to set her protagonist's family and community within a walled suburban city complicates the historical legal mandates of Los Angeles's suburban expansion. This reimagination shows a similar impulse to white flight: blight flight, a longing to escape urban decay. And while *Sower* ends with a possibility for the success of flight, *Talents* reinforces, again and again, the utter inevitability of its failure. In its place, we are left with the need for responsible engagement with our cultural, political, and ecological flaws and shortcomings.

2

TOXIC METROPOLIS

ALEJANDRO MORALES'S *THE RAG DOLL PLAGUES*

Since fifteen hundred and sixteen
. . . their borders and boots on top of us
Pullin' knobs on the floor of their toxic metropolis
RAGE AGAINST THE MACHINE, "The People of the Sun"

This chapter moves from the dystopian SF future of Butler's parable novels to the temporally diverse SF depictions of Mexicana/o and Chicana/o communities in Alejandro Morales's *The Rag Doll Plagues.*[1] Whereas Butler's novels focus on multiethnic communities from an African American point of view, this novel looks at the multiethnic and multiracial elements of Chicana/o communities in and between Mexico City and Southern California. In their apostrophe to Chicana/o identity, "The People of the Sun," used here as my epigraph, Rage against the Machine describes Los Angeles as a toxic metropolis, drawing a connection between the colonial enterprise in Mexico and the economic, military, *and* ecological interventions in Mexico by the United States. In 1516 Charles V ascended the throne of Spain, marking that nation's post-Moor unification and the beginning of Spanish attempts to explore and ultimately gain control over mainland Mesoamerica. The song's reference to "their border and boots on top of us" refers to the United States wresting its southwestern corner from Mexico by military action and laying its border over preexisting Mexican and indigenous communities.[2] As in Butler's texts, we see an emphasis on the permeability of political borders in *The Rag Doll Plagues*, as well as allusions to indigenous American identities. In this case, we also note, however, the historic continuity of Mexican and Mexican American presence in the United States and Los Angeles in particular. That this metropolis is "toxic" connects the cultural and economic domination of Mexican Americans in the United States and that of the rest of the human and nonhuman world, a connection similarly emphasized in *The Rag Doll Plagues*.

While, as I will show, this novel on occasion relies on essentialist notions of Chicana/o identity, naturalized heterosexuality, and an essential human body, that essentialism is also repeatedly problematized by the narrators' frequent refutations of the possibility of purity. Morales's novel takes great pains to show that states of purity cannot exist in the world, that notions of purity are necessarily atavistic or static and, as such, inapplicable to real-world situations. Instead, the narrators constantly emphasize the ways that identities shift, allegiances form and falter, and hope for human survival lies within the most polluted spaces. These positive pollutions illustrate and elucidate the permeability of human selves and cultures and ultimately assert a connection among humans and between humans and the other species with which we live. Furthermore, the reclamation of cast-off communities, cast-off objects, and desecrated spaces becomes possible through recognizing ourselves as members of broad, complex, and inclusive communities. Moreover, Morales, like Rage against the Machine, draws on Mexica tradition as a base for this communal identity with the nonhuman, a base that, strangely, remains unexamined in the critical texts focused on this novel.[3] Finally, I argue Morales's narrative serves as a form of pepenador, retrieving society's wretched refuse (both the waste and people who are thrown away) and desecrated spaces and reclaiming and recycling them back into society.[4]

The Rag Doll Plagues takes place during three periods of time, each told in a sixty-six-page section: book 1, "Mexico City," takes place from 1788 to 1792 in México DF; book 2, "Delhi," in the mid- to late 1970s in Orange County, California; and book 3, "LAMEX," sometime between 2050 and 2100 in LAMEX, a section of the Triple Alliance—a political entity comprised of Mexico, the United States, and Canada.[5] Each book is narrated by a physician named Gregorio, or Gregory Revueltas, who is attempting to treat some manifestation of a recurring, evolving disease: *la mona*, or "the rag doll," so named because it swells the limbs, dissolves bone, and renders the infected immobile.

"First Professor of Medicine, Anatomy and Surgery of the Royal Bed-chamber" and "Director of the Royal *Protomedicato*" (15)—Gregorio Revueltas, a Spanish doctor in Mexico City who attempts to treat a disease spreading throughout New Spain and effecting people of all classes and races, narrates book 1. Over the course of this first book, Gregorio gradually comes to identify with the Mexican people and forsake Spain as well as his betrothed, a Spanish noblewoman named Renata. In order to examine the evolution of the narrator as well as Morales's crafting of a narrative that emphasizes fluidity and permeability, it is necessary to examine the first chapter of the first book in some detail, paying close attention to its historiographic nature as well as the narrative persona of Doctor Gregorio Revueltas. Specifically, Gregorio transforms from a rather generically racist colonist into a compassionate Mexican émigré.

In the first paragraph of this novel, Gregorio marks a contrast between his European nobility and the perceived putrescence of the indigenous and mixed-race populations of Mexico. Discussing architectural features of the viceroy's royal palace he states, "The cherub's golden wings shimmered in the afternoon sun, which passed over the center of the Main Plaza, and contrasted with the filthy central fountain where Indians, Mestizos, Negroes, Mulattoes, and other immoral racial mixtures of humanity drank and filled clay jugs with foul dark water while they socialized" (11). This quote sets the tone for the entire book, as it combines European notions of a polluted space with the non-European population. This passage, the third sentence of the novel, comes even before the introduction of the narrator. We note first that Gregorio contrasts cherubs to the local population. These people, we are shown, are no angels. Moreover, as cherubs are generally (and mistakenly) represented as babies or children, their iconographic innocence contrasts the savages (not the noble kind) with their immorality.[6] Second, this sentence is somewhat misleading as far as what the peasants are being contrasted to. It would seem at first as though Gregorio is contrasting them to the cherubs; however, the sentence structure is more telling than this initial reading since they are in fact being contrasted with the cherub's golden wings, which Gregorio particularly notes are shimmering in the afternoon sun. Reading a contrast between the peasants and the sun is rather more disenfranchising within a specifically Mexica context. As this passage is set in Mexico City—the former capital of the Mexica empire, the primary religion of which revolves to a large extent around Huitzilopochtli, the god of the sun (whom I will discuss in more detail in my section on book 2)—these people are shown in contrast to the indigenously sacred as well. Finally and most notably, this passage sets up a connection that the reader will encounter throughout the novel: the population of Mexico City (which serves synecdochically for Mexican and later for Mexican American populations) is, in every way, a pollutant within the colonial imagination. The narrator calls the individuals by the fountain "immoral racial mixtures of humanity," invoking European constructions of racial interbreeding as miscegenation, a watering down of otherwise pure blood. Moreover, the image of water in a fountain reflects what the narrator sees as a chaotic blending and mixing within an enclosed space. We can read this space as metaphoric for either New Spain or, perhaps more interestingly, the Valley of Mexico, a landscape historically composed of immigrations and mixings between indigenous populations, a geologic bowl filled with liquid identities. Finally, the narrator describes the water as "foul" and "dark" and the fountain as "filthy." These adjectival choices show that the preoccupation with purity and static racial identity in this novel exist from its very beginning. Foulness and filthiness are connected to darkness; all these concepts oppose the narrator's ideals, especially of whiteness, or lightness, as purity.

Morales proceeds to blend a number of historical figures into this novel in order to muddy the distinction between history and fiction. Characters such as Viceroy Don Juan Vicente de Guemes Pacheco de Padilla and Father Juan Antonio Llorente are historical individuals contemporaneous to the period in which the book is set. Morales also focuses most of one chapter on his discussion of Doña Catalina de Erauso, also known as La Monja Alférez (the Lieutenant Nun). By integrating this historical figure into a work of fiction, Morales emphasizes a liquidity between identities, between history and fiction, and among genders and sexualities. Gregorio narrates her story: "La Monja Alférez had taken many lives. Her dueling and killing had brought her into conflict with the authorities, who pursued her until finally she was sentenced to hang.

But she was spared her life when she revealed to the Royal Courts that she was a woman, a nun and a virgin. The latter she proved by exposing a chastity belt that she had worn since her first menstruation. . . . The King gave her a pension for life and the Pope a dispensation to wear male clothing for the rest of her remaining time on earth" (14). This part of the narrative conforms to the extant historical and biographical information we have about Doña Catalina de Erauso, and she serves as an image of positive pollution of static, rigid, or essentialist gendered identities. According to this version of the story, once the woman has proven her purity (read virginity), she is freed by the colonial courts. This could be seen as Morales striking a blow in favor of notions of purity or, at least, being able to assert one's purity, were he to end the tale there. But he does not. Gregorio continues, "Her life came to a climax when she fell in love with the smell, taste, touch and voice of another woman" (14). La Monja's lover is "the Spanish wife of a young *hidalgo*," who finds the two lovers together and accepts a challenge to duel from La Monja, who "skewer[s] the *macho* from his screaming mouth through his bleeding anus" (14). No charges are brought against La Monja Alférez, and she and her lover live, it seems, happily ever after. Morales's novel refigures the very purity that allows for La Monja's escape as the punch line of this story. It figures a transgender nun, who has received the blessings of the crown and the pope, as the murdering, philandering protagonist and even ends the *crónica* with the scatological reference to the bleeding anus of the cuckolded young hidalgo. While Morales imagines purity as a saving grace for La Monja Alférez, he almost instantaneously returns to invert and mock the very possibility of the existence of that purity. Purity here is performative or bureaucratic and political; we can in no way assume it to be essential. The incorporation of Erauso's story serves to overturn heteronormative notions of naturalized gender identities and sexualities.

The Rag Doll Plagues draws on this historical figure to in order to create a usable Latin American past, transforming the narrative to fit Morales's ends. While there are many doubts about the authenticity of her autobiography, La Monja Alférez is a historical person, a noble Basque woman named Doña Catalina de Erauso, born around 1592 in San Sebastian de Guipuzcoa, Spain. She entered a convent at age four and escaped dressed as a man just before she was to take her vows at age fifteen. She traveled to the Americas in 1603 and fought as a Spanish soldier (passing as a man) and was appointed *alférez* (a low officiary rank) (Stepto xxv). During her time as a soldier, she killed a number of men in brawls (including her brother) and was eventually arrested for murder, at which point she revealed her identity to a priest. Erauso returned to Spain dressed as a nun; received Pope Urbano's dispensation to dress as a man and use her masculine name, Antonio de Erauso; and returned to the Americas to work as a muleteer. Alexis Zepeda points out that Erauso was pardoned her cross-dressing because she did so in "the right direction," attempting to become something better than she was, a man instead of a woman. She also notes that Erauso never states her sexual preference early in her memoir but that she falls in love with a woman she is escorting to Mexico City to meet her prospective husband. Erauso pays the bride's dowry, and they join a nunnery and live together, presumably as lovers.

Morales takes certain liberties with the story, especially in changing the ending of the tale. But even this work of creative historiography reinforces his textual emphasis on the liquidity of identity, especially in terms of gender (and within the colonial mindset, in terms of sexuality as well); Erauso's narrative, already a site of contention between historical accuracy and folk tradition (more to the chagrin of the former than the latter), opens up for further imaginings.[7] Marjorie Garber calls such positively polluting historiographic ambiguity a "category crisis," that is, "a failure of definitional distinction, a borderline that becomes permeable, permitting border crossings from one apparently distinct category to another" (xiv). This biological woman becomes, in the eyes of her community, a man. Morales shows that categorization by gender, thought by many to be fundamental to human identity, is easily subverted and, as such, challenged. Not only does the narrative represent the impossibility of fixed identity; the narrative's boundaries become unfixed and permeable.

Doctor Revueltas goes on to describe a number of other pollutive dangers facing the colonial New World early in this first chapter of the novel; one example leads to his quest to bring a more modern practice of medicine to the colony. He hopes "the male and female Spanish-speaking practitioners of witchcraft, the popular *curanderos*, would be forced out of circulation. These *curanderos* were dangerous and had caused the deaths of thousands. Worst of all were the Indian *curanderos* who practiced witchcraft in their native tongue" (16). It is important to note that the worst aspect of these last curanderos is not the idea that they had caused "thousands of deaths"—a dubious assertion to be sure—but rather that some of them were Indians who practiced "in their native tongue." In his analysis of the role of sexual desire as an impulse of colonial expansion, Robert Young likens linguistically hybrid forms of creole and pidgin to miscegenation, a pollution of an otherwise pure language by lesser ones (5). Gregorio imagines Native language by curanderos as a malpractice akin to murder, or at least manslaughter, indicating death as preferable to cultural and linguistic pollution. These references to linguistic pollution and impurity continue throughout the beginning of book 1 as Gregorio looks down upon all things American.

Morales's novel further juxtaposes these fears of linguistic pollution with spiritual and political pollution. Gregorio notes that he has been sent because "the King desired to avoid a spirit of separatism here. He was well aware that the French revolutionary emotion was *contagious* and that the success of the United States independence movement could effect the future direction of the empire" (16, emphasis mine). The king, of course, is right. This period, the reign of Charles IV (1788–1808), marks the beginning of the end for Spain as a great colonial power, with the defeat to Nelson at Trafalgar (1805) and in the Napoleonic Wars (1803–1815). While the independence of the nations of the Americas remains, for the most part, a decade or more away, their seeds are being sown at this moment. Linda Arnold marks the end of the colonial period in Mexico at 1810, corresponding to the termination of the vice-regency (14). Gregorio goes on to conflate bodily health—the health of the bodies of the residents and citizens of New Spain—with the health of the body politic and political strength of Spain itself, a connection present throughout the novel. He concludes, "I was here to quell the fires of revolutionary fervor by extinguishing the illnesses in the fevered populace" (16). The crown understands the correlation between the epidemiological and social, that widespread disease will lead to revolutionary impulses. Of course, the epidemiological is inherently ecological, the interaction of the human and various bacterial and viral species.

Such permeability rests not only in social collectivities but also in the first book's most positively polluted individual body, that of Father Jude, a priest who has been facially mutilated by French pirates and sent by the viceroy to assist Gregorio. Doctor Revueltas describes Father Jude as "the mask of death itself" and "a living skull, a monk from whose face the nose and upper lip had been sliced away to reveal long, deep, opened nostrils and upper gums and teeth" (19). Father Jude is imminently permeable. The fact that most of his face has been sliced away to reveal his facial cavities serves to do more than merely shock the reader. Rather, it shows that we can see inside him; he has no shell to create the illusion of invulnerability and no barrier to separate him from the rest of the physical world. What's more, he is perhaps the most positive figure in the entire novel; his compassion and strength serve as a model for Gregorio's transformation.

Human permeability is largely demonstrated in terms of our olfactory sense, particularly in the smells that tend to occur in Father Jude's presence, though not always because of him. These odors come to illustrate that all people, not only this physically open priest, face constant permeation by outside particles. Smells are, after all, merely airborne fragments of matter, which we receive, smell, and taste. We cannot stop this particulate matter from entering us without a number of high-tech devices for filtering the air. Morales shows that we are always the recipients of particles—be they germs, foul odors, or pleasant aromas—that seem to find us regardless of our efforts (and the narrator takes great pains to try to stop or mask the penetrating odor of death and decay throughout this book). These things seep into and swirl around and penetrate us. We are never impermeable; and as such, we can never be pure. Neither can we ever be isolated or alone.

Morales's novel refigures not only the isolation of the individuated body but also a temporal isolation in its focus on Mexica notions of temporal cyclicality, constructed using not only recurring events but also coincidental encounters. Morales positively pollutes linear and unidirectional time. Martín-Rodríguez states, "*Plagues* presents a vision of history close to the Nietzschean notion of eternal return. In this sense, the three Gregorys are one, as is the plague that reappears with different names throughout the book, and as is the space in which the three stories take place" (91). While I do not assert that Morales denies this Nietzschean concept of time, I think the examples that run throughout the novel show the connection to cyclicality borne out in the Mexica calendar and worldview. The two Mexica calendars, the *tonalpohualli* (or 260-day count) and the *xiuhpohualli* or (365-day count), sync with each other every fifty-two years. Each calendar represents a cycle—the former of ritual and divination, the latter of the solar year. These two cyclical annual systems combine to create a third fifty-two-year cycle. Richard F. Townsend points out, "the succession of 52-year cycles was not calendrically differentiated. It is as if our centuries were not distinguished as being before or after Christ" (135). Centuries cycle back on themselves; years repeat rather than progress (a temporal emphasis we likewise see in *Tropic of Orange*). Such a repetition rests at the heart of cyclical time. Ultimately, Morales moves toward a liquid concept of time in which the past, present, and future are not separate but integrally connected and influencing (as well as repeating) one another.[8]

This image of combination also comes in the form of Papá Damián, the guide who aids the three doctor-narrators throughout the novel and who is coupled with images of religious syncretism.[9] The narrator notes, "While a serpent coiled around Gregorio's body, a man and a woman prayed in my room to the *Virgen de Guadalupe*" (24). At this point Morales draws upon Mexica imagery for the first time, in the figure of the serpent coiled around Gregorio. Serpents abound in Mexica as well as Catholic (and more broadly Judeo-Christian) traditions. However, although vilified in the latter as a trickster (or worse) who talks Eve into sampling the fruit of the tree of the knowledge of good and evil, serpents appear in numerous Mexica stories and images. The most well-known example is Quetzalcoatl, the quetzal-plumed serpent and god of the wind who plays an integral role in the creation of humanity (outwitting the god of death and the underworld, Mictlantecuhtli). Quetzalcoatl is also responsible for the spread of corn throughout Mesoamerica. As Karl Taube points out "*Coatl* signifies both 'twin' and 'snake'" (17), and Quetzalcoatl serves as just one of many figures of duality and flux within Mexica religion.[10]

Gloria Anzaldúa discusses the hybrid form of *La Virgen de Guadalupe* in terms of Tonantzin as well as Coatlicue and Coatlalopeuh.[11] However, for Anzaldúa, "*La Virgen de Guadalupe* is the symbol of ethnic identity and of the tolerance for ambiguity that Chicanos-*mexicanos*, people of mixed race, people who have Indian blood, people who cross cultures, by necessity possess" (30). Morales's invocation of La Virgen builds on this tradition of mixed race and ethnicity in cross-cultural individuals and communities and serves to embody the liquidity portrayed throughout *The Rag Doll Plagues*. We will encounter still more snake imagery with the appearance of Coatlicue, she of the serpent skirt, in book 2.

All these types of positive pollution (linguistic, ideological, religious, temporal, etc.) also mirror the ecological toxicity in this novel. Morales presents an image of permeable human beings and cultures, and illustrates how, through our very corporeality, the human species itself cannot be rigidly, statically, or essentially defined. The physical or ecological toxicity within book 1—apart from la mona—comes in the form of human waste, feces and urine, and dead bodies. Gregorio comments, "As we passed the Palace of the Inquisition, men and women squatted facing each other and deposited excrement and urine into the canal that ran down the center of the street. . . . The windows of the houses along this street were tightly closed in a desperate attempt to keep out the gases of decaying animal and human waste" (26). He goes on to describe children playing in this filth and continues, "The drainage ditch running down the middle of the street was clogged with the manure and urine from animals and human beings" (26). Morales makes a point of noting that Mexico City "was built on top of the destroyed Aztec city of Tenochtitlán in the middle of Lake Texcoco by Indian and Mestizo slave labor directed by Spanish architects" (25). Mexico City grew around Tenochtitlán, an island city, and expanded to cover the lake that was gradually drained to allow for the expansion. Unfortunately for the residents, the soft lake bed did not support the weight of this city, and so the city began to sink. Gregorio states, "We stopped abruptly to find that our path had been blocked by a brown, putrid ooze emerging from the soft bottom of Lake Texcoco. The cobblestone street, pounded for decades by carriages, had cracked severely, allowing the pestilential muck to rise to the surface" (26–27). As Mexico City sank, it fell below the level of the formerly belowground sewage, which spread in certain places. As this sewage dried and evaporated, it became airborne and began to spread disease around the valley in which Mexico City sits. The city fills the volcanic Valley of Mexico and is surrounded by mountains. Compounding these geologic difficulties is the prominence of inversion layers, which literally press the particulate matter—now especially smog and ozone (the two most abundant pollutants stemming especially from energy consumption)—back down on the residents (World Health Organization and the United Nations Environment Programme 163). This problem has continued into the twentieth century and coupled with the increasing population and use of fossil fuels to help give Mexico City the most toxic air in the Western Hemisphere.

Morales pairs this narrative of ecological toxicity with his first descriptions of la mona and again with scenes of sex workers and sexually transmitted diseases. Father Jude and Gregorio arrive at a chapel where Father Jude ministers to "dying male and female prostitutes who [suffer] from the epidemic and/or venereal diseases" (28). In this way, Morales pairs the disease (la mona) with sexuality, and sex workers in particular.[12] After one of the prostitutes dies, Father Jude notes, "She was a mere child of twelve, insane and deformed by syphilis. Just another one of the millions who have benefited from our Majesty's policies" (29). Father Jude conflates the physical and cultural toxins of la mona, syphilis, and child prostitution as products of the colonial enterprise. The poor planning of the city accelerates the spread of la mona; the poverty and neglect of the city, Father Jude suggests, lead to the widespread prostitution, child abuse, and sex trade, just as the Spanish presence leads to the outbreak of syphilis.[13] Young argues that the "focus on hybridity [in colonial discourse] inscribes gender and the sexual division of labour within the mode of colonial reproduction" (19). The racialized agon between colonizer and colonized gets waged over the feminized, sexualized, and queered bodies, themselves seen as penetrable sites.[14]

Father Jude—as befits his namesake, the patron saint of lost causes—says of these sex workers, "I am the only person who treats them. I help them die" (29). What Gregorio says of Father Jude's patients bears some examination: "[Fr. Jude's] lacerations were nothing compared to the physical and mental wounds of the people to whom he ministered. His flock was a diseased, infested population: the prostitutes, the lepers, the abandoned children, the demented homeless people, the disenfranchised who survived in the filthy streets, the dungheaps and the garbage dumps of the city. Along with the laboring enslaved poor, these were Father Jude's patients, who looked to him not only for physical and spiritual remedies, but for an insurgent attitude that made life more tolerable and nurtured a growing desire for change" (29). The words Gregorio employs—*wounds, diseased, infested, lepers, filthy, dungheaps, garbage dumps*—are all terms of pollution and toxicity. These figures do not merely dwell in the waste of this colonial empire; like so many others I study throughout *Positive Pollutions*, they are the waste. They are cast off or cast aside and deemed to be without value. Father Jude recognizes their humanity and helps them not only to survive (collectively, if not individually) but also to find comfort in this life and in death. Beyond that, he shows that their lives can improve; he helps them to find hope for a better existence for change. At this point in the book, Gregorio begins to recognize the humanity of his patients, the Indians and Mestizos he has derided to this point. Simultaneously, Father Jude becomes a pepenador (a concept I will return to in my discussion of book 3), working among the castoffs to reclaim all that is good or useful (we are reminded of the scrap heap in *Talents*).

The conclusion of book 1 discusses the cure to la mona in terms of environmental justice. Father Jude's confessor—Father Juan Antonio Llorente,[15] the general secretary of the Holy Office—tells Gregorio that to cure la mona the Spanish must "simply stop ravaging the resources of Mexico. Leave monies here and designate an appropriate amount of funds for medical services and training. Let the Viceroy know, let the King beware of the possible decimation of the population. . . . This plague will kill at least a million savages" (40). Father Antonio clearly indicates that there is no cure for la mona, no treatment for those who fall victim to it. However, as to what can be done *about* la mona, the first response is "stop ravaging the resources." Here, Morales most clearly states the source of the disease; it is the culturally toxic and negligent treatment of the people of Mexico and its land by the Spanish. General social and specific environmental injustice has led to this crisis.[16] All of this moves the narrative toward its insistence on community in a broad, diverse, and ecocentric sense. In the idealized community of this narrative, hierarchies fail and relationality becomes privileged.

Gregorio comes to feel at home in Mexico City and works hard to ensure a better life for its inhabitants. He speaks of social and ecological improvements simultaneously, showing the close interrelatedness of the two, noting, "After three years, the city was cleaner, safer. . . . The clogged drainage systems received attention. More public baths were installed. Fountains were designated for drinking only. Garbage and death carts circulated through the city streets more often. Doctors and surgeons were required to treat all patients; the university medical school opened its doors to treat the indigent. Botanical gardens were laid out in the suburbs of the capital for the entertainment of the people. It seemed that these improvements helped strengthen the people. *La Mona*'s killing had subsided and seemed to be moving away to the North" (44). Throughout this passage, Morales scatters and intersperses legal and ecological improvements beginning with the fact that the city is "cleaner and safer." Many of these improvements come in the form of hygiene and waste disposal—that is, dealing with the detritus that humans make in the day-to-day process of being. But Gregorio also notes that "the indigent" are now better cared for. They are no longer viewed as societal or cultural detritus but rather recognized for their humanity. This novel reinforces the fact that we are intricately and inextricably bound to our ecological community and to other human beings as these social and ecological improvements lead to the abatement of the plague.

The plague subsides in spring, and Marisela and Father Jude's child is born just as Marisela dies. Gregorio describes the baby, Mónica Marisela, as "a live, well-developed girl, whose powerful little lungs bellowed a cry" (59). This child, with her powerful lungs, presages the immunity of the Mexico City Mexicans of book 3 (as do her initials—MM), and Gregorio notes, "It seemed as if with her birth, *La Mona*'s attacks on the populace had dwindled to nothing" (61). Gregorio works with renewed vigor "for a better world, a better Mexico for Mónica Marisela" (61) just as he "heard the people discuss the future of their country" (62). This vernal period represents that this country is no longer New Spain to Gregorio; it has become Mexico in his mind. The savior children who appear at the ends of books 1 and 3, I argue, also represent pepenadores, as do the various savior figures examined throughout my study. They will be the ones who reclaim the trash of this world (and this trashed world) to make a better future.

The protagonist of book 2, Doctor Gregory Revueltas, works in a hospital in "an old Santa Ana *barrio* called Delhi"—a neighborhood in southern Santa Ana, California (71). Gregory meets and falls in love with Sandra Spear—a wealthy, Jewish, European American, hemophiliac actress who, during the sixty-six pages of book 2, miscarries, tests positive for HIV, and dies.

This book, like the others, contains a number of other-than-human images: jaguars, trees, birds, and snakes among them. However, this second book is the only one of the three that begins with a description of a nonhuman entity. While the first and third books begin with descriptions of architecture, the second commences with "the heroic blue-green cypress" (69). The cypress, genus *Cupressus*, is comprised of around twenty species that grow all over the world—in the Americas, they grow wild in the Western United States, Mexico, and Guatemala (*Botanica's Trees and Shrubs* 298). Morales's novel demonstrates an ecological awareness, setting an endemic genus within its ecosystem. The narrator repeatedly notes that both the cypress tree and Sandra's eyes are blue green, a correlation that bears particular significance as relates to their respective diseases.[17] Cypress trees are disease and insect prone. The most common ailments that affect this tree are juniper scale (*Carulaspis juniperi*) and Seiridium canker, caused by *Seiridium unicorne*; the symptoms of both diseases resemble those of la mona. Juniper scale affects the bark of the tree, causing discoloration and stunting the growth of the limbs. Seiridium canker forms on branches (causing them to die back), and discolored splotches or depressions appear on the bark of the tree and tend to be accompanied by unusual sap excretion. The discoloration of the limbs (they tend to turn reddish brown) coupled with the flow of resin is reminiscent of the liquid flow that accompanies la mona. What's more, like the plagues of this novel, this disease tends to be spread by water, either from splashing on an infected tree then a healthy one or from irrigation. We note the solutions to the causes of la mona in book 1, many of which include cleaning water supplies and improving liquid waste removal. I will return to images of liquids as disease carriers or cures in my reading of book 3.

We gain some more understanding of the novel when we learn about these conifers. First, they are evergreens, as are the sequoias (and some oaks) of chapter 1. Evergreens frequently serve as an image of enduring life in the face of death. Evergreens, as opposed to deciduous trees, do not enter stages of dormancy but continue to feed and grow under the harshest of conditions. Of course, the arboreal metaphor of the evergreen makes sense mostly in places where the winters are cold and long. Such wintry conditions are certainly not present in Orange County with its annual 13.8 inches of rain and average annual temperature of 64.8 degrees (and average high temperature of 75.4 degrees).[18] However, Gregory does show both the tree and Sandra to be endangered. Despite its longevity, Gregory still calls the tree "delicate" and says that it is "forever in danger of being broken, cut down by men and women concerned more with industrial profit than the preservation of natural life" (69).[19] Not only is this a somewhat frail species of tree, but it has the misfortune to have been planted in Orange County, a place where, in general, there is more concern with industrial profit than the preservation of natural life. Moreover, Orange County is also a site associated with varied assaults to human diversity. It is, in fact, the historical California seat of culturally toxic organizations like the Ku Klux Klan and, more recently, White Aryan Resistance. In *Ecology of Fear*, Mike Davis spends several pages addressing crimes that "in another era . . . would have been called lynchings" (406); all these crimes took place in Orange County in the 1990s. Orange County, then, can be read in this context as being as *socially* inhospitable for people of color and of mixed ethnicity as it is *ecologically* inhospitable for the cypress. These material realities counter romantic images of California as an idyllic multiethnic space and reveal some of the cultural toxins that lead to and arise from isolating suburbanization (as we also see in Butler's and Yamashita's novels).[20]

Gregory explains how this tree *grounds* him within this specific landscape. He says, "Here, next to this well-planted tree, I felt rooted in this earth" (69). This tree represents Gregory's relational connection to place. Obviously, Morales's use of "roots" here implies both the nutrient absorbing tendrils of the plant kingdom and human cultural and familial history. But, roots also imply an absence of mobility or, at least, of mobilization.[21] After all, trees do not wander the way animals do. They are directly tied, inexorably bound to a specific location and are heavily influenced by the ecosystems in which they find themselves. That Gregory associates himself with this cypress implies a long-term connection to Santa Ana as a home space and, ultimately, a home land. Morales's Chicana/o emplacement counters what Raúl Homero Villa calls "the centrality of . . . deterritorialization to Chicanos [that] has guaranteed its importance as a theme in their expressive practice . . . most commonly figured through imagery and rhetoric of 'the lost land'" (1). Gregory's ties to the land are not lost but clearly defined in an ecosystemic, familial, and cultural sense.

The cypress, moreover, takes on a vocality as it literally speaks about Sandra to Gregory, telling him, "There is magic in her" (67). Moreover, Herrera-Sobek points out that "Sandra and nature will fuse in Gregory's mind: she will become an Anglo Coatlicue" (103), the Mexica goddess of life and death attributed with serpentine qualities, whose name indeed means "Serpent Skirt." She is the mother of Huitzilopochtli—the god of war, the hummingbird wizard (hence all the hummingbirds and butterflies surrounding Gregory and Sandra throughout the book), and the chief god of Tenochtitlán, which was the Mexica capital (conquered by a coalition of nearby tribal soldiers and a minority of Spanish military who were led by Cortés in 1521) and the site of modern Mexico City.

As Coatlicue's and Huitzilopochtli's stories appear so central to this novel, and to book 2 in particular, some examination and explanation of Huitzilopochtli's birth is appropriate. The story goes: One day, Coatlicue was sweeping out the temple on Coatepec, near the city of Tula. A feathered ball fell from the sky and brushed her breast (in some versions, she held it to her breast). She became pregnant, which was seen as scandalous to her children, the centzon huitznahua (the four hundred southerners). One daughter in particular, Coyolxauhqui (thought by some to represent the moon or the Milky Way), incited her siblings to kill their mother (Taube 47). When they arrived at the mountaintop to kill Coatlicue, Huitzilopochtli sprang "forth from his mother's womb full grown [and] dressed as a warrior" (Carrasco 75). He grabbed his weapon—xiuhcoatl, the fire or turquoise serpent (interpreted as a ray of the sun)—and beat back his siblings, chasing them down and killing them, decapitating Coyolxauhqui with one swing. Those of his brothers and sisters who escaped fled to the south; those who did not, turned into the stars. The Mexica explained their migration southward from Aztlán partially in terms of this story; they were forever chasing Coatlicue's and Huitzilopochtli's attackers. Moreover, Huitzilopochtli serves not only as a god but also as an ancestor—the Mexica are descendants of Huitzilopochtli.

Coatlique's maternal role correlates to Gregory's comment that he imagines Sandra giving birth to the world. He defines her predominantly in terms of her sexuality—describing her breasts, her thighs, her pubic hair. Within an ecologically minded literary criticism, Sandra's HIV-positive status presents an ominous foreboding, as do the facts that she (our earth mother figure) has already miscarried and that she is a hemophiliac (a striking detail in that women are overwhelmingly more likely to be asymptomatic carriers of hemophilia than symptomatically afflicted). *The Rag Doll Plagues* presents an earth mother, a goddess of life and death, who is incapable of reproduction, one who is potentially lethal for anyone attempting to reproduce with her, one who would likely pass on at least one of the diseases that is killing her to her progeny.[22] The earth, the tree (paired as it is with Sandra), Gregory's very roots have become diseased. What's more, if Sandra stands in for or indeed actually *becomes* Coatlicue, it is critical that she bears no young. Coatlicue's son is the god of Tenochtitlán, the capital of the Mexica empire—her infection would seem to unmake the city and its people.

This analysis of Coatlicue, Huitzilopochtli, and Mexico City leads us to look at the actual environment of Mexico City. I have already discussed the problems of Mexico City's descent into its own sewage. And since—like Southern California, in which the rest of the novel is set—it is surrounded by mountains and prone to inversion layers, especially in the summer, there is nowhere for the smog and ozone to go. Coatlicue's toxification does, then, parallel that of her offspring, Huitzilopochtli, the god of Tenochtitlán and Mexico City itself. We can extend this reading, in light of the geologic and textual associations between Mexico City and Los Angeles, to figure Sandra's death unmaking Aztlán, another religiously significant location similarly transformed into a smog-laden sprawl. In fact, Mike Davis draws a connection between Mexico City and Los Angeles, noting, "Only Mexico City has more completely toxified its natural setting, and no other metropolis in the industrialized Northern Hemisphere continues to grow at such breakneck speed" as Los Angeles (318). We note that Davis falls back on the nature/city binary here, but his comments about toxification especially apply to this chapter.

The fact that Sandra's infection, and its paralleling destruction of the goddess of life, represents an ecologically minded statement becomes clearer in book 3, when we learn where HIV and AIDS come from. That book's Gregory explains, "AIDS was caused by a polluted mutant gene that originally appeared in Pittsburgh, had been taken to Africa where it germinated into a stronger lethal virus, and finally had been returned to the United States" (160). Like the other plagues that occur throughout the novel, AIDS comes from pollution—presumably from industrial waste, given the fact that the origin lies within the United States and specifically in a traditionally industrial city: Pittsburgh, with its history of toxic industrial accidents, acid rain, cyanide in the Monongahela, and blood in the Allegheny. That this novel refigures the pathogenesis of the disease to make the point of origin the United States rather than some exoticized Africa serves to make this disease not only less foreign but also the direct responsibility of the United States. He continues, "AIDS, like cancer, was a deforming, hideous infection which slowly transformed the individual into a social pariah" (160). This transformation into a "social pariah" connects all the plagues in the text and ties the diseases to cultural toxins of exclusion and segregation. Finally, Gregory notes, "HIV-positive people were considered polluting factors and extremely dangerous" (160–61). Not only is this mistreatment of the diseased and the Other an act of exclusion; it also recalls miscegenation ideologies, as those with this metonymic disease are seen not only as polluted but polluting, as if active agents in the destruction of an otherwise pure society.

This novel also insists upon an ecological reading of the plagues themselves; plagues are, after all, life forms—usually defined as specifically viral or bacterial ones. This novel shows la mona to be a long-lived, if constantly mutating, entity. This mutation speaks to the evolutionary traits of all life forms but to microorganisms in particular, which adapt and change at stunning rates.[23] Despite the fact that book 2 ends with Sandra's death (while the other two end with bittersweet births—combinations of tears and births), this book shows a note of optimism and an ecologically evolutionary optimism. Señora Jane, who runs a hospital in Mexico City that Gregory and Sandra go to in hopes of treating Sandra's illness, tells Sandra not to fear her failing body. She says, "We see it as a modification. Your body is changing rapidly now. . . . Do not be ashamed of your decaying body. Decay is a natural process" (119).

Señora Jane's is a classic articulation of compost theology, which states that since we are composed of matter and energy and matter and energy are constants (because they are never destroyed, only transformed), death as we conceive it is an illusion. Thoreau is perhaps the most commonly cited example of a compost theologist. He writes, "We are cheered when we observe the vulture feeding on the carrion which disgusts and disheartens us and deriving health and strength from the repast" (339). The vulture—bald, smelly, a creature associated with a kind of opportunism we disparage in humanity—is an extremely positive image in compost theology. It eats death and makes life. Later authors known for their environmental awareness (Mary Austin, Robinson Jeffers, and Lew Welch, for example) take up this theme of carrion as life bearer. Señora Jane continues, "God and the energies of the earth are calling you to join them in their metamorphosis of all of us. I love you. I love your decay. I love your illness. I will marry you and love you to the last day. I will hold you in your putrefaction" (119). Morales's text recognizes that the interactions of the human and the other than human are not always pretty; this is not the pastoral or wilderness that the National Parks, for example, were set up to protect.[24] But it is real; death and decay happen. This novel implies that Sandra's disease is not to be feared; death is not to be feared. Both are merely liquid alterations that are part of the ecology of the world and, as such, are never to be viewed solely negatively.[25] Indeed, despite the fact that these plagues endanger human life, they are part of life and so, not really contamination or pollution at all, but mere transformation. This is perhaps the most idealistically ecologically grounded statement in this novel. After all, ecology does not privilege human life over viral life. Of course, this is not to assert that humans should not attempt to overcome illness, merely that our agonistic relationship to pathogens is nonetheless a relationship.

While disease indicates one of many degrees of human permeability in this novel, the suburbs serve (as in the Butler and Yamashita texts) as emblems of white disassociation from communities of color. Orange County is perhaps the model of suburbia in the United States. Irvine, certainly, has become the exemplar of master-planned communities, entire cities or sections of cities planned to the last yard, the last cul-de-sac, the last tree. Such planning contradicts the evolutionary and microbe-like processes by which most species propagate and migrate. Mike Davis has called southern Orange County (commonly delimited by area code 949, which includes Irvine), "an affluent version of architectural Stalinism" (12). The cities of the area have been built and maintained with the utmost of homogeneity in mind. They are, like the Valley of the parable texts, centers of white flight in Southern California, conservative in terms of their covenants, conditions, and restrictions (CC&RS) to the point of absurdity (as evidenced by Irvine's palette of acceptable housing colors that residents joke consists of one entry: Irvine beige). These are the suburban homes that Lefebvre says "come close to the lowest possible *threshold of sociability*—the point beyond which survival would be impossible because all social life would have disappeared" (316). Not only are these communities closed off to their surroundings; their very makeup allows for a minimum of human contact within their boundaries.[26]

While Orange County serves as an emblem of U.S. suburbanization, its largest and oldest city, Santa Ana, stands as its urban core, maintaining a sizable Chicana/o relationship to and presence in Orange County. David R. Diaz notes that between "1980 and 1990 the Chicana/o populace [of Santa Ana] increased by 111 percent and now constituted 65.1 percent of the city" (86). Morales represents this Chicana/o presence through the locus of Clemente's garden, which serves as an indigenous utopian (rather than heterotopian) image of abundant life. Rather than the garden representing a Judeo-Christian prelapsarian space, within *The Rag Doll Plagues* it serves as a location for Mexica continuance. We see images of abundance as Gregory states, "In Clemente's garden, as in my Mother's, there flew hundreds of butterflies and hummingbirds. The butterflies came and landed on our clothes and the hummingbirds orbited around us like spheres of color" (76). We can infer that this garden contains flowers, which provide food for both butterflies and hummingbirds and which are reproductive plant parts. This space then represents regeneration. But it is also not a rigidly defined place, as the butterflies and hummingbirds (also agents in plant reproduction) fly in and out, permeating or positively polluting the garden space. Diaz asserts, "Chicana/o urbanism's vibrancy is correlated to an eclectic reconstruction of space and the social functions of that space. *Jardins, patios,* and *salons* are the spatial zones that structure everyday life centered on an appreciation of social interaction" (16). However, we must not consider these species outside the Mexica traditions to which Morales takes pains to refer.

I have shown the relationship of hummingbirds to Huitzilopochtli, but it is also important to note that hummingbirds (family *Trochildae*) are, like the other species *The Rag Doll Plagues* portrays, endemic to the Americas. Again, Morales's text shows an awareness and responsibility to portray the species of these landscapes and ecosystems. Because they feed on flowers, they symbolize growth and (re)birth. However, these species are somewhat delicate, as they comprise the smallest bird family in the world. Despite this delicacy, though, Morales shows them to be resilient and likens that resilience to the Mexican people. Gregory says, "The Mexicans suffered the abuse, but because of the extreme spiritual strength, they have survived like the delicate butterfly or hummingbird" (181). The delicateness of the Mexican people, in Morales's text, speaks to what Villa calls their "second-order citizenship . . . compelled by a variety of legal and extralegal social processes that contributed to the 'racial formation' . . . of American society in which they were situated" (1). But it also speaks to a longer history of colonization dating back to Spain and, in the Mexica origin story, Huitzilopotchli's attackers, and hence agonistic indigenous relationships.

Like hummingbirds, jaguars represent a sacred tie to Mexica roots. There are two in this novel, both in book 2. The first is Sandra's car; the second is Clemente's pet. Gregory notes, "Clemente, an ancient man that we went to see, lived in an old dilapidated house. . . . He had a two hundred-pound jaguar as a pet. . . . Strange as it might seem, the City of Santa Ana did not disturb this kind and gentle beast" (76). While the jaguar (*Panthera onca*) is not indigenous to Southern California, it is indigenous to the tropics and semitropics of North and South America. All in all, the biological jaguar is a rather strange choice for this book—not fitting in the contemporary milieu as an indigenous species—unless we consider the implication of the jaguar within the framework of Mexica tradition. Morales's narrative naturalizes the presence of this great cat, especially in light of law enforcement's acceptance of it within the city limits.

Jaguar, the god of the underworld, moves between that world and this one in Mexica religion and plays a central role in human history and spiritual evolution (Taube 34). Like many indigenous religions, Mexica traditions hold that, as it is, the world is merely the most recent manifestation or incarnation of itself. The first era of the earth, or the first sun, is called 4 Jaguar (*Nahui Ocelotl*). During this period, people were giants who did not farm but only gathered food to eat. "This imperfect era ended when a jaguar devoured the giants" (Townsend 127). This devouring jaguar is the terrestrial form of Tezcatlipoca—Lord of the Smoking Mirror and "one of the four creator gods who ordered the cosmos" (Carrasco 88)—who "represents conflict and change" as well as death within Mexica tradition (Taube 31). Jaguar is a terrestrial god, whereas others are related to other elements such as wind or waters. Finally, Tezcatlipoca is also related to the north. Morales blends the ideas of creation, death, the earth, and the north as Sandra returns *al Norte* to die. Jaguar is a god of the dyad of creation and death and destruction, just as Sandra's disease becomes coded as destruction but also as a new form of being. So Clemente's garden serves as more than a pastoral place or an enclave in which to escape. It is instead a space steeped in Mexica religious imagery and tradition and in which Gregory and his family and community rekindle their ties not only to that tradition but to this space that serves as their collective emergence location (Aztlán, discussed below). Moreover, in connecting these images of life, death, and renewal, this garden reinforces cyclicality and compost theology into this narrative.

Gregory speaks, not only to animal species and corresponding ethereal entities, but also to geographic and geologic elements. For example, he describes himself dancing "by the little rivulet that meandered down to what was once my family's home, my *barrio*, Simons" (69). Gregory's sense of home goes beyond that of mere residence. Home, in this case, is less of a specific *place* and more of a *space*, a region, and, in truth, a bioregion (though the codification of one bioregion as distinct from another runs the risk of oversimplifying one space's interrelation to others near and far). More specifically, we see that Gregory identifies his notions of home to the path of this little rivulet. That this is a riparian water body speaks to the breadth of Gregory's sense of home. While Simons is no longer where his family lives, it remains his barrio. He goes on to call this region, "the real Aztlán, the origins of my Indian past" (71). Aztlán is the traditional Aztec place of origin, often conceived of within Chicana/o nationalism to be Southern California—or more generally the Southwest region of the United States, lost by Mexico under the Treaty of Guadalupe Hidalgo in 1848 following the expansionist Mexican-American War.[27] This reclamation invokes indigeneity to bind Chicanidad to local identity. This place is the traditional, if not the ancient, home of the Revueltas family (unlike the mostly recent immigrants to Southern Californian suburban spaces).

Many critics have noted the problems with the concept of Aztlán in Chicana/o discourse. Martín-Rodríguez, for example, notes, "Chicano/a nationalism (centered on the idea of Aztlán as the Chicano/a homeland) struggled to reterritorialize a deterritorialized people, but in doing so, it fixed that people in a static picture that suppressed or silenced most internal differences" (88). Villalobos adds, "Culturally, Morales . . . privileges the Aztec origins of Mexico, obliterating other indigenous groups such as the . . . Yaqui" (135). He calls this use of the Aztec a "false synecdoche" (135). Overuse of Mexica origins elides other Mexican tribal ethnicities. Moreover, claiming Aztlán within Southern California threatens claims of current indigenous populations (Kumeyaay, Tongva, Chumash, and many others) to the lands on which their people have dwelled for millennia and to which they claim a sacred, sovereign, and originary right.

Ultimately, Sandra becomes the hyperpermeable character for book 2 that Father Jude was for book 1. Gregory laments, "She became disease-prone. She seemed never to be free of viruses or bacteria. . . . Sandra was a hemophiliac and suffered from severe aplastic anemia, which caused her infections" (102). Her hemophilia is emblematic of an inability to stop herself, or at least her blood (a fluid that in many ways stands in for identity throughout this novel), from flowing outward.[28] Sandra's bleeding, once begun, cannot be stopped. The fact that she contracts AIDS expands this image of permeability. AIDS brings into vivid detail how our bodies are always being permeated with diseases, although they are diseases our bodies can ordinarily ward off. Sandra cannot stop what goes into or out of her body, just like Father Jude cannot create any kind of barrier between himself and the outside world. However, in Sandra's case, this permeability would seem to lead to her destruction, were it not for Señora Jane's earlier celebration of her transformation.

BOOK 3: LAMEX

Morales sets book 3, LAMEX, in "the Lamex Coastal Region of the Triple Alliance," a futuristic postnation comprised of Mexico, the United States, and Canada; its SF focus most directly mirrors those of the parable novels. The Gregory Revueltas of book 3 serves as the medical director of the "Lamex Health Corridor and a specialist in medical biological environmental genetics" (134). The Lamex corridor itself stretches from "the center of Mexico to the Pacific Coast" (134). López Lozano points out that the Triple Alliance is an early imagination of a post-NAFTA North America in which the flow of goods and people between these three nations has become so fluid as to enable, or indeed necessitate, a political marriage between them (60). These pollutions or permeations challenge static or rigid concepts of nations. But they seem less positive than some spatial liquidities we see in the texts of this study and more closely relate to those in *Tropic of Orange*. The term "Triple Alliance" has roots outside such European history as World War I. Rather, and more appropriately in this instance, "Triple Alliance" refers to a Mexica relationship between the cities of Tlacopan (on the western shore of Lake Texcoco), Tenochtitlán, and Texcoco (east of the lake and a little inland) (Townsend 26).

Of course, the marriage of North American nations to form the new Triple Alliance is not an easy one, and racialized and classed boundaries not only continue but in many cases worsen in this third book of the novel, particularly in terms of spatial segregation. The state locates its citizens based on class. Sites of homes and dwellings, so integral throughout this novel, become segregated into "concentrations" called

Higher-, Middle-, and Lower-Life Existences. The Lower-Life Existence concentrations, or LLES, are "built around old prison facilities." And we are told that "most of the population consisted of the Lumpen, the criminals and dregs of our society. The failure of our nation's penitentiaries to rehabilitate people had created a one hundred percent recidivism" (137). Morales's novel, rather tongue in cheek, casts forward the future of our contemporary prisons, which already partake in a racist and classist justice system, and imagines a future in which those castoffs of our society will always remain cast off, as will their children, a form of cross generational containment. Gregory continues, "The prisoners made the best out of a bad situation and encouraged their families to settle down outside the prison. . . . After ten years of blood riots and just before the formation of the Triple Alliance, our country designated the prisons as self-governing LLES" (137). In this forecast, Morales posits the continuation of the cycle of oppression and criminalization of poverty. Those born into this system of poverty and crime have no hope of overcoming it. The prisons morph into cities that remain, nonetheless, prisons.

Cultural critics including Angela Davis and Dylan Rodriguez examine the racialization of incarceration, advocating "penal abolition." Rodriguez observes, "Prison and penal abolition imply an analysis of society that illuminates the repressive logic, as well as the fascistic historical trajectory, of the prison's growth as a social and industrial institution" (Davis and Rodriguez). Similarly, Davis asserts, "We need to develop and popularize the kinds of analyses that explain why people of color predominate in prison populations throughout the world and how this structural racism is linked to the globalization of capital." The prison–industrial complex disproportionately incarcerates and targets members of marginalized groups, particularly people of color in the United States. Moreover, Rodriguez wonders, "Why have we come to associate community safety and personal security with the degree to which the state exercises violence through policing and criminal justice?" These longings for "community safety and personal security" mirror those of the suburban impulses present in book 2 of *The Rag Doll Plagues*, as well as those in the parable novels as seen in chapter 1, which hope to wall off regions and populations as irredeemable or unwelcome. A containment ideology prevails, calling for the portioning off of certain people in order to disavow them as actual members of the community. However, like the other books of the novel, this one examines the ways in which the people who are cast in such marginalized situations find to survive. By moving to these LLES, the families continue to live on. While the reader might want these LLES to revolt against the forces that relegate them to third-class citizenship, the novel insists on the importance of a communal survival that reclaims society's scraps. This novel advocates the politics of *rasquachismo*, the "practical inventiveness [often in artistic terms] motivated by limited material conditions," a practice akin to Certeau's poaching (Villa 165). Morales's narrative serves as a pepenador, seeking to reclaim the castoffs (the Lumpen) and create a vibrant society from what was thought to be garbage. The protagonists' name, Revueltas, in fact shows that the survival of Mexicanas/os and Chicanas/os *is* a kind of revolt, rather like the survivance we will see in chapter 5.[29]

Like book 1, book 3 begins with a description of an architectural feature, specifically a house "based on Southwestern architectural designs and constructed with mid-twentieth century adobe clay" and built in California's Hemet Valley by the narrator's grandfather Gregory (133). Gregory constructs this place, El Rancho de las Revueltas, as a pastoral haven (like the others we have seen) with "a small barn for a few horses, goats and chickens" and a well that "pumps precious clean water" (133). Morales immediately establishes the dystopic tone of this book by indicating the rarity of clean water: "From where in the bowels of the terrified earth the crystal clear liquid comes, only God knows" (133). The parched landscape of the Hemet Valley replaces the fruit trees of *Sower* and *Talents*. But even more telling is the characterization of the earth as "terrified." In book 2 the narrator describes the cypress as delicate and endangered; the narrator of book 3 seems to indicate the same is now true of the entire planet. As the book progresses, the reader quickly learns that is exactly the case.

Having already constructed Chicana/o belonging within the land of Southern California, it is no surprise that this novel correlates an endangered but surviving Mexicana/o and Chicana/o population within this endangered planet. At the end of book 3, Gregory discovers that Mexico City Mexicans (or MCMS) are immune to airborne toxin-induced respiratory diseases and that blood transfusions from them can cure the recipients. The novel imagines a world in which "one could find at least two Mexico City Mexicans—a female and a male—in every family" (199) and in which Mexicans "live in privileged enslavement for the remainder of their lives" (193). MCM blood is regularly harvested from blood farms, for sale to the rich. Critics are divided on whether Morales posits an essential Mexican identity here, and the emphasis on blood and blood quantum coupled with the liquid and diverse nature of Mexican identity certainly add to that ambivalence. Márquez, for example, argues that in the final section of the novel, "poverty, hunger, and crime have been eliminated and at least poetic justice has been achieved; Morales reverses history and inverts the geopolitical map" (83). But poverty has not been eliminated, as seen in the Lower Life Existences, in the Mexican families living in garbage dumps (as we will see), and in the fact that the European Americans are still the wealthy and that Mexicanas/os and Chicanas/os as well as Asian Americans remain poor. The map has changed, but poverty and the racialization of poverty remain. And with that racialized poverty continues the ecological injustice that has existed in the previous time periods.

We might also note that the abbreviation "MCM" can be interpreted in a number of ways. In biology, for example, McM stands for Mac-MARCKS,[30] an abundant macrophage (mø) involved in processes such as cell division, migration, and phagocytosis. That is, McM plays an integral role in the immune system, as phagocytosis involves the absorption of an antigen (a substance that causes one's immune system to produce antibodies) by the phagocyte and the subsequent destruction and expulsion of that antigen. Similarly, in this novel Mexico City Mexicans become agents of the elimination of toxicity from the body politic, by absorbing the hazardous cells and evacuating them. Also, because these proteins are involved in cell division, the metaphor expands to being one of replication and reproduction. Gregory makes many references to the Mexican population's growth compared to that of European Americans (a contemporary demographic reality) as well as to the biological naturalization of heterosexual reproduction (as we will see in more detail shortly). For example, he comments, "The Euroanglo population has continued to diminish and grow old while the Mexican population keeps getting larger" (199). MCMs become symbols of reproduction and, thus, of survival itself at the most basic level.

We can also take our interpretation of this abbreviation in quite a different direction, one of Marxist criticism. Herrera-Sobek points out that within this novel, "A critique of capitalism and the exploitation of the Mexican in the United States is intertwined with the ecological concerns related to pollutants, environmental contamination, and virulent epidemics" (106). Expanding on this critique of capitalism, one must recognize the similarity of the abbreviation MCM to Marx's concept of an M-C-M economy, in which money is converted into a certain commodity, which is then converted back into money. Marx sees this as an inversion of the "simplest form of the circulation of commodities," the C-M-C equation, in which commodities are changed into money and then back into commodities, or as Marx puts it, "selling in order to buy" (93). The M-C-M model is one of "buying in order to sell," participating in the capitalist process for the sake of further participation rather than for acquiring the goods and services one needs. In this equation the use value of an item is completely replaced by its exchange value. Marx sees this circuit of exchange as leading to even greater commodity fetishism (and ultimately money fetishism) and an increased abstraction of human labor and "Nature."

Reading Morales's abbreviation for Mexico City Mexicans in light of Marx's circuit of exchange, we see the wealthy purchasing Mexicans to breed as well as the creation of blood farms. While the MCMs have secured, in some instances, a higher life existence, they remain little more than commodities, beasts of burden whose sole purpose is the production of blood. Furthermore, MCM's "privileged enslavement" is rather clearly a reconfiguration of the Mexican body as the service foundation on which much of the U.S. economy is based. The agents of this labor become unimportant outside their task of production (a correlation we revisit in chapter 4). Vampiric wealthy families maintain a stock of MCMs for breeding and concern themselves with pedigree. It is not a stretch to liken this trade to that of farm animals and to follow this chain of signifiers back to contemporary agribusiness' reliance on Mexican (among other) labor as an exploitative venture.

Building on this interpretation of commodified humans, we can examine the role of Gabi, a cyborg doctor with whom Gregory works (as well as his romantic interest), whose worth is determined entirely by her use value as a medical service provider. Gregory states, "My personal guide and assistant in work and in life (there was no difference) was Gabi Chung" (135); and just so the reader doesn't get confused by the surname, Gregory refers to her "Asian face" (135). Gregory introduces Gabi as cyborg as he watches her "couple her robotic right arm into the electrical charger. Upon entering the car I had noticed the smell of burning flesh" (135). This smell of burning flesh follows Gabi around throughout the book and echoes the recurrent stenches of book 1.[31] This odor prefigures her ultimate suicide, but it also plays on the role of women as the sites of contagion that runs throughout this novel and much of European and European American literature (including that of Sandra in book 2). As López Lozano notes, "Gabi Chung's biomechanical hybridity creates additional problems and serves as a further demonstration of the futuristic society's lack of humanity" (65). Gabi is not an advancement but a retreat of human development; her altered body marks her as morally lacking. Stephen Hong Sohn works to redeem Gabi as a character, however, showing that she has limited options outside the stereotypical modes set out for her: the hypersexual Asian American, the model minority, and the neo–yellow peril. He argues, "Gabi's own position within the state is perilous, to pun if only briefly, because she is only a 'model,' a prototype if you will, useful as long as she possesses the capability of maximized efficiency granted to her through her computerized appendage."[32] Gabi's cyborg identity could be portrayed as a positive formation within *The Rag Doll Plagues*, but it is not.

This cyborg identity becomes a necessary tactic for human beings like Gabi as the "competition to accumulate knowledge into one brain and one body for immediate access had escalated for fifty years, since the world had turned against humanity" (136). This image of the dehumanized body reflects Hayles's expression of the posthuman mandate: "Humans can either go gently into that good night, joining the dinosaurs as a species that once ruled the earth but is now obsolete, or hang on for a while longer by becoming machines themselves" (*How We Became Posthuman* 283).

Moreover, Morales extends the fear of a toxified global ecosystem to include the cyborg, which is a necessary weapon in this battle with the planet yet not a positive advancement in human physiology. Instead of

showing it to be wondrous, for example, Gregory refers to Gabi's computerized arm as hideous (147). In contrast, Donna Haraway argues that
technology and cyborg identity (like Hayles's posthuman) allow open
spaces for blasphemy, irony (humor and serious play), and that we can
derive pleasure from this confusion of boundaries and responsibility
in their construction.[33] She privileges the cyborg, in part, because it is
postgender and has no origin story in European traditions; and she offers as the final line of her "A Cyborg Manifesto," "I would rather be a
cyborg than a goddess" (Haraway 181). Haraway shows the positive-pol-
lutive possibilities for cyborg identities, for women in particular, while
Morales focuses on the negative.

Ultimately, Gabi's body rejects the cybernetic arm, leading her, as a
now obsolete doctor and surgeon, to suicide by electrocution—death by
her excessive reliance on technology. She "took into her body a voltage
so great that her arms and legs popped open" (197). Gregory uses flowery
imagery in his discussion of this suicide, and Gabi's death and bursting
limbs quite clearly relate to the symptoms of la mona. He further ne-
gates the values of cyborg identity by invoking the guides of the past, asserting, "I would not allow myself to be carved up and shaped onto what
the Directorate considered a model optimum efficient doctor. Voices
from the past and present warned me not to allow them to *deconstruct
my humanity*" (143, emphasis mine). This alteration of the natural body
serves to destroy one's humanity, to "deconstruct" it. Gregory slips into
an idealization of a pure physical state devoid of human manipulation, a
rather paradoxical and ironic response from a doctor so consumed with
the task of altering bodies and blood and from a text that emphasizes
liquid identities and positive cultural, ethnic, racial, and gender pollutions throughout.

It is at this point that the essentialism that many sense in this text
but are unable to totally explain becomes most clearly stated. What is
essential and pure is not just the Mexican body or blood but the human body as a whole. Morales goes on to construct that pure human
body within a context of a naturalized, compulsory heterosexuality (also
ironic, considering the earlier role of La Monja Alférez and her liquid
gender ambiguity). Of the cure to the mutating la mona, Gregory says,
"The agent had gender and the transfusions could not be made from

male to male, nor female to female, but from male to female or female to male. Gender and sexuality allowed it to reproduce *naturally*" (168, emphasis mine). Natural sexuality here is heterosexuality;[34] the narrator privileges biological reproduction (i.e., reproduction coded within DNA) over reproduction coded as culture, which can be passed on through various discursive practices and techniques. That Mexican culture and history become carried in the physical blood of Mexicans indicates that the only method of conveyance of that culture is through heterosexual reproduction via procreation.

Although Gabi's portrayal as a cyborg falls well short of Haraway's goals, Morales posits a form of cyborg identity within this book that meets many, though certainly not all, of her objectives: computer ghosts. These computer ghosts "are individual human lives who have escaped the parameters of time and the limitations of the computers that house the detailed descriptions of history. Computer ghosts are not uncommon; but usually they are not as strong as these two colleagues of mine [Papá Damián and Grandfather Gregory]" (136). This infusion of the technological with the spiritual and physical relates directly to Haraway's description of cyborg identity as "a hybrid creature, composed of organism and machine. [They] are post–Second World War hybrid entities made of, first, ourselves and other organic creatures in our unchosen high-technological guise as information systems, texts, and ergonomically controlled labouring, desiring, and reproducing systems" (1). Gregory comments that his grandfather Gregory's "self-description, once computerized, was so intense that in hours he became a computer ghost and now appeared to assist and guide me through this world which I believed to be real" (141). Like Haraway, Morales indicates that it is possible for humans to move beyond the confines of biological death or socially constructed norms and rules. But rather than using these cyborgs as transgressive figures who serve to move us beyond gendered confines, Morales uses them to replicate ancestors and maintain biologically determined reproductive ancestral connections, especially masculine ones.

In contrast to the gloomy hemispheric forecast the bulk of book 3 offers, Gregory describes a community that grows around a shared existence between Chicanas/os and Asian Americans, as emblematized in the marriage of Ted Chen, a third generation Chinese American, and Amalia, "a native Mexican Californian" (148). Gregory explains, "In order to survive and coexist, the Mexicans and Asians united economically, politically, culturally and racially. The common cross-cultural, racial marriages were between Asians and Mexicans" (148). Ultimately, Ted and Amalia have a daughter who "represents the hope for the new millennium" (200). It seems odd that a child not born to MCMs would serve this role of hope for the future. She would not, one supposes, be born with the immunity required to stave off the rampant infections of this dystopic future. However, the likelihood of an MCM child possessing the mobility and opportunity to represent "the hope for the new millennium" seems slim considering their new roles as interned blood producers. We can read this child as a harbinger of changing times, much the same way Gregorio sees Mónica Marisela in book 1. While the child is not an MCM, she represents a continuing move away from singularity in racial identity and toward a community strengthened by hybridity.

The incarnation of la mona in book 3 is even more lethal than it has been throughout the novel. Our first encounter with the disease occurs as Gregory and Gabi approach one of the victims with the telltale symptoms: "She extended a grotesquely bruised hand. Her feet and legs appeared battered. To the touch, her limbs felt like balloons filled with liquid. The woman rolled to the side, made an effort to push herself up with her hands, which burst and discharged a fetid substance" (138). As in book 1, the narrator opts to describe the manifestations of the disease in gory detail. This serves to shock the reader, of course; but in this book the symptoms take on important meaning. This is the first time a narrator describes the limbs actually bursting; it seems the disease is getting worse. But we also see the fetid liquid emerging. This liquid is likely to carry the disease and thus shows la mona's method of contagion becoming more aggressive. It also shows that the victims are liquefying at a faster rate. We note the reiteration of concepts of liquidity increase in this book, just as the vehemence of governmental segregation increases. The emphasis on segregation and on fears of contagion cycle back to the segregation of book 1 but become amplified. The plague in book 3, named Blue Buster, runs its course in three to four days, versus the nine months of the earlier manifestations of la mona.

The root of these plagues also seems in keeping with book 1 in its relation to sewage, garbage, and general ecological toxification. Upon the appearance of this new plague, characters utter the following: "We've been hit by the living shit" and "It finally has happened. Our waste has turned against us" (150). The reader equates this idea of our waste turning against us with the aforementioned statement that the earth had turned against humanity. But here we also see the relation between human detritus and those cast-off and cast-aside members of society who end up dwelling either in the waste dumps of this and other novels I examine in this project or in the supertoxic spaces not officially designated as garbage dumps but clearly described as de facto disposal sites.[35]

This novel also utilizes a material discussion of Mexico City and its problems with air and water quality. Gregory notes, "As the population grew, the ecological balance of the city was destroyed, its public services overwhelmed and natural resources decimated. . . . I read in grandfather Gregory's books that the city was built on a lake and continued to sink for hundreds of years. Mexicans had lived contented in this quagmire for the last one hundred years" (163). All of this is true, of course, except perhaps for the idea of the contentment of the citizens of Mexico City. The city, like all megalopolises, is too large to be supported by the resources therein.[36] Gregory then refers to the air quality of Mexico City but presents a positive slant upon it: "Daily, a brownish haze covered the Valley of Mexico. This thick smog consisted of thousands of tons of metals, chemicals, bacteria and dirt so thick that it darkened the sky like mahogany. Nonetheless, the Mexicans had lived in this irreversibly polluted toxic air for more than a century. These conditions were responsible for the steady rise of human biological mutations" (163). Air quality is Mexico City's greatest ecological problem. Indeed, "About 52 percent of [children in Mexico City demonstrate] an abnormal amount of interstitial markings in their lungs, changes that may be predictive of future lung abnormalities" (Lang). The air of Mexico's capital city is literally, if slowly, killing its children and negatively impacting their health over their lifetimes.

Of course, a city of this size and with such a large population is bound to produce tons of waste, and this novel continues to show its concern over that physical waste and the people who will live in and with it.

Gregory laments, "Worst of all was the horrid smell of dried excrement and bacteria that the northeast winds brought to cover the valley with an inch or more of virulent dust" (163). This "horrid smell" blows in from the direction of the aptly named El Pepenador, one of the "garbage colonies, where millions of people scavenged and lived off the salvageable waste" (164). Néstor García Canclini calls such activity (which I have already discussed in terms of rasquachismo) "cultural reconversion," as subaltern groups reclaim and reuse objects and circumvent the mediation of the state (López Lozano 40). Gregory later states, "That night I found myself wrapped in a wonderfully baroque cover made from a multitude of colorful waste materials" (168). This cultural reconversion, the rasquache art of the pepenador, is the same form of recycling we see throughout this project. It is a way of taking the things that other people claim are without value and putting them to use, an inversion of the model that privileges exchange value over use value, a reclamation and empowerment that works outside the system; and it is implemented by castoffs dwelling amid that which is cast off. Of the children of El Pepenador, Gregory states, "If they lived beyond nine months to a year in the severely polluted environment of El Pepenador, survival was ninety percent certain" (164). This Darwinian struggle in El Pepenador is one source of the immunity of MCMS. MCMS, and metonymically all Mexicana/o and Chicana/o people, demonstrate a similar survivability. Having endured ecological and social toxins since at least Spanish colonialism, they now appear capable of overcoming anything and outlasting everyone.

In weaving Mexica traditions into this modern narrative, *The Rag Doll Plagues* reinforces a somewhat laudable connection to an indigenous and precontact history within Chicana/o heritage. Although this connection can be troubling (as discussed earlier), this text's narrators use it to illustrate the existence of a community across time as well as space. In Morales's reclamation of this community, this novel posits the pepenador as a key image to Chicana/o identity, all the while emphasizing the fluidity of all identities. It praises figures who will sort through and find the innate value of, by recasting and reusing, the objects and traditions that others have left behind.

3

RIDDING THE WORLD OF WASTE

LOUISE ERDRICH'S *THE ANTELOPE WIFE*

I'm an Indian with a buzz cut now. . . . Plain living. Hard work. The simple life, unadorned, ridding the world of waste. "People You Can Count On." Our motto in garbage management. My belief.
LOUISE ERDRICH, *The Antelope Wife*

Ojibwa sanitation engineer Klaus Shawano, one of the many narrators of Louise Erdrich's 1998 novel *The Antelope Wife*, embraces his role in the business that he and his on-again, off-again friend Richard Whiteheart Beads have founded.[1] Within this novel, the focus on garbage rests primarily on these two central figures.[2] However, Erdrich extends her portrayal of waste, excess, toxicity, and pollution, through her use of these two men as foils for a number of other characters. In so doing, she discusses the changing conditions of American Indian people; their relationships to all people, the nonhuman, and supernatural worlds around them; as well as changing cultural and financial patterns within Indian communities. *The Antelope Wife* addresses and comments on the most prescient issues in Indian country today, including environmental justice and urban Indian identities. Ultimately, Erdrich offers an adolescent young woman, Cally, as a contrast to Richard and Klaus. Like Mónica Marisela, Ted and Amalia Chen's child in *The Rag Doll Plagues*, Cally emblematizes the hope for (in this case, Native) success in the cities and the end of a centuries-old curse on the interrelated Shawano, Roy, and Whiteheart Beads families. Finally, Erdrich's use of multiple narrators in this novel, as in much of her work, serves to place the reader within a space of liquid and shifting identities and histories and, like Butler's multiple narrators in *Talents*, positively pollutes singular or absolute narrative power. I have divided this chapter into two main sections. The first examines the specific correlations between members of the Roy, Shawano, and Whiteheart Beads families and waste, toxicity, and positive pollution; the second details the hope for the urban community represented in this novel as well as the permeability of identity as presented in its characters.

SECTION 1: THE ROY, SHAWANO, AND WHITEHEART BEADS FAMILY

The Antelope Wife details the connection between the Roy and Shawano families, which serves as a microcosm of vast matrices of human interminglings that can become impossible to separate from one another. In the case of this novel, these interminglings become obvious a century in the past, when Private Scranton Teodorus Roy of the U.S. Cavalry takes part in "a spectacular cruel raid upon an isolated Ojibwa village *mistaken* for hostile" (3, emphasis mine). The fact that this raid is a mistake, that the killings that occur are taken out of the realm of warfare and placed within that of murder and cruelty, matters a great deal as the narrative unfolds. Scranton Roy bayonets "an old woman who set upon him with no other weapon but a stone picked from the ground" (4). As he kills the woman (who turns out to be the mother of Midass, the matriarch of what will become the Roy and Shawano families), she says, "Daashkikaa" (4). The reader encounters this word on the third page of text, but it is not defined for another two hundred. The term, it turns out, is an old name that means, "cracked apart" (213). In *The Antelope Wife*, this name speaks to things being broken or out of balance. When read along with the strains of ecological community within this novel, the theme of being out of balance takes on a deeper meaning than a dying woman finding her mortal wounding to be a mistake (which, of course, it is). The word, the name, speaks to the state of the world, to Ojibwa culture seeming to be cracked apart, the human and other-than-human (including the divine) orders appearing cracked apart, the families and clans being cracked apart, though they are certainly not destroyed. Similarly, these connections and orders have never been static but always in the process of being re-formed. Instead, we note that these patterns are irrevocably altered; but as we will see as the novel progresses, alteration should not be read as a tragic end. This alteration may seem like destruction, but the characters of this novel constantly take broken pieces, fragments, and ingredients to combine them into new wholes that are no less authentic or important than those predating contact (which themselves were never static or unchanging). Indeed, these new wholes reassert the preexisting connections between the elements that comprise them. The dying grandmother also speaks a curse upon the man responsible for her death. He will be cracked apart (he removes the bayonet and begins to run, deserting the U.S. military and turning his back on his entire life in the process), as will the lives of his descendants. The novel then moves into the present, discussing the complex web of family that stems from the earlier interaction of Scranton Roy and the Ojibwa village. Specifically, it focuses on the thoroughly interconnected Roys, Rozin and her daughter Cally (as well as Cally's grandmothers Mary and Zosie); the Shawano brothers, Klaus and Frank—who eventually weds Rozin; and Rozin's first husband and Klaus's one-time business partner, Richard Whiteheart Beads.

The Antelope Wife establishes its focus on an urban Indian community immediately following the section about Scranton Roy. This focus challenges mainstream assumptions about static Indian identities, ones that imagine Native people relegated either to the past or to rural containment sites called reservations. The reader quickly encounters Klaus Shawano, and it is through him that the novel introduces the eponymous character, the Antelope Wife (also known as Sweetheart Calico). In this very early moment, Klaus both establishes a distinction between woods and plains Indians (challenging pan-Indian categories) and speaks a word for the city and for urban Indians as potentially healthy. He notes, "I used to make the circuit as a trader at the western powwows, though I am an urban Indian myself, a sanitation engineer" (21). Klaus offers a number of categorizations here that he believes conflict one another. Klaus's first distinction is between western Indians (or at least those who frequent western powwows) and urban Indians. He contrasts Minneapolis to big sky country. Klaus sees these two settings as fundamentally distinct throughout this text. He continues, describing his home, "Minneapolis, Gakahbekong we call it, where everything is set out clear in lines and neatly labeled, where you can hide from the great sky, forget" (25).

The second distinction Klaus draws, though this one is more implicit, is between those same western Indians and himself as a sanitation engineer; a part of the contrast seems to be Klaus's ability or willingness to work in waste removal or treatment. His employment in waste disposal, however, does not preclude him from questioning the alarming production of waste within contemporary societies. He notes of Native people, "We mill around. We eat more. Used to be us Indians had nothing to throw away—we used it all up to the last scrap. Now we have a lot of casino trash, of course, and used diapers, disposable and yet eternal, like the rest of the country. Keep this up and we'll all one day be a landfill of diapers, living as adults right on top of our own baby shit. Makes sense in some way. Makes sense to me" (44). Klaus speaks to the negative aspects of wealth, especially in terms of the changing economic realities for many Native people, drawing on the prevailing idyllic notion that Indians never wasted any part of any animal (though he couches it in terms of never having *had* anything to throw away). Klaus points out that waste comes with material excess. When we have more than we need, we tend to cast away the objects deemed to be lesser. But of particular interest are the two types of excess and waste that Klaus names. The first is casino trash, though he never specifies what, exactly, comprises this detrital genre. We can infer the general trash that accompanies any large-scale entertainment center: leftover food, cleaning supplies, napkins, paper and plastic cups, cigarette butts, and the like. Mainly these stem from the sheer number of visitors to the reservation and the amount of waste they leave as vacationers not necessarily concerned with the status of the attraction after their departure (seeing it as distinct from themselves or their homes). I would also argue that "casino trash" refers to the less than desirable human elements that often surround gambling in contemporary U.S. life, addicted gamblers as well as organized crime.[3] If this is the case, it may also refer to the individuals who become overwhelmed with greed as relates to the money to be made from tribal gaming. These people, then, become "casino trash."[4]

But the casino trash in the above excerpt is mentioned in passing;

more interesting to Klaus are the "used diapers." Like *The Rag Doll Plagues*'s Gregorios, this narrator shows the connection between humans and the fecal detritus piling up around us. This is not the waste these characters have inherited from generations that have come before them; neither is it the waste that has trickled down from dominant society onto Native peoples. In this case, it is their own and that of their progeny. As such, this waste is their own responsibility. Klaus notes that this simply "makes sense" to him. After all, we cannot distinguish ourselves from our future generations or our waste—these things we make are part of us. The diapers we use, called "disposable," are, as Klaus points out, nothing close to biodegradable. They are, in fact, the third most common waste product found in U.S. landfills and are estimated to take five hundred years to decompose (Beil). Klaus calls them "disposable and yet eternal, like the rest of the country." The United States, then, becomes the avatar of the disposability—which is not really disposability, or at least does not imply disappearance—that has overtaken Indian lands. The problem, Klaus suggests, is that Indian country is becoming a little too much like the rest of the country. The diapers emphasize the myth of ephemerality—the truth is that any attempt to simply discard any thing (as we have seen again and again) opposes the fundamental truth that we live with our cast-off objects and communities for far longer than the discarders would like to believe. Finally, Klaus notes, "We'll be a landfill of diapers." Klaus likens *we*, Indian selves, to a landfill. Native Americans will become the very emblems of excess and waste, of misuse and overspending.

Statements like Klaus's counter essentialist notions of ecopiety; this novel refuses to show Native people as any more ideologically or ecologically pure than anyone else. Nonetheless, his narrative does lament contemporary Indian ecological shortsightedness. However, Klaus also points out that the bulk of the waste that his and Richard's business processes does not come from Native communities, casinos, or reservations. He explains, "Our main business is that we deal with other people's garbage. We're now the first Native-owned waste disposal company in the whole U.S. and proud of it. Proud of our management expertise and good old-fashioned ability to haul shit. Not to mention stabilize it. That's the real question" (44). Klaus focuses again on the fecal aspects of waste removal, and this is one of the few instances in which the exact nature of Klaus and Richard's "trash collection concern" is addressed (43). The most visible part of their business is hauling shit. Certainly this is not the most glamorous job in the world, though we can all agree it is a critical one. But the metaphor here needs unpacking as this passage has not been examined by critics. These Ojibwa men are, in effect, dealing with the United States' shit. To some degree, this image could be considered a case of Native people being the unwitting victims of environmental racism and injustice. But Klaus and Richard see an opportunity to take advantage of, if not entirely invert, this top-down fecal structure. Rather than Native people being dumped on by the United States, these Indian men are charging that nation to deal with its shit for it. We can read this work as serving in a domestic capacity, certainly, as people of color are once again charged with cleaning up after a predominantly white society. But this is an Indian-owned operation; Native people are profiting economically from this exchange. What's more, this company is recognized for its ability to "stabilize" the toxic human waste. That is, they are not merely releasing sludge into an aquifer (as we will see in chapter 5), but they are also not the reactive recipients of waste like the people of El Pepenador in *The Rag Doll Plagues*. Instead, they are proactive, taking advantage of a societal niche that needs filling, profiting from it, *and* doing so in a manner that appears, or that Klaus at least believes, to be socially and ecologically responsible.

Erdrich's focus on the future within this novel comes in her consideration of other socially pressing concerns such as responsibility, connection, and permeability. Characters learn that their actions carry certain tangible repercussions and that they must behave as though they are members of a broad community. One example comes as Klaus talks to Jimmy Badger, who admonishes Klaus to return the Antelope Wife to her people. Jimmy tells Klaus, "Our luck is changing. Our houses caved in with the winter's snow and our work is going for grabs. Nobody's stopping at the gas pump. Bring her back to us! . . . There's misery in the air. Fish are mushy inside—some disease" (33). These negative material events are the consequences of Klaus's selfishness. A whole community suffers, a community comprised not only of people and their homes and businesses but of the creatures of the water that become toxic with a disease that affects them to their very cores, which become liquefied.

However, while Klaus shows some concern about ecological balance, Richard lies further still from the ecological steward of environmentalist stereotypes. As Julie Tharp points out, Erdrich's portrayal of Richard "deals a deathblow to the environmentalist romantic fantasy about Native Americans" (124). We learn, for example, that Richard "dumped toxic waste way back when. Took the payoff. Used the money" (205). Not only does he illegally dispose of waste, presumably on tribal land, but he also uses the money for himself, instead of sharing it. He poisons the land without regard for it or for the other life on it. This is the kind of selfishness that the reader comes to expect from Richard; and like many of the characters in this novel, his selfishness is his tragic and toxic flaw. Along these lines, Tharp notes, "As a product of the city and reservation corruption, Richard typifies the larger harm done to Native people through their assimilation into European-American culture" (126). And while Richard emblematizes a certain corruption, to be sure, I am unconvinced that Tharp's assertion as to the cause of that corruption is accurate. If Richard represents the windigo, as Tharp (rightly and insightfully) argues he does, then at least a part of his character stems from precontact traditions.

The windigo is defined in *The Antelope Wife* as a "bad spirit of hunger and not just normal hunger but out-of-control hunger. Hunger of impossible devouring. Utter animal hunger that did not care whether you were sober or brave" (127). One version of an Ojibwa windigo story begins as a skilled and successful hunter goes out during an especially long and cold winter to find food. However, game grows more and more scarce, and the hunter struggles to find enough to feed his family, which has taken to subsisting on boiled tree bark and what few roots they can find. The hunter comes to a village, reconnoitering it from the tree line. By some turn of events (in some versions he is cursed by dark magic; in others he simply goes mad from isolation and hunger), he sees the people of the village transform into beavers. The hunter, not questioning what he perceives to be his good fortune, slaughters all the beavers and sits down to gorge himself on their flesh, saving none to bring home to his family. These are the hunter's great sins: his cannibalism and his failure to provide for his kin and community. From this point on, the hunter craves human flesh, transforming into a monstrous embodiment. This story serves as a cautionary tale about greed, obsession, and excess. With that in mind, I argue that Richard may not have become corrupt because of his contact with white people. Greed did not only arrive in the Americas with Europeans. If it had, then the cautionary tales of the toxic windigo would have been unnecessary. Throughout this novel, multiple characters take on windigo-like characteristics in terms of their refusal to acknowledge their responsibilities to the broad communities of which they are part.

The Antelope Wife demonstrates that those who engage in toxic lifestyles invariably damage the lives that intersect and interpenetrate with theirs, especially, though not surprisingly, those closest to them. By another act of selfish poisoning, Richard inadvertently kills his own daughter, Deanna (one of the many twins who dot the landscape of this novel). Faced with Rozin's infidelity and her decision to leave him, Richard decides to kill himself by carbon monoxide inhalation. But after he has started his truck in the garage, he longs for a glass of whiskey (this novel also portrays alcohol as generally toxic); while he is inside, Deanna hides in the back of the truck cab. Richard proceeds to lock himself out of the garage. Rather than break in or find another key, he decides, "Let the shit come down. Let the truck run out of gas. Let it go. Let the truck run all night" (71). Deanna's death, poisoned in the back of Richard's truck, then, is the result of his failure to poison himself properly. He realizes, ironically, that he "will always be a father" (70) and that leaving his daughters without a father is unacceptable. He concludes, "He seems too much trouble, even to himself, to kill" (71). Richard's penchant for toxicity not only affects some seemingly vague, broad environmental safety and health issue, one which will be especially felt in future generations; he also kills children right now, today. Erdrich makes a statement about the inherently suicidal aspects of toxicity: even if we realize that it is wrong to poison ourselves, especially because of our children and their futures, we may have already done such damage that their health may be compromised.

Richard's toxicity likewise spreads to his ex-wife, Rozin, as she realizes, during the events surrounding her and Frank's wedding, that she and Richard are and will forever be inexorably enmeshed, comprised of one another. In the hustle and bustle preceding the ceremony, Rozin receives a letter from Richard. Recognizing his toxic nature, "Rozin ripped [it] open with an air of contempt and read [it] holding the edges as though the paper was coated with a dangerous virus" (174). To some degree, everything that Richard touches becomes infectious with poison, guilt, and failure. In this letter, Richard falsely claims to have poisoned the wedding cake Frank has prepared for his and Rozin's wedding. Richard's windigo ways will not allow him to let go of his former wife or accept that she has moved on. But this poisoning goes beyond idle threats in this world. The death that accompanies Richard throughout his troubled time on this earth seeps into Rozin's life.

The liquid seepings between Rozin and Richard do not even end with his death. If anything, they grow more apparent. Richard finds Rozin and Frank's honeymoon suite; knocks on the door; and when Rozin opens the door, shoots himself. Rozin attempts to stop him, lunging to grab the gun. As she lands on him, memories "flood . . . into her," memories of their lovemaking and the "the whole unread substance of his love pour[ing] into her, bloody and pure" (180). This passage speaks, of course, to an exchange of bodily fluids during sex, but also to the joining of selves in moments of intimacy. This is not to say, however, Rozin's and Richard's blending ends at the moment of his death. If anything, the two become even more permeable to one another, and in ways that invert the image of woman as penetrated body.

Rozin receives a visit from Richard's apparition after his death. She realizes, "Death has hollowed and scoured him out inside so that there is room . . . for her to enter" (189). Rozin enters Richard and spends a week recognizing that "Richard is knit so far into her that she is the only person alive who can keep him alive and keep him safe" (193). It is not that Richard has penetrated her, physically and spiritually, but that they have penetrated and fused with one another. This fusion is not only about sex but about relationships more generally. We blend with those with whom we share our time: family (chosen or otherwise), friends, lovers, as with all the forces in our lives. When they pass, we carry them within ourselves. In this way, our communities perpetuate themselves, not only in terms of the many but in terms of the single self, which is, in fact, never singular. Ultimately, Erdrich points out that each of us houses those who have influenced our lives. We carry them within us; and in order to do away with them, we would have to destroy ourselves.[5]

These former spouses continue to be intertwined, as Rozin makes use of ecological images for her connections to Richard long after his death. Rozin tells Frank that "she sometimes thinks of herself as an unwitting host and of Richard's personality as something like kudzu or zebra mussels or wild cucumber, a weed that advances daily or a sea lamprey, so that if she wants to purge herself of him she must poison the waters" (192). Erdrich's choice of similes within this passage relates very closely to the ecological issues of balance that thread through the novel. Her first example, kudzu (*Pueraria montana*) is a Japanese climbing vine, introduced to the United States in 1876, and is also known as "the vine that ate the South." This plant can grow up to a foot per day and is known to cover houses, barns, tractors, cars, road signs, and even whole forests, smothering them beneath its weight and the shade of its leaves. Most pesticides prove ineffectual in killing this invasive plant, and grazing can only keep it somewhat at bay. Similarly, wild cucumber (*Echinocystis lobata*) is a climbing, smothering vine, though it is found primarily throughout northeastern Minnesota. This plant is also known as "man root," because its root can weigh up to one hundred pounds. Like kudzu, the only pesticides that seem capable of killing this plant also kill everything else around it; they toxify the soil itself.

Erdrich also selects a pair of water-dwelling species for this analogy: the zebra mussel and the sea lamprey. Like kudzu, each of these species is nonendemic to the inland waterways of North America, though they have found their way to those waters and caused considerable damage to the preexisting species and ecosystems within them. Zebra mussels (*Dreissena polymorpha*) were transported to the Great Lakes sometime around 1988 in ballast water from ships from the Caspian Sea. These bivalves filter out nearly all the phytoplankton from their lakes and rivers, starving native species from the smallest to the largest. These species are also known as biomagnifiers or bioaccumulators, because they ingest and concentrate sublethal toxins in their bodies before excreting them into their aquifers or being eaten by other animals. Sea lampreys (*Petromyzon marinus*) are eel-like parasitic fish, native to the coastal regions on both sides of the Atlantic Ocean. However, they have found their way into the Great Lakes via the Welland Canal, built in 1921. These fish prove especially dangerous to trout and whitefish populations and, as such, to the fishing economies of the Great Lakes. Unlike native lampreys, which are established members of these waterways, these endanger preexisting populations. Various methods have been attempted to destroy or decrease in number these invasive species, but the only successful methods (chlorine, for example) also destroy the endemic species at the same time.

Within these images, we see a complex series of metaphors of invasive native, seminative, and nonnative plants and animals. Some smother from sheer biomass, from their comparative number of organisms. Others are greedy eaters, taking food from the endemic species of their new ecosystems. Still others are parasites. All, I argue, are nonhuman windigo figures. As Rozin relates these images to Richard, she realizes that in order to do away with his presence, she will have to do away with herself. But we can extend Erdrich's use of native and nonnative plants to Native and non-Native peoples. The implication is that just as these ecosystems must evolve in relation to these introduced and, to some degree, highly destructive species, so must Native people continue to adapt to the ongoing contemporary occupation of the Americas by the non-Native governments and inhabitants of settler colonialism. Indeed, we must also recognize that some of the destructive elements within our landscape are indigenous species (like the wild cucumber) and indigenous individuals (like Richard). The invasive elements do not have sole claim to destruction and imbalance. These species, individuals, and elements cannot simply be plucked out of the ground; they are already enmeshed and can be treated, worked with, worked around, and even overcome. But while some elements may be eliminated, remnants and effects of their presence will always remain. If we pretend otherwise, we deny our own complexities and attempt falsely to contain and refuse elements seen as contaminants to an otherwise pure identity.

Klaus extends Rozin's comparisons of Richard as toxic. While traveling in Hawaii (a U.S. state with a distinct settler colonial history), Klaus is accosted by federal agents, who have mistaken him for Richard and seek to question him for environmental crimes. Klaus vows to roll over on Richard, asserting, "I'll rat, I'll speak. Things get dumped, terrible poisons in endless old wells. Nothing's endless, though. Every place has limits. Everybody. Toxins. Resins. Old batteries. Lead. Mercury. And Whiteheart. And Whiteheart" (50). Richard's name is included, indeed emphasized by repetition, in the list of toxins that destroy ecosystems, that test the limits of an ecosystem's ability to mend itself. The list begins with elements that do not biodegrade and that seep into groundwater supplies. That is, like the other toxins examined in this project, they are neither locally nor temporally bound. They remain and they work their ways into the aquifer to be carried around the world. The heavy metals listed are particularly relevant in terms of warnings about their presence in fish. These toxins serve as microcosmic of the concept of the inter-connection of species as they are absorbed by plant species, which are eaten by bottom-feeding fish species (which, like zebra mussels, are also bioaccumulators), which are then eaten by larger fish species. The heavy metals accumulate and, when eaten by humans or other animal species, can cause a host of health concerns, including birth defects, cancer, and intestinal and kidney disorders. Yet it is not Richard's first name that Klaus summons for this list, but his last, his surname, his *family* name. Richard's toxicity is not just in his business dealings or just in the fact of his caustic personality but based on the curse that simultaneously binds and cracks apart the Shawano and Roy family.

In fact, Richard's very name invokes images of the kinds of greed this novel avers lead to toxic relationalites. His family derives its name from "the ruby red whiteheart beads," which "were hard to get and expensive, because their clear cranberry depth was attained only by the addition, to the liquid glass, of twenty-four-carat gold" (183). Richard's name con-jures a certain lust for this precious metal, Marx's universal equivalent form. Within an indigenous context, this lust invokes the history of gold as a motivating factor for the conquest and, when read alongside Klaus's admonition of "casino trash," also suggests greed among Native peoples and contemporary money grabs that are seen as destructive to tribal identities and continuance. These bouts of greed—generated at least in part by centuries of economic marginalization, creating the conditions in which financial windigos are likely to be born—have led to an increas-ing reliance on blood quantum as the single most important method for identifying Indianness and for the practice of detribing or disenroll-ment, in which individuals are removed from tribal registers and en-rollment because of changing blood quantum requirements (thus de-creasing the number of pieces into which profits are cut), or simply for voicing opposition to tribal leadership and government.[6] Such methods rely on the cultural toxin of purity discourse we have seen throughout this project. These exclusionary practices can be seen as self-sabotage by Native nations, however, as decreasing numbers can adversely affect political efficacy and future survival.

Not all toxicity within this novel stems from these forces of greed or possessiveness—indeed, not all toxicity stems from personal dysfunc-tion. Frank's toxicity, for example, comes from a combination of cancer, a cellular mutation that can kill the body, and chemotherapeutic agents applied to kill that cancer. Richard comments, "Frank Shawano is a man shot through with cancer killing chemicals, hanging on by sheer terror, by the tips of his nails, a man doomed" (64). Cancer is a disease that the body makes, often as the result of exposure to genetically toxic chemi-cals. The chemicals we use to treat it are also toxic. Frank's body, then, becomes a battleground of toxic agents, being carefully controlled and manipulated in order to preserve his life.

Ultimately, Frank survives his bout with cancer, albeit in a partial sort of way. Cally observes that Frank has changed, that some part of him seems to have died. She notes that Frank "used to be ironic and jolly, always with a sly humor and a broad goofiness we kids loved, until he had the radiation treatments. From what I understand, the rays killed the tumor and also zapped his funny bone. . . . He lost an Indian's sev-enth sense. He lost his sense of humor. Now he is the only Indian alive without one. . . . It is a terrible burden" (114–15).[7] Erdrich is playing, ap-propriately enough, with notions of Indian humor as discussed by Vine Deloria Jr. (Standing Rock Sioux), Kenneth Lincoln, and Gerald Vizenor, among others. Deloria notes, "Humor, all Indians will agree, is the ce-ment by which the . . . Indian movement is held together. When a people can laugh at themselves and laugh at others and hold all aspects of life together without letting anybody drive them to extremes, then it seems to me that that people can survive" ("Indian Humor" 53). Moreover, Deloria wonders "how anything is accomplished by Indians because of the apparent overemphasis on humor within the Indian world" (39). Erdrich's portrait of Frank, though, is quite the opposite of Deloria's portrait of Native humor. Indeed, Frank focuses primarily on accomplishing things: baking, timing recipes, running his shop. However, Frank has forgotten how to laugh, though it is supposed to be an autonomic response and one that Native people privilege a great deal. This lack of humor could be seen to make Frank no longer Indian, but his condition is temporary and ultimately cured in a moment of ribald comic embarrassment.[8]

But while Frank is to some degree temporarily toxic, his brother Klaus is infinitely more so. The windigo dog, who narrates several sections of the novel, says at one point to Klaus, "You are the most screwed-up, sad, fucked-in-the-face, toxic, scwaybee, irredeemable drunk I've talked to yet today" (126). Of course, windigos are not exactly to be trusted; they are less than reliable narrators. When he calls Klaus "irredeemable," we needn't believe him. Indeed, we see that Klaus is redeemed eventually and saved by the same windigo dog. But in the meantime, Klaus serves as an image of Native alcoholism.[9] Philip A. May notes that "17.0 percent to 19.0 percent of all Indian deaths are probably alcohol related . . . —substantially greater than the general U.S. average of 4.7 percent" (228). However, he likewise notes that these figures vary tremendously from community to community, family to family. This point is critical to note in order to both acknowledge alcoholism as a physically and culturally toxic threat to Native people and communities and to counter the culturally toxic stereotype of all Indian people as alcoholic—or genetically predisposed to alcoholism. Moreover, rather than only examining Klaus's failings and disease, Erdrich focuses a great deal of attention on his redemption and healing. In so doing, this passage not only reexamines the drunken-Indian stereotype; it also complicates the static binary between the healthy and the sick, the polluted and the pure, showing instead the liquid natures of these dualisms. Klaus fluctuates back and forth between these poles, eventually regaining a balance he has struggled to find.

Erdrich demonstrates parallels between certain specific environmental justice concerns and Klaus's worldly struggles during this, his lowest period (one of homelessness, loneliness, and alcoholism). She portrays

Klaus constantly calling for water, *Nibi* in Anishinaabemowin. He even says of himself, again and again, "I'm sick" (94). And Klaus *is* sick, addicted, toxified, diseased, crazy, selfish, jealous, and dehydrated. As he tries to quench his thirst, he begins to drink directly from the river. But Richard notes that the water he seeks, the attempt to dilute the toxins in his body, to bring something pure back into himself, is also just as poisonous as the alcohol he drinks. He says, for example, "That's Prairie Island nuclear water" (97), referring to the nuclear power plant that borders the Mdewakanton Dakota reservation in Red Wing, Minnesota. There have been ongoing conflicts between the tribal community and the Northern States Power Company (and its later manifestation Xcel Energy) about the storage of solid nuclear waste within close proximity (six hundred yards) of residential areas of the reservation. Erdrich relates real issues of environmental justice—which affect many Native communities, reservations, and nations—to the characters of her novel. But Richard rightly points out that Prairie Island is "down the stream farther" (97). Trying to determine how the water might be polluted, Richard quips, "Some beaver might have pissed up near Itasca." Richard complicates ideas of purity and pollution, as excreted elements of endemic species are shown to be toxic and even correlated to nuclear waste. Noticing that Klaus won't stop drinking, Richard continues, "For sure, . . . they dump the beef-house scraps in it up at Little Falls" (98). Little Falls, Minnesota, apart from being Charles Lindbergh's childhood home, is one of many towns with slaughterhouses alongside the Mississippi River's headwaters in Minnesota. Factory farming and slaughterhouses are known to release waste and offal with such food-borne pathogens as E. coli (*Escherichia coli*) and salmonella. Placing such sites along the largest river in the country invites toxic events.

Klaus's repetitious calls for water also indicate a recognition of his need to be cleansed. *Nibi*, within Midewiwin traditions, "represents the life blood of Mother Earth that purifies and gives life to our bodies" (Benton-Benai 70).[10] The fact that Klaus calls out for water in Anishinaabemowin, when the rest of his dialogue is in English, emphasizes the centrality of this moment. At this point, Klaus becomes traditional, returning to a Native healing practice (as his brother Frank has also done). This is the first step, perhaps, on his road to recovery. Klaus longs for the purgative and healing cleansing of water and specifically of the waters of the Mississippi, *Mizi zipi* in Anishinaabemowin, a name that means "the big water," the source of all water and, as such, of all cleansing. In light of this fact, Richard's reference to toxic beaver urine "up near Itasca" takes on further resonance because Lake Itasca marks the source of the Mississippi River.

Klaus's healing continues as he comes to understand his own erroneous conflations of waste and Indian identity. He gets his life back together after a close call with a lawnmower (as we will see) and checks himself into rehab. While he is there, he becomes angry at Richard for keeping him up with his wailing, saying, "I have an industrial cleaning job I have to be awake for, two alarm clocks, plus trying to get my own failures into some new order is itself the job, the real one. Just staying in my life is hard" (153). Klaus is trying to turn his life around, coping with his addiction, working. Indeed, he is making reparations for the crimes of his past, taking a cleaning job after having toxified tribal land. His reparations further come through a realization about waste. He notes:

> When I came here, entered in alongside my buddy, Richard, I didn't own shit. We used garbage bags for clothing and comfort and shelter. . . . I brought all my stuff in my Indian suitcase. . . . Garbage belongs in these things—i.e., me. That's what I thought at the time.
> "God don't make trash, Richard." (153)

Klaus notes that he used to equate Indian identity and Indian possessions with garbage. The fact that garbage bags serve as Klaus's and Richard's shelter, clothing, and luggage certainly reinforces such a view. If these are garbage bags, then whatever is placed inside them becomes garbage. Whoever is forced to use such bags for these purposes is seen as garbage, is cast in the role of waste, and as such, is cast off by society at large.[11] But in this statement, Klaus accepts responsibility for his own out-of-balance existence. He realizes that "God don't make trash," that waste is a human or, at least, an animal or terrestrial invention. Trash, within the worldview of this text, is the product of excess, as with Klaus's discussion of diapers above. All the trash we have comes from the excess and ephemeral condition of contemporary life.

Zosie (Cally's maternal grandmother) makes a similar observation in terms of contemporary Native life, relating society to a body of water.[12] Zosie begins by noting the gendered relationships between the production of waste and the responsibility that comes from dealing with that waste: "'The men fish,' says Zosie very quietly. 'The women end up cleaning the damn things'" (205). She goes on to share her thoughts on the issue of fish and waste with Cally and recalls looking at a fish tank from her childhood in a boarding school, explaining, "Down at the bottom there was a fish that ate the ka-ka. Yesterday, my girl, you know I had this awful thought—us Indians are turning into the bottom-feeders of white culture. Too much television sports. Eating all the fake puffed-up flavors and watching all the cranked-up images and out of our mouth no real humor only laugh tracks" (213–14). In the first of these images, people clean the fish, scraping out the internal organs and scaling the skin. This narrative shows woman dealing with the physical, literal blood and guts of life and death. Women are on the ground in the day-to-day life of the family, just as women very frequently play the most-prominent roles in environmental justice movements (Adamson). The second fish image, though, equates people with fish and Indians with bottom-feeders, a hierarchical framework of racialized humanity laid over a belief that those fish that remove, process, and stabilize waste are lesser. Relating this to the passage above, we see that women having to clean fish parallels the women of this novel being in charge of healing people and of dealing with the bulk of the dirty work. One could think of Klaus and Richard and their business, ridding the world of waste, as an example of this assertion not holding up. But they are convicted of illegal and, we assume, improper dumping. We note, then, a difference between processing waste (as Klaus and Richard were supposed to do), dumping waste (as they actually did), and internalizing waste (as the fish and, Zosie argues, Native people have done). That waste, when dumped or internalized, becomes toxic. If we are not active agents in dealing with our waste, with whatever and whomever we cast aside, its toxicity will only grow and spread.[13]

Zosie sees this transformation into bottom-feeders occurring because of two main products: unhealthy foods and mass-produced entertainment in the form of television. This latter is dangerous because of its "theft of Native irony" and humor, as Vizenor notes, and because it eliminates the importance of community in storytelling (*Postindian Conversations* 90). The former reflects the role of "real foods" throughout this novel, whether they are in the form of the simple, earthy foods of Ojibwa tradition, the cakes and pastries that Frank makes and sells, or the massive grocery store that Rozin works in. Klaus, for example, asserts, "We are people of simple food straight from the earthen earth and from the lakes and from the woods. Manomin. Weyass. Baloney. A little maple sugar now and then" (139). *Manomin* is wild rice; *weyass* is meat, generically. These simple foods contrast the "fake puffed-up flavors" above.[14] But we also note Erdrich's pun on boloney, a sausage that is less instinctively related to the simple foods listed. This text calls into question the veracity of its claims immediately upon making them, utilizing the other meaning of "baloney" as a statement of disbelief. Klaus calls his own claims baloney (and interestingly, not bologna). Claims like his with idealized images of Indian people as simple and pure misrepresent the diversity and complexities of Native lives and ever-evolving cultures.

The Antelope Wife connects multiple forms of cultural and chemical toxins, all embodied as forms of greed or a need to control human and other-than-human Others. We see Klaus's revelations on this front as he realizes he must release Sweetheart Calico, at which point she finally begins to speak. Klaus's epiphany comes as he lies in the park, passed out from drinking Listerine (a sterilizing toxin meant to target oral bacteria). He is nearly run over by a lawnmower that comes "screaming" toward him. The windigo dog barrels out of nowhere and dives into the mower's blades. In this moment, Klaus recognizes the need for greater balance in his life and the importance of moderation. He also realizes something about the lawn mower that nearly killed him; he muses on its scream: "That's what his lawn mower was—one long scream of protest—the world of grass was never meant to be shortened to a carpet so that the outdoors is like one big wall-to-wall room" (225). In the process of coming to terms with his own issues of control, specifically of his socially and personally toxic need to control Sweetheart Calico, Klaus recognizes that other nonhuman species (monocotyledonous species in this case) ought not be forced to be something they are not.

Sweetheart Calico goes on to illustrate the parallel between ecocide and economic oppression. She begins to speak as Klaus realizes he must set her free and return her to the antelope people of the plains. With her first utterance of the novel (twenty-two pages from its conclusion), she tells Cally, "They're selling Christ's coffin at Pier 1. . . . And it was made of raw teak strips deep in a third world jungle and made of sharp bamboo by children in China in a stinking backwater polluted by coal fumes and in Borneo from delicate and ancient barks of trees that never will again grow on earth and it was made by young virgins and their hands are scabbed raw and bleeding so an American has to hose those coffins down when they are shipped over here before they are displayed" (218). In all of this, Sweetheart Calico reveals the union of ecological and human rights issues much like those in all the novels I examine (we are especially reminded of Arcangel's litanies in *Tropic of Orange* and the cure for la mona in book 1 of *The Rag Doll Plagues*). These issues become one, as "children in China" and laboring "virgins" whose hands "are scabbed raw" correlate to Christ, who correlates to "trees that never will again grow" and a "stinking backwater polluted by coal fumes." Sweetheart Calico shows how the bondage suffered by slaves and wage slaves is akin to that suffered by an ever-threatened nonhuman world, both of which are inexorably bound to a spiritual realm that, perhaps because of these threats, is quite literally dying (hence the coffin) at the hands of global capitalism. Indeed, this global capitalism provides the ultimate commodity fetish (in the religious sense) in Christ's coffin, sold by a corporate import franchise. With this zenith of commodity fetishism, we will see the same increased alienation from labor and nature that I discuss throughout this book.[15]

SECTION 2: GAKAHBEKONG/MINNEAPOLIS, NATURAL NATIVE PRESENCE AND PERMEABILITY

Cally, the youngest Roy–Shawano–Whiteheart Beads of *The Antelope Wife*, seems to be the family member most capable of living in the book's urban setting and dealing with the family's cracked-apart curse. Indeed, she has little choice, as she hears the words, the utterance of the curse, all the time. She comments, "It is as though I am on two channels all at once, flipping back and forth . . . hearing an Ojibwa word, over and over,

as the ice shifts, as the snow cracks . . . Daashkikaa, daashkikaa, daashkikaa" (196). She continues later, "Daashkikaa. Daashkikaa, I keep thinking. . . . I see my father's bloody forehead as he lies in the hallway; his
tears come up under my hands" (212). When she asks her grandmother
about this word she keeps hearing over and over, her grandmother re-
plies, "Cracked apart. . . . How do you know that old name?" (213). Most
scholars point out that "cracked apart" refers to a curse of cultural and
personal upheaval. But it is also a name, and this fact requires some
examination that has not yet been undertaken.

The novel emphasizes Cally's importance as she asks her grandmother Zosie about this name she keeps hearing. Zosie, "all of a sud-
den, . . . shows great interest. 'Magizha it is you . . . who gets the names'"
(213).[16] Zosie's interest comes from acknowledging the power Cally possesses. The fact that Cally is a young woman who is six or seven generations removed from the speaking of this name is of great importance.
First, we note that Cally becomes connected to the moment of the fissure
of old ways, the moment at which the traditional life becomes cracked
apart. This is not to say that precontact American cultures were ever
static. But the change that comes with the rapid advance of the U.S.
military into Ojibwa country represents a new kind of change. The previous balance that is supposed to have existed (albeit in constant flux)
is fundamentally changed by this new cultural and military presence.
Moreover, Cally's place within the family and clan unit becomes further
established through this connection. Her importance is emphasized, as
she becomes a powerful figure who plays a critical role in this familial
curse. Cally accepts this role, endeavoring to find a place for the city in
her life, in the lives of her family, and by extension, I would argue, in the
lives of Native people. After all, this quest is not one that Cally accepts
merely for herself but for her extended family as well as her community,
which is not only intertribal but also interethnic and interspecies.

Cally's importance is further clarified as she comes to understand one
of her mother's dreams to be about Minneapolis, where she decides to
remain and to work to understand the role of the city in her life and in
the lives of her family, extended as it is. This understanding equates to
wisdom, and Cally is likely to become a powerful figure. She explains:

My Mama, she once blackened her face with charcoal around when she was my age. She went out in the woods for six days. There, she had a vision of a huge thing, strange, inconceivable. All her life she told me she wondered what it was. It came out of the sky, pierced far into the ground, seethed and trembled. I see this: I was sent here to understand and to report. What she saw was the shape of the world itself. Rising in a trance and eroding downward and destroying what it is. Moment through moment until the end of time if ever there is an end to this. Gakahbekong. That's what she saw. Gakahbekong. The city. Where we are scattered like beads off a necklace and put back together in new patterns, new strings. (220)

We note several key elements about contemporary and mobile Native identities throughout this passage. First, the narrative perspective becomes expanded here. We begin with Cally describing her mother's dream, but the first person seems to see through Rozin's eyes. This story, this dream, becomes shared by mother and daughter. Second, we note that this expanded, dual self-as-narrator has been sent to make sense of the city and to explain her findings. She is entrusted with serving as a messenger, a harbinger of the city itself. Cally/Rozin sees the city as it is, a space of flux within a world of flux. The city's roots have "pierced far into the ground," but remain in motion as they seethe and tremble. The city may erode in time; but most importantly, the people will not be destroyed. Instead, the people are rearranged, placed within new contexts, within new matrices, on new trajectories. Cally sees the reality of Native place in the city, recognizes the fact that Indian people are forming liquid identities in urban settings across the Americas as well as specifically within Minneapolis (a favored site of BIA-sponsored relocation).[17] But these new types of identity need not imply Native destruction. I read within this passage an image of urban continuance, as all people exist (and always have) within the contexts of ever-shifting evolutions. These characters have agency enough to move about their worlds. Their constructions of their own identities and communities remain mobile, liquid, and, above all else, adaptable.

Cally's reclamation of the city notwithstanding, *The Antelope Wife*, like many of the texts in this study, communicates an ambivalence toward urban spaces. Sweetheart Calico's relationship to the city and its willing denizen, Klaus, is quite overtly antagonistic. A third person narrator notes, "Klaus, she never dreamed about or remembered. He was just the one she was tied to, who brought her here. Thongs of fabric, his need, tied to a stake and driven deep into the Minnesota earth. She found that no matter how fast or how far she walked, she couldn't get out of the city. The lights and car panic tangled her. Streets opened onto streets and the highways roared hungry as swollen rivers, bearing in their rush dangerous bright junk" (51–52). As in Rozin's dream of Minneapolis, we see here the image of the rootedness of the city, a stake "driven deep into the earth." We also note that Sweetheart Calico sees the earth beneath the city, into which the city is anchored. Minneapolis is a largely constructed space but one that is recognized for its connection to the land underneath. Moreover, she sees the city in riparian terms; the streets are like rivers.[18] But unlike rivers, which carry water, the life force of the planet (as well as the recurring metaphors of fish and cleansing throughout this text), the cars that make up and shape the city comprise a "rush" of "dangerous bright junk." These cars, subjects of so much urban longing and striving (as Klaus and Richard earlier celebrate their purchase of a new truck), are dangerous for their material threat: they can crush someone or poison them, as in Deanna's case. They are also, ultimately, just junk. They will almost all end up in the junk piles and scrap heaps and are deemed useless by the Antelope Wife. Although she appears to be the ultimate in natural characters, she fails to recognize the use value of objects and urban space in her wholesale rejections. She would cast off these objects that she has no use for as valueless. The Antelope Wife participates in the purity discourse of urban flight and the refuse tropes we have seen throughout these novels.

She continues her critique of the city in terms of the excess of accumulation, of "stuff," lamenting, "I'm drowning in stuff here in Gakahbekong. In so many acres of fruit. In warehouse upon warehouse of tools, Sheetrock nails, air conditioners, and implements of every type and domestic and imported fabrics, and in the supermarkets and fish from the seven seas and slabs of fat-marbled flesh of warm-eyed cows who love and nuzzle their young. And Klaus" (219). We note a correlation between Klaus's earlier inclusion of Richard in his list of toxic elements as the Antelope Wife includes Klaus in this list of stuff in which she is drowning. Her first critique, strangely, is of an excess of fruit, natural images of fecundity, reproduction, health. As we compare this to her later examination of the supermarkets' abundance of fish and beef, we ascertain that the real problem is with *over*abundance. This is a common critique of urban spaces, especially from an environmentalist perspective: the sheer mass of humanity within cities is unsustainable in terms of the resources available to any given landscape. As such, they require the importing from other places with their own evolutionary patterns, which are altered by that exporting. Finally, we must read urban overabundance alongside Sweetheart Calico's mention of other manufactured goods. Ultimately, the problem with the city is with the excess of stuff, the greed of the place for more than it needs and more than in can provide. And the person within this section who emblematizes that greed, that possessiveness, is Klaus, who thus becomes paralleled with Richard and the windigo in his desire to possess more than his proper lot.

Erdrich's use of multiple narrators allows for multiple perspectives on urban Indian identities, a move which also places this novel within a tribal and communal context. Because this novel lacks a single narrator, no single narrative voice is privileged. Sweetheart Calico is lost in the city. For her, it *is* a place to be fled. Cities are confusing. Unlike Klaus, who welcomes the impeded vision of urban spaces, Sweetheart Calico longs for the plains specifically because she feels she cannot see far enough in the city. From Sweetheart Calico's perspective (unlike the others'), *The Antelope Wife* serves as a homing plot (Furlan).[19] She must escape the city's evils and isolation and return to her people in order to be healed.

The city, however, is marked as positive throughout this novel. This is not only because the text is set, for the most part, in the Twin Cities but also because a number of the characters confront their urban identity quite explicitly. Cally, for example, speaks to the value of the city. Although she knows that Rozin "is hoping [she'll] miss the real land," namely that of the reservation, Cally recognizes the tradition of the city itself (103). She comments, "Gakahbekong. That's the name our old ones call the city, what it means from way back when it started as a trading village. Although driveways and houses, concrete parking garages and business stores cover the city's scape, that same land is hunched underneath. There are times, like now, I get this sense of the temporary. It could all blow off. And yet the sheer land would be left underneath. Sand, rock, the Indian black seashell-bearing earth" (124–25). This city, Gakahbekong, which was renamed Minneapolis, has always been a center of commerce.[20] As Jack Forbes points out, cities are not some new force that Indians never dealt with before contact.[21] But like many of the precontact cities of North America, the modern ones are temporary, can fall and fade away. And still the land beneath will be there, providing the miigis shells for the people who live there.[22] The land and the Indian history *anchor* the modern city in its place rather than pressing it down, repressing, or suppressing it.

Both Cally and Rozin recognize the nonhuman community within the city-space of Minneapolis. While she is mourning Richard, Rozin cooks and afterward "removes the plates and brings the food out into the backyard, where the squirrels will eat it, and the city raccoons and the ravens with their glossy arrogance" (190). She maintains ties to the nonhuman through rituals that survive in the city. Similarly, Cally sees Ojibwa traditions surviving through a rather unexpected urban interaction. While watching a pair of Hmong grandmothers working in a community garden, Cally muses, "Every time their hands go to the dirt, I feel better. More peaceful with each movement they make in their cages of tomatoes. . . . As they move and as the sun grows hot on the dirt, so the scent of it rises, same even in the city, that dirt smell, I know they are digging for me" (219). The physical earth of the city connects people across time and ethnicity, to precontact Native ways that have never ended, only evolved. Cally remains connected to her ancestors by the dirt, the soil itself. That smell, as we also see in *The Rag Doll Plagues*, permeates and penetrates, so the earth fills Cally's lungs and becomes part of her. This passage also speaks to broad, interracial human connections. Cally recognizes a connection between herself and these Hmong grandmothers, older, relatively recent immigrants to the area.[23] It also connects all grandmothers, mothers, women, and girls as a continuum of life—life bearing and life support (especially via farming)—stretching across generations, oceans, continents, and centuries. We note another example of pastoral imagery here (as well as biological reproduction), which we see particularly in the parable novels.

Many critics see the city as a negative space within the narrative of this novel. Thomas Matchie, for example, sees an "age-old dichotomy of country vs. city" within this text (31). He considers cities to be distinct from the natural and continues, "Erdrich is rooted in myth and insists we need to learn from our mistakes," which "may take the support of one's own kind and a closeness to the earth as distinct from the dysfunctional life in the city" (35). Julie Tharp, rather than contrasting the urban and the natural, contrasts the urban with the traditional. Tharp argues that "Sweetheart Calico's complete inability to understand or adapt to urban life indicate her . . . connection to traditional Native culture" (118). But we must also read Sweetheart Calico's contempt of the city in relation to Klaus.

Klaus kidnaps the Antelope Wife, taking her from the plains and into the city. Before he does, however, he seeks the advice of Jimmy Badger, "an old medicine man spoken about with hushed respect" (26). Klaus explains, "I'm an Ojibwa, I say to him, so I don't know about the plains much. I am more a woods Indian, a city-bred guy" (26). He continues, later, "I'm just a city boy. . . . I don't know what you people do, out there, living on the plains where there are no trees, no woods, no place to hide except the distances. You can see too much" (33). Klaus views the plains as somehow removed from the positive powers of the woods and city. The city is like the forest, and so it is a naturalized place for a "woods Indian" like himself. Both the woods and the city provide places to hide and break up the vision and prevent the people from "seeing too much." Tharp has argued that "Klaus' response [to the people on the plains] only makes sense if we draw the connection between city living and self-centered behavior" (124). But I assert this connection must be examined on more of a case by case basis. Tharp further argues that "Gakahbekong creates a set of illusions" that are not created elsewhere in the natural world. However, her argument overlooks the fact that Klaus also says that he is a woods Indian and that the plains are overwhelming because, unlike both the woods *and* the city, there is nowhere to hide. And while this idea of hiding might seem like a cop-out to certain critics, it does not seem to be so in this case. Yes, Klaus is a weak character, and one given to obsessive behaviors. But his comment also reflects cultural distinctions that stem from the physical settings of certain cultures. The city reflects the woods; both are crowded places that impede vision (both in terms of seeing and also being seen). Indeed, most articles regarding *The Antelope Wife* generally portray the city only as a site of Indian downfall. But the novel's conclusion, which describes Cally's continuation of her mother's visions in and of Minneapolis, shows the city to be a place of Native regeneration, continuance, and even success. Moreover, as I have already argued, Erdrich's use of multiple narrators allows for these multiple points of view. Within Klaus's thread, the city is home. All of this works to complicate the stereotype that Native people do not, cannot, or should not live, survive, and thrive in urban settings.

I, rather, side with Julie Barak's assessment of this novel, which states that the characters, despite being somewhat migratory, are "nesting" in the city. She asserts, "Nesting, especially in a new environment, means surviving—moving on, making the necessary adjustments for continuance" (2). While the characters in the novel may not see themselves necessarily *of* the city (though some, like Klaus, certainly do), they find themselves living *in* the city and raising children in the city. And those children recognize the homeliness of the city, the fact that it is a place where many people, including Native people, will spend the bulk of their lives. If the city is where we live, for whatever reason, then we had better get on with finding and creating our places in the city. Erdrich's embrace of relocation centers may be complicated, but she still sees the need for recognitions of liquid Native identities in light of contemporary urban existences. As Furlan demonstrates, "Erdrich challenges the notion of a fixed Indian identity, rooted in the past, unable to adapt to modern living" (66).

Erdrich extends her portrayal of urban survivance within this novel to the animals who serve as kin for the people, especially in the forms of dogs, antelope, and deer. Indeed, dogs play a pivotal role throughout this novel. Almost Soup, a dog so named because he narrowly escapes being boiled in a pot for food (Cally thinks he is too cute to cook), is the direct descendent of Sorrow, a dog who appears in the novel's first section detailing Scranton Roy's raid on the Ojibwa village. He is also known as the windigo dog, and he tells us that "Original Dog walked alongside

Wenabojo, their [the Ojibwa's] tricky creator" (81). When Wenabojo (or Naanabozho) asked the creator why he was alone in his journeys, the creator sent him the wolf, Maengun, "to walk, talk, and play with" (Benton-Banai 7). Moreover, Benton-Banai notes, the "linkage of man and dog was very important because it combined the intelligence of man with intuition of the dog. If a man was to get lost in the wilderness, his dogs could lead him back home" (27). Thus, it is no surprise that dogs serve as guides and protectors throughout so much of this novel. They are fulfilling a role that has been theirs since the dawn of time, not merely as kin, but as collaborative escorts, leading themselves and their lost people back home. Such a portrayal positively pollutes human families with canine relatives. Almost Soup saves Cally when she is sick, noting "Rozin feels me put her daughter's life inside of her again. Unknown to her, I have taken it with me to keep it safe" (90). This dog cares for his family. He also saves Klaus, as we have seen, from a lawnmower and talks to him about his problems: "Klaus had thought windigos were strictly human until this dog came to visit him on a rainy afternoon not long after his ass got rightly and properly canned" (126–27). Finally, Almost Soup tells us that death comes in the form of "the great black dog" (82). This final point draws a connection between human stories (which frequently present anthropomorphic animals) and dog stories (which here present canidpomorphic ones).

This interrelatedness persists throughout the novel, but it is also paired with the recurring images of the in-between or the horizon or dividing line. We see characters struggle to find a middle ground rather than a space of greed, control, or excess. Ultimately, the in-between is seen as a space of tremendous power or transformation, such as Klaus's circling lawnmower blade. Klaus oscillates for most of this novel between health and illness, settling down in one or the other. Indeed, he even dwells on the image of the in-between, the line or lack of line between poles. Within that dividing line, the physical embodiment of the in-between space, he attains a new level of clarity.

As he is saved by the windigo dog, Klaus reflects upon his own greed and selfishness: "In the extraordinary light Klaus made a thousand decisions. Two of them mattered. Number one, he would finally stop. Just stop. And he knew . . . that he was done drinking. The other of his important decisions was not so consciously settled. It was just that he knew . . . the next thing to do. . . . *Bring her back. Bring her back to us, you fool.* . . . Getting sober. Letting her go" (226). At this moment, Klaus recognizes the importance of balance, of his own responsibilities as a person and as a member of a community. He recognizes that Sweetheart Calico's presence in the city is a crime. She is trapped, kidnapped, and caged in the wrong place. Unlike Klaus, she is supposed to be where the sky and the earth meet, the line of the horizon. Similarly, Klaus's alcoholism is toxic; it is a dependence of excess, a self-medication for a psychic imbalance. In his near-death experience with the lawnmower, Klaus receives a scar, and the narrator notes, "His drum face wore the sacred center stripe" (225). As the stripe divides his face, he realizes the need for that balance. He can want Sweetheart Calico, but he cannot hold her, cannot possess her. He can want to drink, but he cannot let the alcohol hold and possess him.

The Antelope Wife's calls for balance ought not be confused with calls for purity, however. We see the refusal of discourses of purity in this novel particularly as they relate to racial or blood purity and authenticity. Klaus, for example, expresses the difficulty in identifying Native people by phenotype, noting, "It's hard to tell what tribe people are anymore, we're so mixed—I've got Buffalo Soldier in my own blood, I'm sure, and on the other side I am all Ojibwa. All Shawano" (23).[24] Similarly, we learn that Rozin is "descended of the three-fires people and of an Ivory Coast slave" (34–35). Erdrich is confounding the notion that mixed-bloods, especially from the northern United States (as opposed to the southeast), are products of intermarrying of Native and European or European American people alone.[25] She illustrates the common traditions of acceptance of outsiders into tribal communities. These traditions challenge essentialist or racial conceptions of Native people and communities, emphasizing instead the importance of cultural belonging and intermixings.

Likewise, Cally spends some time discussing variables in Native mixed-blood identities, presenting the outcomes of a number of combinations. She expounds, "Some bloods they go together like water—the French Ojibwas: You mix those up and it is all one person. Like me. Others are a little less predictable. You make a person from a German and an Indian, for instance, and you're creating a two-souled warrior always fighting with themself" (110). She goes on to describe Swedish, Norwegian, Hmong ("so beautiful you want to follow them around and see if they are real"), and Irish Indians, the last of whose creation is "like playing with hot dynamite" (110–11). This section shows a Native perspective on different ethnicities encompassed by the notion of whiteness, French, German, Swedish, Norwegian, Irish. From this perspective, there are essential differences between these ethnicities. Mixing their blood with Indian, particularly Ojibwa, blood creates certain predictable outcomes. I do not think, however, the reader is intended to place great stock in Cally's equations. This is a section that includes the humor in Erdrich's work that, as Robert A. Morace points out, "non-Native American readers often miss" (37). These are the musings of an adolescent (one who shows her own blood mixture as essentially positive, naturalized by its comparison to water) whose critical role in the novel, and indeed in the very future of her family, has not yet developed. Moreover, although she clearly conceives of blood and personality as related, these various mixings do not make any of the concomitant offspring any less Indian. In fact, Erdrich later describes Rozin's and Frank's wedding as a family reunion that displays a community of all shades of mixed-blood identity: "children and grandchildren of varying tones from palest laughing blond to swirls of ocher and obsidian, all poking, eating, tasting, organizing" (171). This portrayal of a positive, happy family and community of mixed-bloods reminds us of those throughout all the novels I examine in this project. If, as Louis Owens posited, mixed-bloods are the future, then the future, at least as portrayed within this novel, looks bright indeed (*Other Destinies* n. pag.).

4

"AN EERIE LIQUID ELASTICITY" KAREN TEI
YAMASHITA'S *TROPIC OF ORANGE*

To everything there seemed to be an eerie liquid elasticity. How
far must she race? How far must she reach to touch her Sol?
KAREN TEI YAMASHITA, *Tropic of Orange*

Some folks didn't even have a suitcase, to pack anything in,
So two trash bags is all they gave them,
When the kids asked Mom, "Where we goin'?"
. . .

Ken . . . said . . .
. . . we have to live in a place called Manzanar"
FORT MINOR, "Kenji"

In "Kenji," Fort Minor describes an Issei shop owner in Los Angeles
whose family is relocated to the Manzanar internment camp during World War II. Based on the history of Fort Minor front man Mike
Shinoda's family and the sampled interviews with his father and aunt,
this track details the forced removal, internment, and loss of home suffered by many Japanese Americans. Manzanar, California—the site of
the Manzanar internment camp, which operated from 1942 to 1945—
lies about seventy miles east of Fresno and about two hundred miles
north of Los Angeles. Interestingly, Manzanar was available for setting the internment camp because it had become a ghost town after
water from the Owens Valley (in which Manzanar sits) was relocated,
via the California aqueduct, to Los Angeles, Shinoda's father's home
and the major setting of the novel this chapter will detail, Karen Tei

Yamashita's *Tropic of Orange*. This draining was created under the auspices of the Los Angeles Department of Water and Power, headed by William Mulholland; and the aqueduct was completed in 1914.[1] The Owens Valley, to that point an agricultural center, became virtually unarable by 1930. We note a parallel between this passage's description of trash bags as luggage to Erdrich's discussion of Indian suitcases in *The Antelope Wife* (chapter 3). The belongings of these people, placed in receptacles for trash, become trash. But even more, in this case, a containment ideology prevails, as Japanese Americans, deemed a pollutive threat, were moved (primarily) from the West Coast of the United States to inland depositories. As John Beck notes, "Wartime removal of Japanese Americans stands as a moment of wish-fulfillment in the history of American waste management in the West" (87). It is fitting, then, that Yamashita names her homeless character Manzanar Murikami, as the homeless in this novel are closely related with trash on a number of fronts: they are, like so many groups I examine throughout *Positive Pollutions and Cultural Toxins*, seen as disposable members of their urban communities; they are cast off by administrative society; and they both dwell in garbage-laden spaces and make use of the waste of more economically advantaged groups.[2]

Tropic of Orange follows seven primary characters over the course of seven days. Each character either lives in, has fled from, or is moving toward Los Angeles, California. The cast includes, in order of appearance, Rafaela Cortes, a Mexican woman who has been working in the United States but has returned to Mazatlán; Bobby Ngu (not his birth name), an apparently, but not actually, Vietnamese American refugee and Rafaela's estranged husband; Emi, a Japanese American television producer; Buzzworm, an African American "Angel of Mercy" with a penchant for portable radios and timepieces; Manzanar Murikami, a homeless Japanese American former surgeon who spends his days standing on overpasses conducting LA freeway traffic like a symphony; Gabriel Balboa, a Chicano newspaper reporter, Emi's longtime boyfriend, and Rafaela's current employer (he owns the home in Mazatlán she is taking care of); and Arcangel, a Latino street performer, prophet, and narrative voice of reason. The main action of the text involves a massive traffic accident on the Harbor Freeway, Interstate 110, in Los Angeles. After this pileup, drivers abandon their vehicles, only to be replaced by an "army" of homeless people who repurpose the stationary vehicles as places to sleep, sit, and in the more luxurious cases, watch television and make phone calls. Alongside this traffic snafu, *Tropic of Orange* details a massive warping of the landscape that occurs on the summer solstice and the week that follows. An orange, being transported from Mexico to the United States, is somehow attached to the Tropic of Cancer, and its transnational movement is pulling on the planet's gravitational forces. For example, while Emi and Gabriel sit in a Japanese restaurant, the world begins to bend: "For some reason, the entire sushi bar seemed to tilt and sag with an indescribable elasticity. Gabriel's elbow lost its surface, and that seaweed, rice, crab, and avocado delicacy tumbled and tumbled" (129). The delicacy being described is a California roll, as Yamashita puns on California's rolling land. The earth is on the move, but not in the jarring shake of an earthquake. Instead, we see a liquidity that allows geography to warp and bow without cracking. Finally, the novel culminates in a massively hyped Lucha Libre–style wrestling match between the archetypal representations of Latin and Anglo America: respectively, El Gran Mojado (a persona adopted by the liquid-trickster Arcangel) and SUPERNAFTA.

Throughout this chapter, I argue that Yamashita's novel challenges absolutes of purity as they relate to space and place (especially as examined by borders, boundaries, and cartography), while examining the interrelated role of time, individuated selves, and waste, toxicity, and castoffs. All boundaries—whether between nations or territories; between past, present, and future; between the self and the other; or between humans and other species—are positively polluted, recognized as porous, and constantly permeated and penetrated. While the overwhelming majority of ecocritical attention to Yamashita's work centers on her perhaps more obviously environmentalist first novel *Through the Arc of the Rain Forest* (see, for example, especially the works by Heise and Buell), themes of waste, contamination, and ecological destruction lie heavy in *Tropic of Orange*. This text's predominant setting of the urban core of Los Angeles makes it an ideal subject for ecocriticism as it grows beyond studies of wilderness and rural spaces.

The novel itself (like *The Antelope Wife*) foregrounds collectivity in its multivocality, with each chapter being told from a different narrative perspective. To that end, Kandice Chuh asserts, "Commitment to a thematic and generic eccentricity and formal elasticity, whereby protagonists transform into minor characters and the latter enlarge into central actors, characterizes Yamashita's work" (621). She continues, "Yamashita's characters . . . might better be understood as character-spaces." The intersections of selves with space and time occupy central positions throughout this text, as do spatial permeations. Rachel Adams asserts that "the novel insists that [the] meeting between North and South is inevitable" and "will further contribute to the Latinization of Southern California" (266). I would extend Adams's assertion to contend that the meeting of North and South has always been happening; indeed, the two concepts mutually constitute one another so that one cannot be understood without the other. Moreover, I argue that Arcangel's movement marks less a Latinization of California than an impending end to the very brief period of Anglicization of California (1848 to the present). Finally, Sue-Im Lee further recognizes, "Contesting the discourse of purity (of blood, race, ethnic, nation, or culture), Yamashita's novels explore and celebrate the porous categories of identities emerging from the phenomena of globalization. Conversely, her novels explore the ways in which the unmooring of identities and affiliations translate into formations of *new* moorings" (503).[3] As we will see, those invested in old moorings fight tenaciously to constantly reassert them, while those who become unmoored often work to create new stabilities. Nonetheless, each of the characters in *Tropic of Orange* in some way or another embraces the liquid realities implied by Lee's metaphor of mooring—a seemingly solid and fixed device of attachment in a liquid body.

Tropic of Orange recognizes a liquidity of the human social self that relates to names; Manzanar's may be the prime example. The fact that Manzanar is homeless reflects the loss of home suffered by interned Japanese Americans (including Kenji in this chapter's epigraph). However, Gabriel posits, Manzanar "was not his real name. . . . He had created his name out of his birthplace, Manzanar Concentration Camp in the Owens Valley. He claimed he was born there during the war" (110). It is difficult to ascertain the truth of Manzanar's naming—perhaps it is given to him by his parents, perhaps he gives it to himself. Nonetheless, his name speaks to a critical element about him. He is born of the cultural toxins of forced relocation, internment, and dispossession, in a site of prior relocations and dispossession (of indigenous people by Mexican and later U.S. settler colonists, of Mexican Californios by Anglo squatters, of family farmers by superwealthy urbanites, and of Japanese Americans by a xenophobic and racist federal government). Manzanar's name speaks to a liquidity of identity that belies the administrative containment ideology that led to its generation.

If Manzanar does change his name to recognize the space and place of his formation as a marginalized partial citizen by the state, he is not alone. Bobby Ngu crafts a name to appear to be Vietnamese, though he is in fact ethnically Chinese from Indonesia: "Real name's Li Kwan Yu. But don't tell nobody" (15). Yamashita's text consciously puns on *Ngu* and *new* to explain, "They all got Ngu names" (15). Bobby's nominal liquidity marks his tactical mobility, as he pretends to be Vietnamese in order to seek out a more economically stable life in the United States, immigrating with other Southeast Asian "boatpeople" refugees following U.S. military incursions of the 1960s and 1970s. In the cases of Manzanar and Bobby, the change in name is deeply tied to place and loss of place, expulsion from home due to U.S. military and economic forces (part of Bobby's leaving has to do with his father's bicycle factory being put out of business by a U.S. one). Each name demonstrates ways in which the self is altered by movement. Likewise, the novel's two arguably Chicana/o characters, both of whom draw on Mesoamerican privileging of hybrid, part-indigenous roots, are also nominally related to figures of the European conquest of those lands. Rafaela's surname is Cortes, linking her to Hernán Cortés, as I will revisit later (see also chapter 2 for more on Cortés's relationship to the Mexica). Gabriel's last name is Balboa, aligning him with conquistador Vasco Nuñez de Balboa, the first European to see the Pacific coast of the Americas (where this novel is set). Again, each of these figures is related to a loss of homeland as well as to the taking of that homeland. Both Rafaela and Gabriel also share the names of Catholic archangels, a theme that continues throughout the novel as each character is likened to an angel (in the City of Angels) at one point or another.[4]

Yamashita establishes the tenor of her novel with her choice of three epigraphs detailing Southern California as a liquid landscape that is and has always been blended and positively polluted with the other liquid landscapes of the Americas and the Pacific Rim. The first of the three epigraphs to this novel, all of which have been to this point understudied, comes from Michael Ventura's essay "Grand Illusion":

> A city named after sacred but imaginary beings, in a state named after a paradise that was the figment of a woman's dream; a city that came to fame by filming such figments; a city existing now on sufferance from the ever-hotter desert and the ever-rising sea, and that feels every day, to so many of us, like a mirage as it waits for its great quake. Its suffering is real enough, God knows. But its beauty is the beauty of letting things go; letting go of where you came from; letting go of old lessons; letting go of what you want for what you are, or what you are for what you want; letting go of so much—and that is a hard beauty to love. (N. pag.)

In Ventura's estimation, Los Angeles exists as a real place defined, more than most other places, by its self-fashioned illusions (its filmed figments, for example). The City of Angels was always already imaginary in this sense—as is California, named for the island of the Amazons ruled by Queen Califia. However, Yamashita's choice of epigraph reinforces, as does the body of the novel, the fact that despite this illusory nature, LA is nonetheless very real. The desert and sea that define the city with their (and correspondingly, the city's) boundaries and borders are material, natural elements, both of which face the effects of anthropogenic global climate change. These elements threaten the city's existence, as waking threatens a happy dream. The city is likewise defined by its seismic activity, which waits below the surface (and LA here is all surface) to destroy it. The suffering of the city, the people of which are not mentioned within this passage, is given short shrift. Instead, the focus here is on beauty, albeit a beauty without connection, without retention, without maintenance. It is a new and youthful beauty, a constantly shifting beauty that can and must never remain in one place. While one can understand why such a beauty of letting go would be hard to love (one can think of a lover who is forever letting go rather than holding on), Yamashita's text in many ways privileges the act of releasing ideas and ideals of control (as in *The Antelope Wife*) and boundary and embracing flux and liquidity: the positive pollutions that stem from the liquidities of time and space, of self, of cultures, and of nation.

Letting go figures deeply within *Tropic of Orange*. Each character must release some toxic, self-destructive, unhealthy, or erroneous notion of stability and simplicity in order to grow or survive. The novel concludes not with the battle between El Gran Mojado and SUPERNAFTA but with Bobby as he watches the crowd. After having taken the orange that has been dragging the Tropic of Cancer northward, Bobby feels the weight of that line and of all dividing lines. At this moment of letting go, Bobby realizes that his family is safe, that its members are not as utterly reliant on him as he had previously assumed: "Wasn't there to protect his family after all. . . . What's he gonna do? Tied fast to these lines. Family out there. Still stuck on the other side. He's gritting his teeth and crying like a fool. What are these goddamn lines anyway? What do they connect? What do they divide? What's he holding on to? What's he holding on to?" (268). The boundaries Bobby constructs between himself and his family become permeated. In assuming their differentiation from himself, the solid self/other boundary, he neglected himself, not realizing that in so doing, he was damaging them because they are all part of one another. Bobby begins to question the barriers that he, like all of us, has received. We are taught, and in fact we may depend on, the differentiation of objects, subjects, selves, nations, everything. But the supposed boundaries between these things aren't real. While they seem to help us understand, they in fact mislead us. The truth is that whatever is supposed to be encapsulated, bound, or contained within those borders, those "goddamn lines," always leaks, seeps, and bleeds out. But because these imaginary lines are so culturally ingrained, they become invisible, tacitly assumed. As such, Bobby's clinging to those lines, lines that divide, appears from the outside to be an embrace:

> Anybody looking sees his arms open wide like he's flying. Like he's flying forward to embrace. Don't nobody know he's hanging on to these invisible bungy cords. That's when he lets go. Lets the lines slither around his wrists, past his palms, through his fingers. Lets go. Go figure. Embrace.
>
> That's it. (268)

Ultimately, Bobby concludes, as the novel concludes, that he can release these lines, though they might at first have seemed to bind him. Once he does, they simply slither off him. The fact that they slither, however, rather than, say, slide, demonstrates an activity if not an agency about the borders that construct and misconstrue us.

The third epigraph, from Guillermo Gómez-Peña's poem "Freefalling toward a Borderless Future," lays out the understanding of the Americas as a single, united landmass through the image of a whole—though hardly static—body, undifferentiated by the borders that Bobby ultimately releases.[5] This poem addresses several of the central ideas underlying *Tropic of Orange*, especially in terms of the role of maps (and changing maps) and in terms of interconnection. It reads:

standing on the map of my political desires
I toast to a borderless future
(I raise my glass of wine toward the moon)
with . . .
our Alaska hair
our Canadian head
our U.S. torso
our Mexican genitalia
our Central American cojones
our Caribbean sperm
our South American legs
our Patagonian feet
our Antarctic nails
jumping borders at ease
jumping borders with pleasure
amen, hey man (n. pag.)

Gómez-Peña's map is one of his "political desires," a reshaped and reinterpreted understanding of the landscape as it is. It is a hope that people will reimagine the Americas as a single space, naturalized via the image of a single and unified body. The image of Caribbean sperm might seem to be an expelling of Antillean North America, but it is also a reaching out into the sea, to bind it to American genetic material. We can also consider the Caribbean as the generative site of the Americas when we recall that it was there that Columbus landed and thus there that the Americas began to become the Americas and became global in an expanded human and ecological sense. Gómez-Peña describes jumping borders with ease and pleasure, to signify not only the pragmatic nature of downplaying borders, positively polluting nations, but also the reality that borders, by reifying administrative rule, counter a certain *jouissance* made possible in the free play of borderlessness. Modeled after Gómez-Peña, Arcangel—a performance artist and trickster-savior—speaks to, lives, and demonstrates a united America devoid of its pre- and post-contact borders.

Tropic of Orange maintains a deep concern with representations of geographic space, particularly in demonstrating the failures of maps and of cartography generally. The text continuously returns to discussions of how we understand space and place, and particularly the multiple, overlapping, intersecting, and positively polluted human, cultural, economic, physical, and ecological forces and factors that must be taken into consideration in order to craft any understanding of space. The reader encounters this cartographic focus within the earliest pages, with a section titled "HyperContexts," a grid formed by the seven character names in a column on the left, the days of the week with subtitles across the top, and the corresponding chapter numbers and titles for each row and column intersection point. We are reminded of Los Angeles's geometric grid pattern, and Yamashita has commented to that very end: "The hypercontext at the beginning is sort of the map of the book. You have your map, you're in LA, and you have to drive" (Cheung 339). "HyperContexts" serves in the stead of the ubiquitous Southern Californian's *Thomas Guide*, the map that so many motorists keep in their cars to help them navigate the city (these are increasingly being replaced by GPS units by those with the means). However, this grid, while appearing linear and fixed, proves to be far more circuitous and in flux than one might expect. The very fact that "HyperContexts" takes a novel, already a fairly linear narrative form, and places it within a grid that does not conform to the reader's experience of the book challenges its accuracy and utility. Moreover, this novel, in which time and space are in constant motion, demonstrates the challenges of understanding space and place in such rigid and fixed terms. The text explains, for example, "Once again, the grid was changing" (239). The grid, which expresses a longing for a solid place, demonstrates spatial liquidity, as what is in truth a gradual but constant liquid process of geologic and political change is imagined here as a weeklong event.

Arcangel understands these liquid interconnections between people (including our economies) and the rest of the world. Moreover, his narrative persona grasps an understanding of deep time and the singularity of the Americas as a geographic body. He speaks to the role of time as a liquid instability rather than a linear progression:

> There is no future or past.
>
> . . .
>
> There is no aging. There is only changing.
> What can this progress my challenger speaks of
> really be? (258).

Rather than seeing time as a progression from worse to better, from savage to civilized, or from inchoate to developed, we can understand that the world is merely in flux, that all things are moving from a present state (itself not a solid condition but a process) to another state. Arcangel continues by querying who is served by the master narrative and myth of progress:

> You who live in the declining and abandoned places
> of great cities, called barrios, ghettos, and favelas:
> What is archaic? What is modern? We are both.
> The myth of the first world is that
> development is wealth and technology progress.
> It is all rubbish.
> It means that you are no longer human beings
> but only labor.
> It means that the land you live on is not earth
> but only property.
> It means that what you produce with your own hands
> is not yours to eat or wear or shelter you
> if you cannot buy it. (258–59)

Those who live in the abandoned places represent the abandoned people and communities of the capitalist state. They are the lumpen, the wretched refuse. But Arcangel overturns such an ideology of casting off to refer to the myth of progress as "rubbish." This neoliberal ideology labels the land itself and human bodies as nothing more than machines of commodification. Even the most basic of material needs, food and shelter, are not rights guaranteed to all, but luxuries afforded those who can pay for them. Any ties to space and place beyond titled ownership are also severed, creating a landless and homeless populous, cast off to their containment barrios, waste dumps of capitalism.

Such an ideology of containment fails in comparison to the novel's attention to the fluidity and permeability of boundaries, particularly as they relate to the border between the United States and Mexico, which the text refers to as "the line in the dust [that] became again as wide as an entire culture and as deep as the social and economic construct that nobody knew how to change" (254). Although many of the characters of the novel figure into this examination of the border, Arcangel is its most vocal and overt analyst and critic. Much of his commentary addresses labor and environmental injustices faced by a collective Latin American poor at the hands of moneyed outsiders. Arcangel's vision encompasses the broad geography and deep time of the Americas *en toto*. For example, he can simultaneously see:

> the woman who sold him the nopales in the plaza
> and this Juan Valdez picking Colombian coffee
> and Chico Mendes tapping Brazilian rubber.
> *He could see*
> Haitian farmers burning and slashing cane, workers stirring
>   molasses into white gold.
> Guatemalans loading trucks with
> crates of bananas and corn.
> Indians, who mined tin in the Cerro Rico
> and saltpeter from the Atacama desert, chewing coca and drinking
>   aguardiente to dull the pain of their labor.
> . . .
>
> *He saw*
> the mother in Idaho peeling a banana for her child. (145)

As he often does, Arcangel pays particular attention to people who work the land: working with plant life in the form of nopales, coffee, rubber, sugar cane, bananas, and corn as well as mining tin and saltpeter. We can also note that these activities grow more and more technologically mediated over the course of the passage, from cooking a plant to picking and tapping, to the more complex and involved preparation of molasses, to loading trucks, to mining. But the passage concludes with the transnational flow of goods, as the bananas picked and crated earlier in the passage are consumed in the United States. We also note a parallel between the opening image, a woman preparing food for sale, and a woman preparing food for her child, complicated by the economic necessities of each.

Such collectivity belies the boundaries that states imagine and construct to differentiate themselves from others. The border as an actual place comes under the lens of this narrative as do lines in general. Buzzworm, for example, is described as "taking a hard look at the urban front line, trying to figure where exactly that line might be drawn. It was all war talk. Even the years he'd been in Vietnam, never was clear. . . . Line wasn't something drawn on the ground" (217). The lines that appear on maps, that demarcate one place from another, are absent in the actuality of space. Battle lines, drawn on military, gang, or police maps, are imaginary, never real. These borders are designed to separate communities, but their boundaries are always both porous and in motion. On a similar note, Bobby, while crossing the border with a cousin he is smuggling into the United States from Mexico, observes, "Border's nothing but desks and lines of people on linoleum floors" (204).[6] Bobby's description transforms the border from a physical location in the landscape but also from a militarized battleground. Instead, the border becomes framed, as indeed it is, as a bureaucratic zone. The line is not a stripe in the sand but a queue on a prefabricated plastic floor. The border is a sterile administrative place, not a lived space.

Yamashita's novel speaks to a liquid understanding of time and space. Time here is not linear and progressive, and it's not strictly circular, though elements of the cyclical play a major role. Instead, the emphasis throughout *Tropic of Orange* is on all time existing at once: moments from the past interpenetrate moments of the present, ebbing, flowing, surging, diving deep beneath the surface, and rising in unexpected places, like lava or tectonic plates.[7] To that end, Buzzworm contends, "Time could heal, but it wouldn't make wrongs go away. Time came back like a reminder. Time folded with memory. In a moment, everything could fold itself up, and time stand still" (86). Buzzworm's understanding of time represents a single liquid temporality like that present in each of the texts studied here. Time is not a linear progression from wrong to right, nor do we ever move away from the past. The image of time folding with memory represents both a combination of time and memory, an emphasis on the subjective nature of time, as well as time and memory warping around one another. Beyond that, time has the capability of slowing down to the point of stopping, such that we can become moored within that temporal liquidity.

Tropic of Orange begins with an understanding of time and space in a cosmological sense, taking place at midday on the Tropic of Cancer on the summer solstice, the moment and location at which the sun lies directly overhead. Arcangel refers to it as "the Tropic of Cancer. That is a border made plain by the sun itself, a border one can easily recognize" (71). The date, presumably June 21, is conspicuously absent, emphasizing a cosmic interaction of earth and tilt and sun over the limits of the Gregorian calendar. The English word solstice comes to us from Latin, from a combination of sol ("sun") and sistere ("to stand still"). The solstice is the day on which the sun stands still. To that end, Buzzworm notes, "Time stood still momentarily. Time stood still eternally. Whatever it was doing, it was standing. Just standing. . . . Twelve noon just standing there" (137). Within a solar calendar, such an understanding of the solstice indicates that it is not only the sun but time itself that stands still. And considering the mutual constitutive correlation between time and space, the former's freezing is bound to alter the latter. In the case of Tropic of Orange, time, ordinarily understood as constantly on the move, sticks, while space, which is imagined as a relative stasis, bends and warps wildly. Yamashita's text demonstrates that the spatial element of time and space is always in motion. Her selection of the Pacific coast of North America as this story's home (though this habitus expands over the course of the novel, especially and fittingly to encompass the entirety of the Pacific Rim) makes use of a geography that is prone to startling illustrations of just how liquid space always is. Indeed, the fact that the rim is defined by the Pacific Ocean rather than a body of land reinforces this emphasis on liquidity.

The earthquake remains the foremost natural disaster fear about California generally and Los Angeles in particular; fires, floods, and mudslides are a few others. As Emi explains, "*El A* is *A*-pocalypse. It's bee ess I tell you. Earthquakes. Riots. Fires. Floods. It's just natural phenomena: earth, wind, fire, water" (162). Each of these geologic and geographic alterations emblematize the liquid nature of the supposedly solid ground on which we stand, on which we have built the global center that is LA.[8] The earthquake demonstrates, without regard for what we may or may not want, that the land, the earth on which we draw boundaries and which we assume to exist in an absolutely solid stasis, is itself always moving, or moving toward moving, always in the process of becoming something else. The plate on which Los Angeles sits continues to creep northward (the idea that LA will fall into the sea is a myth that misunderstands the strike-slip nature of the San Andreas fault, though rising sea levels may rework this cataclysm in a more gradual temporal framing). Such a questioning of geographic and geologic permanence challenges all mythmaking of static or solid structures laid over the ever-shifting land and water.

As the entire Pacific Rim shares this characteristic shifting, it behooves us to understand the role of this enormous range within the novel. The great showdown between SUPERNAFTA and El Gran Mojado takes places at the Pacific Rim Auditorium, and the final section of the novel is simply titled "Pacific Rim." Moreover, Manzanar's narrative describes, "Encroaching on this vision was a larger one: the great Pacific stretching along its great rim, brimming over long coastal shores from one hemisphere to the other" (170). The Pacific Rim comprises an enormous stretch of the planet, one which houses or borders four continents and, apart from Europe and Africa, all those inhabited by humans. Centering the Pacific Rim for the conclusion of the novel (and eschewing Europe in particular) counters the black/white binary of commonly imagined U.S. racial constructions. Moreover, because *Tropic of Orange* includes no white central characters, it further resituates assumptions of a correlation between U.S. citizens or residents and whiteness.

Perhaps the character with the greatest understanding of a deep ecological community, one that attempts to understand a global interrelationality between all elements of nonhuman and human existences, is
also the character whom society deems the easiest to dismiss: homeless freeway conductor Manzanar. His importance as a knowing witness
to the city is reinforced as the novel notes that "only Manzanar could
see the undulating patterns and the changing geography corrupting the
sun's shadows, confusing time, so that all events should happen and
end at the same time" (206). The narrative speaks of a simultaneity of
all time—all things have always really been happening at the same time,
and we are only occasionally able to understand or comprehend that
reality. Beyond his deep temporal understanding, Manzanar also recognizes the parallels between the human-made city and other bodily phenomena: "He bore and raised each note, joined them, united families,
created a community, a great society, an entire civilization of sound. The
great flow of humanity ran below and beyond his feet in every direction,
pumping and pulsating, that blood connection, the great heartbeat of a
great city" (35). Manzanar sees the human city and the humans in it for
their collective life force. They comprise the circulatory system that ani-
mates, makes animate, and makes animal the concrete exoskeleton of
Los Angeles. Moreover, Manzanar occupies a position much like those
of many nature writers, including Thoreau, Muir, Aldo Leopold, Wendell
Berry, Edward Abbey, Annie Dillard, and Barry Lopez. He comes to see
the space where he lives as home in an all-encompassing sense: "To say
that Manzanar Murakami was homeless was as absurd as the work he
chose to do. No one was more at home in L.A. than this man" (36). For
Manzanar, the entire city and county of Los Angeles becomes home,
rather than a single dwelling or even a neighborhood.[9] Manzanar dwells
in a Heideggerian sense that relates living in relationship to place with
being open to existence, and he comes to recognize the vital forces that
swirl in their respective and collective liquidities. His understanding of
the ecologically complex city is underscored as the novel explains, "The
freeway was a great root system, an organic living entity. It was nothing
more than a great writhing concrete dinosaur and nothing less than the
greatest orchestra on Earth" (37). While the metaphor is a bit mixed,
Manzanar's worldview recognizes the organic in the city's infrastruc-

ture, as the freeway is the root, the nutrient grabbing subsurface, as well as the giant creature (this dinosaur is not extinct but alive in its writhing). The freeway is also the collective artistry of the city, a high-end music-making group that bows and blows and drums the background soundtrack of LA's urban life.

Manzanar not only understands the city as a living entity; he also recognizes an alternative cartography within it. The novel explains, "*There are maps and there are maps and there are maps.* The uncanny thing was that [Manzanar] could see all of them at once, filter some, pick them out like transparent windows and place them even delicately and consecutively in a complex grid of pattern, spatial discernment, body politic*" (56). In short, Manzanar represents one of a very few who can see the world, or in this case see the microcosmic city, in ecological terms, with an understanding of various positively polluted strata, intersections, muddy liquid mingling, and all, always interconnected and moving but also localized in time and space. Hsu argues that the images of Los Angeles in *Tropic of Orange* "seek to decenter the dominant Anglo Euro-American narratives about Los Angeles" by "appropriating and re-deploying hegemonic tropes of cartography and geography in ways that map Western colonialism and the buried sites (longitude and latitude figured in the parole of history) of prehistoric rivers, flora and fauna, and 'native' resistance as well as the ongoing transgressions of African Americans, new Asian immigrants, Latino/as, just to name a few" (77). Hsu alludes to the fact that Manzanar recognizes layers that "began within the very geology of the land, the artesian rivers running beneath the surface, connected and divergent, shifting and swelling. There was the complex and normally silent web of faults" (*Tropic of Orange* 57). Even in one of the most sprawling, seemingly entirely human-made spaces on the globe, the bedrock of geology still flows, still shapes the land, and will continue to shape, to bend and shake and alter, the land over which people lay our physical and cultural structures. The physical structure of the city *concretizes* difference and hierarchy (though we must remember that concrete is shaped in its liquid form). But those structures are no less a part of the landscape or part or our lives. The narrator continues describing, "Below the surface, there was the man-made grid of civil utilities: Southern California pipelines of natural gas; the unnatural waterways of the Los Angeles Department of Water and Power, and the great dank tunnels of sewage; the cascades of poisonous effluents surging" (57).[10] While these underground waterways are deemed "unnatural" here (though notably juxtaposed with "natural gas"), they are paralleled with all their sewage and effluents to the artesian rivers of the previous sentence; they exist at a similarly unregistered level by most of the city's inhabitants and visitors and play a literally vital role in the health of many of the species in the urban area. But "ordinary persons never bother to notice . . . the prehistoric grid of plant and fauna and human behavior, nor the historic grid of land usage and property, the great overlays of transport—sidewalks, bicycle paths, roads, freeways, systems of transit both ground and air, a thousand natural and man-made divisions, variations both dynamic and stagnant, patterns and connections by every conceivable definition from the distribution of wealth and race, from patterns of climate to the curious blueprint of the skies" (57). Yamashita weaves a dizzying array of elements into a hint at the ecological complexities of urban spaces, but also one that can be found in countless spaces of the earth. There exist the seen and unseen layers of human and nonhuman creation: sidewalks and beaten paths; heavily human-mediated aquifers; transmissions of power in electrical, hydrological, thermal, economic, cultural, and bodily senses. These are always in process, even if the process involves growing stagnant (stagnancy, after all, allows for certain kinds of life to thrive).

Manzanar's understanding of the inseparability of the human and other than human persists in discussions of the homeless, as Manzanar demonstrates their integral role to their ecosystems and economies. Near the conclusion of the novel, exterminating the homeless is seen as a positive alternative to jailing them, casting them aside in penitentiary disposal sites (we recall the Lumpen in book 3 of The Rag Doll Plagues). This novel describes this casting away, this making into trash of this population, as "the utterly violent assumption underlying everything: that the homeless were expendable" (123). Moreover, Buzzworm later demonstrates his recognition of the administrative process regarding the homeless: "Everything's colliding into everything. No place for these people to go. What they gonna do? Put us all in jail? At forty thou per head, doesn't seem too cost effective" (192). The forces that ultimately invade the accident scene with military might, including helicopters with guns blazing, are not going to "waste" such capital on incarcerating a homeless population that is already devoid of financial resources.[11] Human lives are reduced to a bottom line of financial expense, and these lives, already occupying a cast-off positionality on a reclaimed geography, become nearly devoid of exchange value.

But Yamashita's novel offers an alternative to a framework that casts a binary distinction between the new, shiny commodity and the used piece of trash, through the far more ecologically and socially sound practices of reclamation, reuse, and recycling. Recycling in this instance, however, is not only a human activity; rather, it is a process in which many of the most accomplished and successful species excel. "Manzanar imagined himself a kind of recycler. After all he, like other homeless in the city, was a recycler of the last run. The homeless were the insects and scavengers of society, feeding on leftovers, living in residue, collecting refuse, carting it this way and that for pennies. In the same manner, who would use the residue of sounds in the city if Manzanar did not?" (56). Considering Manzanar's recycling within an environmentalist framework, we recognize acts of composting (beyond his composing) in his activities. Like the pepenadores of *The Rag Doll Plagues*, he utilizes cast-off objects, reclaiming them both for their use and exchange values. One might not generally take being likened to an insect as a compliment; but in this instance, the narrative recognizes insects for what they are, seemingly insignificant organisms that, in fact, fuel their ecosystems by engaging in processes of scavenging. This cleansing is by no means altruistic but a carved-out methodology of survival. Nothing, not even the fleeting excess sounds of the city, goes wasted in this inordinately complex system.

The homeless village that grows out of the abandoned vehicles on the 110 embraces the recycling of the characters bound to waste throughout these chapters. It makes use of reusable objects but also emphasizes sanitation. The "valley of cars" becomes enough of a media curiosity that the mayor visits. While he is there, one of his aides notes, "Actually, I'm surprised to see how clean it is down here" (217). The outsider assumes the valley of the homeless will be as dirty as the homeless are assumed to be—as if by choice. The valley's cleanliness is contrasted to the LA

River, a mainly paved aqueduct that houses a large homeless population. "The L.A. River. . . . Shit floating down the river. Car parts, hypodermics, dead dogs, Neanderthal bones, props from the last movie shot down there, you name it" (41). The homeless population dwells amid the cast-off objects of the city and the entertainment industry. Ultimately, all this waste is simply lumped together as "shit," as are the homeless people themselves. However, one of the valley's residents (who are in many ways no longer homeless) explains, "We got regular trash pickup once a day. Bottles, cans, and plastic already get separated" and "We carted the outhouses from the construction work and distributed them at regular intervals, but we could use more. We're gonna be needing running water and a sewage system" (217–18). The residents are settled into this space, providing for themselves an infrastructure that they would otherwise be denied: "A commissary truck opened for business, as did a recycling truck" (121), "creating a community out of a traffic jam" (156). This community has established routines of waste management and recycling, but we must also remember that this entire neighborhood is a reclaimed space in which motor vehicles, abandoned by their prior owners, are repurposed according to the needs of those who have reclaimed them.

Near the end of the novel, Manzanar's point of view again focuses its attention on garbage and waste. After a massive explosion, every airbag in every car in the city inflates. Traffic has stopped and Manzanar's symphony comes to an end. We note that this chapter takes place on "The Rim," setting this chapter on the coast, the seemingly liminal space between sea and land (though both permeate one another far more expansively than the littoral zone might suggest). This passage examines the ocean's role on human ecologies of Los Angeles. Manzanar sees himself emerging from the sea, awakening to the terrestrial and aquatic life around him: "Slowly his head rose above the foam and floating kelp. He walked from the rim and looked back at the waves of natural and human garbage thrown back again and again. Everything would churn itself into tiny bits of sand, crumble there at the rim—the descending sun one gigantic blazing orange dipping behind, boiling the sea into steamy shades of blood" (255). The orange, a challenging image to understand throughout the novel, is paired with the sun, such a central image of Southern California. Meanwhile, the sea becomes the great composter.

Everything gets chewed up, unified, and reassembled here on the rim. Human garbage (which can refer to humans who are garbage as well as to the garbage that humans make) and natural garbage (the waste of the rest of the world that I would argue is no more or less natural than that of the humans), all become part of the geologic forces that are forever shaping all landscapes, though those actions may be more visible here in Los Angeles or here on the rim. The broken-down components are mixed up and reassembled, much like the beads at the end of *The Antelope Wife* as discussed in chapter 3—though the latter's image maintains a structural unity absent in Yamashita's metaphor. Nonetheless, the rim serves as a global center in this novel as it does in contemporary reality. Emphasizing the centrality of the Southland, Buzzworm explains to Gabe, "I myself don't go nowhere. Hell, L.A. don't go nowhere, and look at this. Shit just comes to us" (114). Despite LA's physical mobility, it remains both margin (rim) and center, material but nonetheless liquid.

The aforementioned orange plays a critical role in the settling of the Southland as it does within this novel. Historian Douglas Cazaux Sackman writes, "From the 1880s through World War II, the citrus industry was the primary engine of the growth machine in Southern California" (5). The citrus industry, synecdochically represented by the orange, played multiple roles in fueling this growth machine, from ecological and horticultural changes to the physical landscape of the Southland, to economic structures: agricultural jobs, millionaire landowners, railroads, irrigation, roads in and out of the groves, and travel, investment, and relocation propaganda declaring California to be an Edenic setting of eternal sunshine. Sackman continues:

> the Orange Empire was more than just an industry. It established hegemony over peoples and places. It recruited and managed thousands of laborers from across the globe. It also created millions of consumers, colonizing public and private spaces across the country to convey its alluring advertisements. The Orange Empire's spheres of influence stretched over nature as well as culture[;] earth, water, trees, and fruits all were transformed under its governing hands. (7)

The orange-growing enterprise, which Sackman refers to as an empire, serves as an emblematic starting point for Southern California's role as the consumer cultural center of the world, a global locus of capital, labor, and mythmaking. Sze alludes to such mythmaking when she asserts, "Yamashita puts race and class at the center of her definition of Los Angeles, as opposed to the historical development of Los Angeles, which operated on an ideology of L.A. as a 'natural' and utopic escape from the problems of urbanization and humanity that plague the older cities of the eastern and Midwestern United States" (27).

The eponymous orange of Yamashita's novel comes from a navel tree that Gabriel brings from Riverside, California, which may be "the descendent of the original trees first brought to California from Brazil in 1873, and planted by L.C. Tibbetts," though Gabriel acknowledges that it is "probably a hybrid" (11). In fact, oranges arrived in the Americas with Christopher Columbus, and they migrated to Mission San Gabriel in what would become California in the early 1800s. Tibbett's Brazilian trees were seedless Bahias, also known as Riverside, Washington, or navel oranges; and they were agricultural game changers. Though Yamashita's text credits L. C. Tibbetts, many consider his wife, Eliza, to be the original cultivator of California's orange industry. The plants were, in truth, shipped to the Tibbettses from Washington DC by William Saunders, who had received them from Bahia, Brazil. As seedless fruit, they represent a genetic dead end, kept alive by human hands grafting a scion to a rootstock. The rootstock is a preexisting root system of one species; the scion is the bud of the plant the botanist wishes to grow. These trees are, in fact, the product of human mediation; they are constructed, as it were, but live and grow based on their own adaptive and symbiotic capacities. All these Riverside oranges were and are clones of the originals, with the exact same genetic makeup.

The role of cloning further comes into play in *Tropic of Orange* in its discussions of the combatants in el Contrato con America.[12] Arcangel's narrative explains, "National heroes like SUPERNAFTA were usually replicants of some sort" (257), while "international heroes like El Gran Mojado were usually freaks of nature" (258). The nationalistic ideal, personified by SUPERNAFTA, is one of replication, a process of reproduction that subverts the processes of differentiation and mutation that occur through biological reproduction. International heroes, by contrast, are the products of such mutation, genetic border crossings that redirect the original body process. We can think of the navel oranges along these lines, as they are crafted and grafted asexually, in a manner more akin to SUPERNAFTA. However, the species is itself a product of nonhuman-induced mutation, the engine of evolution, though this mutation would present an evolutionary dead end were it not for human intervention. Human and nonhuman forces meld in this orange species.

The orange that drags the Tropic (and the tropics) north is an ecological aberration in another sense as well. Gabriel's tree fruits "too early"; Rafaela suspects global warming or the industriousness of African bees. As such, this tree marks an intersection of multiple global influences in the forms of transcontinental trade and colonialism—which led to the introduction of the orange (originally an Asian plant) to Europe; plantation economies in South America; importation of African, or more accurately Africanized bees, to the Americas; and the effects of global climate change. These Africanized bees are themselves hybrid species, descendants of the African honey bee (*Apis mellifera scutellata*) and European honey bees such as the Italian or the Spanish/Gibraltar (*Apis mellifera ligustica* and *Apis melliferia iberiensis*, respectively). In fact, all of these are subspecies of the Western honey bee. It is worth noting that European bees are seen as becoming Africanized, rather than African bees becoming Europeanized. This nominal difference corresponds to their designation as "killer bees," with more aggressive tendencies than their European counterparts. Moreover, the discursive threat of these killer bees in the 1990s stemmed from their increasing presence in the southwestern United States, as they began to migrate in increasing numbers from Mexico and the rest of Latin America, where they had been cultivated for their high yields of honey. We note a parallel between these Africanized and hybrid "invaders" from the south and the novel's fixation on U.S. xenophobic border security and ideals of racial purity. Yamashita's novel demonstrates the complex and liquid interrelationalities spanning time and space over both thousands of years and thousands of miles.

Oranges, however, become bearers of toxicity as smugglers inject them with cocaine in order to sneak them into the United States. The rhetoric around these toxic oranges gets ramped up over the course of the narrative, eventually echoing the hegemonic concerns of national and ethnic purity and impermeability. The description of the events surrounding these toxic oranges begins as a "*spiked* orange alert" (138). The oranges are spiked, an intentional act by someone, but the event itself is merely an alert. The next manifestation is an "*illegal* orange scare" (139), followed by the xenophobic "*illegal alien* orange scare" (140). Each of these terms, of course, alludes to immigration, while the text challenges how exactly a piece of fruit can be illegal. We can extrapolate this commentary to other border-related discourse, especially in terms of drug trafficking. Arcangel calls this "the war over an innocent indigenous plant," while a Mexican man he is speaking with ponders, "It all goes north to the gringos. If they want it so much, why don't they plant it in their own backyards?" (both marijuana and coca are indigenous to the Americas) (146). On a similar note, Arcangel later wonders, "Is it a crime to be poor? Can it be illegal to be a human being?" (211). We are reminded of the term "illegal" as it refers to undocumented workers in the United States, a term that denotes an essential bodily illegality. The scare tactics of naming reach a crescendo with "*Death oranges*" (141). A heretofore healthy plant part becomes a carrier of death, the ultimate toxic commodity. People respond in predicable ways: "Oranges went underground. The word was emphatic: All oranges were suspect. And deemed highly toxic. Waste companies hauled the rotting stuff by the tons to landfills. Environmental experts declared them toxic waste. . . . The poison could leach into the water system. Fruit flies could spread it too" (141). The corresponding frantic reactions to this public health crisis reinforce the interrelationality of ecological existence. However, the majority of people here find this interrelationality terrifying. Oranges are treated as if they were toxic, whether they are or not. As such, they are cast away, buried away from populated areas in disposal sites. But, of course, landfills are inhabited by myriad species as well as the usually marginalized human communities, who, by the very nature of their proximity to waste, become regarded as societal detritus themselves. However, such segregation or containment can never succeed, as all spaces are bound together both by their interconnected aquifers and by their species (here, fruit flies, an allusion to California's battle against the incursion of Mediterranean fruit flies, *Ceratitis capitata*, themselves an invasive species in the 1980s). Humans can pretend they are not utterly permeable elements of their ecosystems only up to a point.

Later, the narrative returns to the subject of oranges and the ecological connections between living things. "Some're saying it's orange trees growing in poppy fields in Bolivia. Others say it's a dangerous tropical virus, like flesh-eating bacteria. Can you believe it? Oranges with cancer" (163). In these instances, the dangers from the oranges do not stem so much from human manipulation as biologically occurring cross-pollinations and mutations. The tropics become vilified as a dark and foreboding place where lurks not only moral but also epidemiological evils. The invocation of cancer nods to the tropic being pulled closer but also to the disease, which itself is a problem of mutation. While mutation allows for evolutionary adaptation, most mutations are not beneficial for the survival of a body or population.[13]

The oranges in *Tropic of Orange* come to represent, rather than the health and vitality of the Southern California landscape, physical toxins whose effects are made most lethal by corresponding cultural toxins. Buzzworm notes that one young man's medical report reads, "Direct cause of death: high doses of a very pure form of cocaine and unidentified chemicals found in the stomach and digestive tract, probably ingested orally" (104). The physical toxin in play here is cocaine, but Buzzworm points out that the injection of physical toxins arises largely from cultural ones, utilizing the term "running" to refer to running with a gang: "It was mostly an *overdose of hormones and poverty* made them run. Running fast, but not fast enough. Things were aiming to catch up with them: drugs, petty theft, assault, robbery. But it wasn't time for homicide, Buzzworm thought. Wasn't time" (105, emphasis mine). Buzzworm's calculations of the intersections of drug use, gang membership, and murder are temporally spatial. People subjected to overdoses of poverty, combined with temporally age-specific hormones, reach certain markers at certain moments: they follow a map with estimable travel times. But in the warping landscape of this novel, understandings of time and space grow increasingly liquid, and physical and cultural toxins become more lethal, more quickly.

Of course, the ecological interconnection present in this novel also includes the human made and the exchanges of transnational or globalized neoliberal capitalism. The United States likens the crossing of its boundaries by Mexican objects and agents to the constantly permeated boundaries between human settlements and their refuse. Bobby describes, "Gifts from NAFTA. Oranges, bananas, corn, lettuce, guarachis, women's apparel, tennis shoes, radios, electrodomestics, live-in domestics, living domestics, gardeners, dishwashers, waiters, masons, ditch diggers, migrants, pickers, packers, braceros, refugees, centroamericanos, wetbacks, wops, undocumenteds, illegals, aliens" (161–62). This narrative begins with produce, natural objects exchanged between the nations that produce them and those that consume them (much like Arcangel's passage discussed earlier). Next come human-produced objects, growing from the more handmade and materially necessary guarachis, clothes, and shoes to the more luxurious and technologically mediating radios and electrodomestics. The transition here moves from the machines or objects that perform household chores to the human bodies that do so, from objects to agents and subjects. This harvesting of agricultural commodities and trafficking of bodies develops over the course of the novel into the harvesting and trafficking of human organs. If the body can be commodified and moved, particularly within a discursive tradition of metonymic cancelation (the people become strong backs, hands that pick, etc.), then its parts can become literally parsed in the same ways they have been figuratively parsed.

The agriculturally grounded discourse of *Tropic of Orange* describes wealthy people paying for organs harvested from disenfranchised Latin American children. We generally think of *harvesting* as the reaping of a botanical crop. The former surgeon, Manzanar, looking at a human child's heart that is transported around in the novel, supposes, "I imagine it was harvested for transplant" (216). We note the botanical diction here as well in Manzanar's use of both terms: *harvest* and *transplant*. And Manzanar would know. The novel explains, "Long ago, Manzanar had been a skilled surgeon. His work had entailed careful incisions through layers of living tissue, excising tumors, inserting implants, facilitating transplants" (56). Manzanar is well acquainted with the permeability of human bodies; his former career consisted of little else. But the "baton replaced the knife," and Manzanar comes to penetrate human selves in a different way—sonically, aurally. However, unlike the voluntary procedures administered by Manzanar, those taking place in *Tropic of Orange* are ghastly. A child is found, killed, and butchered. The conversations that introduce the subject of organ harvesting take place in Mexico at

Gabriel's neighbor's house, surrounded by cornfields. Indeed, the narrative moves back and forth between its discussions of an infant heart in a cooler and the corn crops and ears of corn being held by Sol.

Corn plays a central role in this thread in particular but also in the novel as a whole, representing an indigenous crop (and a heavily human-engineered one) to counter the imported hybrid species of the novel's title. Similarly, indigenous stories and histories intersect with this particular thread in the novel. Rafaela discovers that her neighbor's son Hernando (whose nominal similarities to Hernán Cortés—Cortes is Rafaela's last name as well—must not be missed) is an organ smuggler, and he (driving a black Jaguar) begins to chase her and Sol. At one point, he catches her, and they begin to fight. He transforms into a jaguar (more on this shortly); and she, into a snake. Many have noted that Rafaela becomes Quetzalcoatl, who is renowned for having brought corn to the people.[14] The novel demonstrates the cyclical nature of this fight, rejecting a finality to its conclusion: "As night fell, they began their horrific dance with death, gutting and searing the tissue of their existence, copulating in rage, destroying and creating at once—the apocalyptic fulfillment of a prophecy—blood and semen commingling among shredded serpent and feline remains" (221). This transmogrification of people into animals and gods pairs seemingly disparate activities like creation and destruction, birth and death, in order to show that they, like north and south, like conqueror and conquered, cannot be understood outside each other. The Spanish and the indigenous meet here, battling over Rafaela's son Sol—whose two-year-old body would provide Hernando with the organs he needs to harvest. The very sun (sol) is at stake, but so is the source of Mexica power, in the form of Huitzilopochtli, as discussed in chapter 2. Jaguar, the god of the underworld, moves between that world and this one in Mexica religion and embodies Tezcatlipoca, Lord of the Smoking Mirror, who is related to the north. Jaguar is a god of the dyad of creation and death and destruction. We are reminded of the novel's culminating fight between El Gran Mojado and SUPERNAFTA, which becomes coded as destruction but also as a new form of being. Sadowski-Smith asserts that the "simultaneous deaths of [SUPERNAFTA and El Gran Mojado] not only signify the increasing degree of hemispheric interdependence, they also symbolize the possibility that when the signifiers of First-World and

Third-World under-development destroy each other and the borders they represent, new ways for imagining a different kind of continental future may emerge" (106–07). We must also keep in mind that the pairings of Rafaela and Hernando and Quetzalcoatl and Jaguar also participate in cycles of death and birth, creation and destruction, in Mexica stories and cultural-religious constructions.

Ultimately this battle between the indigenous, mestizo, Latino figure of El Gran Mojado and the U.S. Anglo male figure of SUPERNAFTA becomes a new round in the cyclical battle between Quetzalcoatl and Tezcatlipoca, chasing each other across earth and sky, each bound to take the lead for a period, only to be overtaken by the other in due course. At the novel's conclusion, El Gran Mojado seems to defeat SUPERNAFTA, until the latter launches a Patriot missile into the former (the name of the missile has importance, of course, but we should also bear in mind that the Patriot is a defensive weapon and represents the United States defending itself from the invading Gran Mojado). As such, neither proves entirely victorious or defeated. Both seem to perish, though the finality of such a perishing remains in question, allowing for the possibility of their return via some far-fetched but nonetheless certain-to-occur plot twist.

Rafaela further represents the novel's demonstration of such ecosystemic sustainability and recurrence from the opening paragraph, as she is shown sweeping various species that creep into Gabriel's Mazatlán home each night. She brushes these "dead and living things from over and under beds, from behind doors and shutters, through archways, along the veranda," in short, from everywhere in the house (3). The house is not a closed system but a permeated space crawling with life. However, this presence of the other than human in the house and home does not mark it as a diseased or infested place: "Every morning, a small pile of assorted insects and tiny animals—moths and spiders, lizards and beetles [an] iguana, a crab, and a mouse. And there was the scorpion, always dead—its fragile back broken in the middle. And the snake that slithered away at the urging of her broom" (3).[15] Each day begins with this same routine, and the process takes on a cyclical nature not only for its recurrence but from Yamashita's wielding of the definite article, particularly as pertains to "the scorpion" and "the snake." These specific creatures take on a mythical resonance for their repetition not as examples of one of a species but as exemplars for their species. One scorpion, always there, always dead. Reborn and rekilled again and again. And always the same snake. We remember the correlation between Rafaela, the snake, and Quetzalcoatl in this text and understand that the ecological community becomes subsumed within an ecospiritual one. The realms of the human, the natural, and the supernatural are shown to be interpenetrating, undifferentiated, and ultimately undifferentiatable.

Rafaela, like many characters studied here, is a cleaner by occupation. However, Yamashita's novel shows differences in cleaning Gabe's Mazatlán house and cleaning office buildings in the United States. In the latter, she makes use of electronic devices and harsh chemicals. But in Mexico she finds other methods more reliable: "When she first came to the house, she couldn't find a broom to accomplish this daily ritual . . . Gabriel had left an American vacuum cleaner in a closet" (4). The vacuum fails as a useful tool in this instance for a variety of reasons, the primary one being the fact that the electricity to the house is unreliable. Replacement bags are also required, and as anyone who has ever attempted it can attest, "recycling these bags was nearly impossible" (4). Rafaela "did not have the heart to dump them without releasing the trapped animals inside" (4). Pieces of crab (the zodiac symbol for Cancer) jam the gears of the machine, and it ceases to work entirely. Rafaela's broom, on the contrary, works perfectly well for shooing the creatures, living and dead, out of the house. One might be tempted to read in this a neo-Luddite impulse; but considering the connections made between people via technological means throughout this novel (particularly in Gabe's epiphanies near the novel's conclusion, as we will see), reading such a stance would seem misguided. Instead, Yamashita's text offers, not only in this moment but elsewhere, analysis of the vacuum not only as an appliance (as in "vacuum cleaner") but also as a physical state. Most notably, the text demonstrates that after any calamity, "in a matter of minutes, life filled a vacuum, reorganizing itself in predicable and unpredictable ways" (121). The vacuum implies an emptiness; that which seeks to clean, to impose order via the vacuum, cannot function in a place as full of life as Gabe's land, or indeed any of earth's spaces. *Tropic of Orange* describes a return to a recognition of the life that abounds but frequently goes unrecognized within even the most urban of spaces.

Gabriel attempts to create an idealized slice of the heavily irrigated Southern California landscape in Mexico, but the ecosystemic space continues to reclaim the house and its property. He strives to establish plants he idealizes, while Rafaela's garden is replete with those that will succeed in their setting. Rafaela plants cacti, peppers, "my herbs," and sunflowers. "Now the roses were twisting along the ground and up a banana tree. The idea of having fruit trees was a nice one too, except that the soil was sandy and required a lot of dung and compost." While the banana tree "knew how to make use of fresh refuse . . . composting trees like peach and plum was a more delicate business" (10). Rafaela, the cleaner, recognizes the role of waste in the generative processes of growth and food production. These plants, particularly ill-adapted for the climate and soil in which they are placed, require extra waste just to survive. In the ecosystemic struggle for survival, "the fittest were the mango and papaya trees," and Rafaela wonders "why Gabriel insisted on planting trees that couldn't survive in this climate" (10). Gabriel does not engage with Mazatlán or Mexico as an actual lived space but as a mental image colored by nostalgic longing for an ancestral home with which his family does not identify. Gabriel explains, "No one in my entire family had ever bothered to come here. They called it Gabe's Folly. 'Hey ése, what about investing in the homeland—East L.A.?' they snickered" (224). Gabriel's family, his actual ancestral root system, recognizes a homeland in the United States, rather than abiding Gabriel's diasporic subjectivity longing for Mexico. Rafaela's plants are endemic, successful in this climate, and useful for food and health. Gabriel recognizes even in himself an ineffectual longing in this space. On the contrary, Rafaela eschews tragic agonism for a comic pragmatism.

The focus on human and plant relationships moves to LA's urban core in the form of Buzzworm's attention to palm trees. The novel describes Buzzworm as a "big black seven-foot dude, Vietnam vet, an Afro shirt with palm trees painted all over it, dreds, pager and Walkman belted to his waist, sound plugged into one ear and two or three watches at least on both his wrists" (27). While Buzzworm may seem to be one of the novel's more technologically mediated individuals (and he is until the text's conclusion—though such a concept may imply a differentiation between technology and the nonhuman that need not exist), he is nonetheless deeply interested with the nonhuman, particularly as relates to palm trees. His point-of-view narrator describes him expounding, "Family Palmaceae. Four thousand species. Tall ones called Washingtonia Robusta or Mexican Fan Palm. Similar ones with thicker trunks were called Washingtonia Filifera" (30). The two species Buzzworm mentions, the *Washingtonia robusta* and the *Washingtonia filifera*, are closely related, known as the Mexican Fan and California Fan Palms, respectively. The choice of these two palms, considering the privileged geographies of California and Mexico in this novel, marks these species bearing particular import. The latter palm is also the only one indigenous to Southern California, a critical detail in light of the popular cultural iconography of the region as relates to these trees.

In describing more about these native plants, Buzzworm explains, "You understand the species of trees in the neighborhood, you understand the *nature* of my work" (31, emphasis mine). Buzzworm shows himself a student of these trees, knowing which are male and female, which produce what kinds of fruit, and so forth. But the residents of the neighborhood mostly just know the trees "made a mess when the dead fronds fell, the orange fruit got all over the sidewalk and the birds made a mess nesting and squabbling about" (31). Palms represent little more than problematic and annoying incursions on the ordered human realm, by way of both the plants themselves and their avian denizens. Nonetheless, Buzzworm contends, "These trees're like my watches here, markin' time. Palm tree's smart, knows the time for everything. Knows to put out flowers and fruit when the time's right, even though out here don't seem like there's any seasons to speak of. Suppose we could all learn something from a palm tree that knows the seasons better than us" (31). Buzzworm, the exclusively inner-city urban resident, acknowledges in these monocots a kind of knowledge and wisdom that correlates particularly to an understanding of time that is greater than that of the people of the city (or people from outside Los Angeles who often make the erroneous statement that LA lacks seasonal climatic changes). What's more, these trees are also indicators of space and place in Los Angeles: "That was what the palm trees were for. To make out the place where he lived. To make sure that people noticed. And the palm trees were like the eyes of his neighborhood, watching the rest of the city, watching it sleep and eat and play and die" (32). Plant organisms become sentient viewers, simultaneously agents and subjects of the gaze, observing and marking human society's animal behaviors (sleeping, eating, playing, and dying). They are watchers as well as watches. He continues, "There was a beauty about those palm trees, a beauty neither he nor anybody down there next to them could appreciate, a beauty you could only notice if you were far away" (32). We note the novel's return to a distant kind of beauty, like that discussed in the first epigraph. The trees not only indicate space; they mark an interrelationship with the humans who planted them. Buzzworm concludes, "Everything going on down under those palm trees might be poor and crazy, ugly or beautiful, honest or shameful—all sorts of life that could only be imagined from far away. This was probably why the palm trees didn't need any water to speak of. They were fed by something else, something only the streets of his hood could offer. It was a great fertilizer—the dankest but richest of waters. It produced the tallest trees in the city, looking out over everything, symbols of the landscape, a beauty that could only be appreciated from afar" (32). The palms become recyclers in a manner somewhat akin to Manzanar, or like the composters we see throughout these chapters; they grow and thrive on the composted waste of the city, taking the detritus of the poor, crazy, ugly, and shameful to produce fruit as well as to guide the people in their understandings of time and place. This detritus serves as fertilizer that a "cleaner" product would not be able to match. Their fertilizer, otherwise a toxic element, becomes reused as a positive force for growth.

Buzzworm continues his reclamation project in relation to his watches (already likened to the palm trees), all of which he has "picked out at flea markets. Buzzworm swore by the swap meets where life and death meet, he liked to say. Life for a set of pink Bakelite dishes left by your dead Aunt Polly. Life for a bunch of has-been watches" (27). The swap meet represents a reuse-and-recycle program akin to those I identify throughout this project: resquachismo, salvage piles, and composting. But Buzzworm takes this reclamation to the level of compost theology in likening swap meets to a meeting, a union, or a joining of life and death. Soon after he makes this comparison, he tells a story about the ghost of a dead man going into a pawn shop to reclaim his old watch. Buzzworm concludes, "Points is: Dead come back" (29). Again,

Buzzworm understands temporality not as a linear progression. Such a worldview welcomes the dissolution or positive pollution of the imagined boundary between the living and the dead.

The bonds between people within *Tropic of Orange* exist in varying degrees in the face of technologically mediated interactions and bodies, particularly within Friday's section, titled "Artificial Intelligence." This portion of the novel opens from Emi's point of view and emphasizes her cyborg nature. In a chat session between Emi and Gabriel, she asks him, "*HAVE YOU LOST YOUR C-DRIVE?*" (177) and tells him, "Oh god, Gabe, you've lost a chip." Emi places herself as well as Gabriel within a technologically mediated corporeality, viewing all people as, at the very least, computer-like. Emi is constantly associated with television, forever concerned with programming schedules and, later, with getting the shot (until she actually gets shot). Perhaps the clearest figuration of Emi as cyborg comes in her possible (perhaps even probable) death scene: "Emi's voice sank to a whisper. 'Abort. Retry. Ignore. Fail . . .'" (252). Emi becomes a computer with a glitch. But her technical mediation also fittingly affects her relationships with other people. At one point, she has cybersex with someone other than Gabriel, and she wonders if it counts as infidelity. Later, she is video chatting with Gabriel, another technologically mediated interaction. The narrative explains, "They saw the same simultaneous image, give or take for satellite lag and time code correction. Did their eyes therefore touch? Did this count?" (180). The question, "Did this count?" refers to whether this video-mediated contact counts as contact. Do eyes that meet each other via cameras count like (or as much as) eyes that meet each other via only their biological and physical processes (mediated by light and gravity, for example)?

It might appear at first that the answer to this question is no. After all, the most cyborg character meets with what appears to be a fatal gunshot; Buzzworm, who has been defined in relationship to the ever-present radio in his ear and the watches on his wrist, relinquishes them all. He describes the last radio show he listened to, which talked "about mythic realities, like everyone gets plugged into a myth and builds a reality around it. Or was it the other way around?" (265). Rather than continuing to be tied to this mythmaking apparatus, he becomes "unplugged and timeless," but "thinking like this was scary, Buzzworm gritted his teeth. . . . Solar-powered, he could not run out of time" (265). While relinquishing the airborne voices is scary, he recognizes an alternate method of existing in time, one tied to the apparent movement of the sun through the sky. Such disassociation from technological mediation appears necessary as the narrative explains, "The virtually real could not accommodate the magical. Digital memory failed to translate imaginary memory. . . . There were not enough dots in the universe. It other words, to see it, you had to have been there yourself" (197). The novel discerns a difference between observing an event from a mediated distance and from the lived experience of being there. Of course, what comprises being there is never clearly defined. The novel further notes, "If they didn't see it, they didn't see it. Like the homeboy said, anyone on the ground'd know. These folks weren't on the ground. They were on-line somewhere on the waves" (190). Again, *Tropic of Orange* privileges place-based, local knowledge. Just as the city cannot be understood from maps imagining a depopulated aerial view, the life of the place cannot be properly understood when viewed onscreen as a digital replication.

However, Gabriel becomes a convert not only to the connections between people that digital technologies can allow or facilitate but (through them) also to an acceptance of the muddy liquid connections and interminglings that exist in the world. The narrative puns, for example, "World Wide Web, that a so-called Local Area Network is traditionally designed to provide maximum capabilities, flexibility and growth for the future" (179). The contrast of the World Wide Web and the local area network reminds the reader of the environmentalist credo, Think Globally, Act Locally. Of course, ecologically speaking, there has always been a world wide web, although the solidity of the web metaphor might not account for the full complexity of ecological connections. Nonetheless, in this global web, the *local* area network still serves as the ideal device for connection. Gabriel comes to understand this liquid complexity, recognizing that all things are interconnected, that there are no neat conclusions to be drawn. He expounds, "I no longer looked for a resolution to the loose threads hanging off my storylines. If I had begun to understand anything, I now knew they were simply the warp and woof of a fraying net of conspiracies in an expanding universe where the holes only seemed to get larger and larger. . . . The picture got larger and larger. I could follow a story or I could abandon it, but I could not stop" (249).

The metaphor of the web as net combines the human with the nonhuman, as we correlate webs to spiders in particular and nets to human creations. Still, the two products parallel each other closely, both being woven patterns especially used to catch prey. The web or net is a trap for food or, in its internet usage, for information (though the web-net metaphor stems more from nodes being connected).[16] Gabriel recognizes that digital communication can serve a useful purpose but also that, like following hyperlinks from page to page, truth is comprised of infinite connections between information, beings, and communities. He concludes with a longing to comprehend the world in its entirety, asserting, "The connection begs to be understood" (236). He goes on to call upon "the rest of the net; it was a big borderless soup and I was cooking. There were miles and miles of text stacking up at my address; I couldn't be alone ever again" (246). Gabriel recognizes the global communities of which he is part only when he recognizes them online. Nonetheless, he does come to realize that he is connected to everything else, as the digital technology behind the internet facilitates an ecological awareness.

We note a contrast here between Gabriel's acceptance of enormity and circuity to his earlier frustrations in dealing with Manzanar and Buzzworm. Gabriel explains that Manzanar "might just look like one more crackpot homeless figure who got stepped on by the system. But his was a case where the man had side-stepped the system. . . . I hurried back to my desk, tried to reconstruct the interview, reorganize Buzzworm's circuitous style. It drove me nuts. I was always the hunter, calculating my moves, getting ready for the kill. Of course, finesse was involved; I was subtly brutal. I'd be out of there before anyone remembered what happened" (108). Gabriel narrates himself as an assassin: cold, calculating, exact, and planned out. He is linear, driving a beeline to his desk and cursing Buzz's circuitousness. But Manzanar does not facilitate Gabriel's attempts to record his story in any linear or permanent manner. Manzanar's symphony is not recorded, but uttered, and collectively, before it passes out of existence, save in our memories. The fact that Gabriel evolves from needing this kind of linearity to appreciating the liquid, unfinished narratives that his internet communities maintain represents the positive possibilities of technologically mediated contact.

Although *Tropic of Orange*'s urban setting might preclude some readers from considering it an environmentalist text, I would argue it is no less so than her Brazil-set first novel, *Through the Arc of the Rain Forest*. The focus of this text consistently lies in a recognition of the ways that humanity resembles the rest of the world, particularly because we are inseparable and indecipherable from it. The same impulses that lead to ecological destruction also lead to cycles of social inequality. Both stem from a tendency to see the rest of the world, whether defined as other species, other cultures, or other nations, as something outside our self or our selves. *Tropic of Orange* rejects such constructions. And this understanding that the social and the environmental cannot be differentiated from one another is a statement of profound ecology.

5

"OUTCASTS AND DREAMERS IN THE CITIES"

GERALD VIZENOR'S *DEAD VOICES*

She said the past was stolen, the tribe was invented and recited in dead voices, and the present was hunted and driven with the animals and birds from the treelines. The animals and birds, and their shadows of creation, she insisted, had become outcasts and dreamers in the cities.

GERALD VIZENOR, *Dead Voices*

In this passage from his 1992 novel *Dead Voices: Natural Agonies in the New World*, Gerald Vizenor laments the difficulties in discussing urban Indian experiences.[1] His novel attempts to find a place for Native people in the cities and a place for the cities in Native American stories and traditions. Vizenor mourns a stolen past and bemoans a hunted present, a temporal threat that leaves Indians with only the safety of the future. In this future, Vizenor finds hope for the survival of Native people and narratives, challenging the widespread assertion that they cannot thrive in the cities, that their only refuge is on the reservation. And while Native people in the cities within this passage may be "outcasts," seemingly shut off or removed from whitestream society as well as their nations, tribes, bands, and clans, they also remain "dreamers," actively forging new ways to exist and flourish in the urban settings in which they find themselves. These dreams locate positively polluting, intertribal, and interspecies communities in the cities. Vizenor's text also focuses on a number of toxic elements, like the other texts I examine throughout this project, querying the possibility of any kind of purity while confronting those elements and agents of toxicity. Vizenor's portrayal of toxicity and waste within this text represents a major confluence of these themes and illustrates a recognition of the amorphous and liquid qualities of human perception (as one interrelated species among many) and of reality.

In *Dead Voices* Vizenor illustrates a way that Native people can come to feel at home in the city. As such, *Dead Voices*, like the other texts I read in *Positive Pollutions and Cultural Toxins*, is not only a literary text but also a theoretical treatise, in this case refiguring contemporary Indian identities within urban communities. This novel refuses the models of the tragedy of urban failure so common in homing plots, in which protagonists must seek out ancestral lands in order to reconnect to their families, cultures, and selves.[2] Instead, it offers a way in which we can form and embrace relationships with our surroundings and come to see cities as positive spaces. In its examination of garbage and waste, this novel refigures human relationships to what we discard, arguing for an expanded notion of the communal self that includes our detritus. *Dead Voices* focuses on and reclaims a number of ecological toxins and waste (e.g., garbage, swill, sewage) as well as cultural toxins like static, universalizing images of Indians held by both European and Native Americans. Analyzing these waste products and toxins, I discuss the potential for mobility and community that Vizenor presents in this novel. This text argues against the static—against the possibility of anything ever being static—and offers one of the two narrator-protagonists, Bagese, as exemplar of the shifting identities that this text privileges in its theorizing urban space and existence from a Native American perspective.

Dead Voices is divided into eleven chapters that describe the interactions between Bagese, a cross-blood Anishinaabe trickster, and Laundry, a mixed-blood professor so named because he smells like soap to Bagese, who calls soap a "dead voice."[3] Seven of the chapters detail the events that occur while Bagese (we think) takes part in a wanaki game. This wanaki game is one practice that the characters of the novel use to move across the supposed borders that separate humans from the nonhuman, "pure blood" from "mixed-blood" Indians, and city Indians from reservation Indians.

THE WANAKI GAME, CHANCE,
AND BAGESE'S POSITIVE POLLUTION

Each of the cards in the wanaki meditation game portrays an animal:
bear, beaver, squirrel, crow, flea, praying mantis, and the trickster, which
is "a wild card that transforms the player into an otter, a rabbit, a crane,
spider, or even a human" (17). The instructions for the game are as follows: "The player arises at dawn, turns one of the seven cards, meditates
on the picture, and imagines he has become the animal, bird, or insect
on the card for the day" (28). Bagese explains to Laundry, "The players
must use the plural pronoun *we* to share in the stories and become the
creatures on the cards" (17).[4] The wanaki game is the way Stone, one of
the first three manidoos (or spirits) and Naanabozho's brother (as I will
explain in greater detail later), wages war with loneliness that comes
when humans imagine themselves distinct from other life (29).[5] In the
final chapter of the novel, the narrator reiterates, "The wanaki game is
our war with the wordies and the peace of their dead voices. Our seasons
are the same at last. We must go on" (140). The wanaki game is a method
of survival, a way to continue living and reinforcing the process of recognizing our relationships with the nonhuman world and the places in
which we find ourselves.

Bagese goes on to teach Laundry that players are "not to pretend, but
to see and hear the real stories behind the words, the voices of the animals in him/her" (7). As the narrators assume the form of the animals
and figures on the cards, they *become* those animals, hearing the voices
of the animals that already exist within them. This use of the first person
plural speaks to the ways that the characters are encouraged to recognize
their communities. These characters are not static or partitioned individuals; instead, they learn to hear the voices that have always been there,
the voices that come from the fact that "their shadows once shared the
same stories" as the other animals (7). The Wanaki game's first person
plural also indicates not only that there is no separation between the human and the nonhuman but also that all creatures should carry multiple
communities within their consciousnesses. This seeming transmogrification amplifies human connections we see throughout this study—we

can think of Lauren's hyperempathy or Señora Jane's compost theology as demonstrations of these extra–self connections. Within such a world-view the flora and fauna of any space or place cannot be viewed as unimportant or even as Other. Instead, they are and must be seen as integral parts of the self, always shifting, changing, influenced by and influencing interactions and foundations of identity.

The game itself is a reinterpretation, reimagination, or, as Kimberly M. Blaeser (Anishinaabe) calls it, a "fictional adaptation of an Ojibway dish game" (192). Indeed, Bagese's name translates to "the one who plays the dish game." Dish games are played in various versions across North America, often with seven dice, colored balls, carved figures, and other items tossed in a dish in order to make a certain symbol or color come up on all the game pieces or to make the carved figures stand. Within one Anishinaabe narrative (which Vizenor publishes elsewhere), this game of chance and skill, *pagessewin* in Anishinaabemowin, holds special significance as humanity is saved when Naanabozho, the trickster in Anishinaabe emergence or creation stories, among others, defeats the evil gambler, *gichi nita ataaged*, by summoning the winds to knock down the carved figures on the gambler's toss (*Summer in the Spring* 129–31).[6] This defeat of the great gambler befits Naanabozho's role as a hero within Anishinaabe tradition as he frees the souls of those whom the gambler had defeated in the past. This game in *Dead Voices* also builds on Vizenor's emphasis on *chance* in life. Within his rich oeuvre, *chance* connotes more than the occasional luck of the draw that comes with games of chance. Rather, life, when lived (or perhaps *played* is a better word) correctly, *is* a game of chance, and the urban setting of this text provides a tremendous number of variables to such a game.[7] Paul Pasquaretta notes that this summoning of the gambler is common in contemporary Native-authored literature, in which, frequently, "a good gambler is pitted against an evil opponent. The evil opponent is associated with both European American culture and the evil gamblers of Native American tradition" (21). Good fortune, sometimes in the guise of what could be considered cheating (or poaching), lands on the side of the good guy, an underdog who defeats an opponent whose dark and mysterious power has, to this point, tyrannized the people. Vizenor's novel is permeated by these recurrent themes in Native literature, placing it in conversation with other texts in a manner akin to the talking book discussed in chapter 1.

But gambling and chance within *Dead Voices* take on a further significance in terms of the permeation of our lives by chance events and relationalities. The narrator explains, "Chance is an invitation to animal voices in a tribal world, and the word 'wanaki' means to live somewhere in peace, a chance at peace" (17). Vizenor recasts this game of chance as an invitation to animal voices and a possibility of living in peace. Chance, within Vizenor's textual worldview, expresses the need for adaptability rather than casting ourselves into molds to which we feel we must adhere. Chance, above all else, is a method of being open to possibilities that do not present themselves to those who live by what Vizenor calls "terminal creeds," static and absolute ("terminal" here puns on *final* and *fatal*) concepts about reality. He has said, "Chances, not causes, are my stories" (*Postindian Conversations* 57). While many view human existence as a sequence of causal chains, we really live out a series of incomprehensible chances, a chaotic, liquid happenstance. Vizenor also says of his work, "Memory is my chance, nature is chance, so the eternal tease is chance, and we are much wiser by nature and chance than by traditions and terminal creeds" (*Postindian Conversations* 19). These terminal creeds are those of the hegemonic dominant society, of course, but also those of ethnic subcultures, those of anyone who would attempt to rigidly codify human identities. Like the other texts of this study, *Dead Voices* insists on liquid identities that refuse differentiation of the Other or of privileged fixed racial or ethnic constructions.

The first example of chance we see in *Dead Voices* comes as Laundry is unable to keep up with Bagese in his first attempt to follow her. He finds her apartment by chance, once he stops looking: "I rested on a bench at a bus stop, and it was there, in a most unusual manner that I found her apartment. . . . When two students boarded they commented on the crazy bear behind the hedge" (15). Of note here, too, is Vizenor's use of the term "manner"—a term similar to "terminal creed" throughout Vizenor's work, but one which encapsulates the hegemonic expected behaviors of all people, including those described with the misnomer "Indian." Bagese tells him, "Nothing comes around in chance when the best moments are lost to manners and the clock" (16). The narrator further adds, "Bagese has tried to lose me every time we got together" (14). While this passage describes Bagese physically ditching Laundry, it also alludes to Bagese forcing him into a state of defamiliarization, the condition of being psychologically lost that enables a person to experience something anew, without the preconceptions and preformed thought patterns that impede cognition.[8] Bagese teaches that people must be ready and willing to shift their expectations as well as their personae in order to experience life fully. While this openness to new experiences differs to some degree from Certeau's ideas about tactical mobility as a tool for political gains (if only fleetingly), the commonalities between Bagese and Certeau's concepts of poaching within the city space cannot be overlooked.

As I discuss in my introduction, Certeau argues that planners and administrators of cities seek to codify the lives of the people who live in the city in order to maximize order and that "rational organization must thus repress all the physical, mental and political *pollutions* that would compromise it" (94, emphasis mine). Those who monitor and attempt to control the people view nonconformity as pollution (we are reminded of Manzanar in *Tropic of Orange* here as well). Bagese's role within the Oakland of *Dead Voices* is to show the possibilities of the positively polluting contradictory movements Certeau describes. The city is not designed as a place for shape-shifting Indians to assume the characteristics of all these animals, to run around acting "crazy," and to speak of themselves in the first person plural. The city opens up to new, unforeseen possibilities by the wanaki game, and these possibilities are subversive; empowering; and, to administrative eyes, pollutive.

Indeed, Bagese can be seen as a pollutive element in a number of senses. First of all, her physical appearance falls outside the realm of what would be considered hygienic by normative standards of the United States. The narrator notes, for example, "Bagese reeked of urine" (6). She also calls the narrator Laundry and decries the smell of soap as a dead voice. Later, the narrator adds, "He reeks of perfume and laundry soap. Even the crows move back, out of his poison scent. How can we remember who the wordies are when they smell the same, as if they came from the same box of soap? Their animals are lost, and no one can hear the stories in their blood" (31).[9] Bagese uses the same word for Laundry as he uses for her, saying he "reeks." To her, soap's smell is a toxin that communicates a false cleanliness. Soap sterilizes (or gives the illusion of sterilization), and this sterility marks, not an environment in which life thrives, but one in which diverse forms of life are covered, ignored, or destroyed. Soap also covers the scents by which other species recognize and greet one another.

Bagese's home is also littered with bits of what many would call garbage. In her apartment, the narrator finds an interior that "came alive with mirrors, and a collection of stones, many stones, birds, leaves, flowers, insects, and other mysterious things spread out like a map on the floor" (15). Bagese has brought elements from the outside—cast-off objects, animal and plant waste—into her home space, positively polluting the human domestic sphere with nonhuman remnants. The reader also encounters the vision of Bagese's apartment as a somewhat dirty place: "The city buses rattled the aluminum dishes in the sink, and overnight bits of paint and plaster were shaken loose from the ceiling and covered the table. The kitchen walls were touched with shadows of mold, the corners held their own natural traces" (8). This apartment is disintegrating, crumbling down on itself. Bagese does not seem to clean it, and mold grows on the walls. Many would call this place filthy and the mold a health hazard. But Bagese seems to discount such charges on two fronts. First, as we have seen, she calls attention to the negative aspects of extreme cleanliness and sterility, welcoming nonhuman life and eschewing the permanence of the structure in which she lives. Second, she points out that trash seems quite appropriate in the urban setting of this novel and to her persona as bear.

Bagese continues this thread of reflection over the discarded as a fundamental element of urban locations, describing the scene at street level in the city: "Beer cans and chicken cartons at the bus stop. Cigarettes buried in the concrete. Printed flowers on a wet scarf distract us from the trees and flowers behind the building . . . , the wet red flowers and leaves on the scarf seem more real than the trumpet vines that decorated the center of the cedar trees across the barrier. The cedars were moist and gentle in the rain, but the cotton flowers bound a culture that made more sense in the cities" (33). All these images denote garbage, the discarded trash of people who have moved on and left behind what they had no use for. The first are examples of things that have been consumed: beer, chicken, cigarettes—all bereft of their use value and tossed aside. Next, Bagese notes that they are "distracted" by the printed flowers on the scarf. Note that it is not the scarf itself that is distracting, but the images of the flowers. They draw attention away from the actual trees and flowers. These reproductions appear to replace their referents and come to "seem more real" than the gardens in the city. But Bagese adds one final note to this supplementarity of the natural. She contrasts the cedars, which are gentle, to the cotton flowers, which bind culture. One suspects that Vizenor is playing with the word "bind" here. Binding includes tying together, tying up or restraining, making to cohere, securing. Bagese could be saying that the cotton flowers keep the culture together or that they restrict civilization or both. At any rate, these cast-off flowers on this cast-off scarf represent an integral aspect of the civilization in and of the city. One might expect this commentary, especially in a Native-authored text, to ring with irony and aspersion, but Bagese works to undermine such expectations. She notes, "We tried to avoid the trash on the streets. Anyway, bears were never known for their tidy nests" (39). While Bagese seems to recognize some problem with the trash, something about it that ought to be avoided, she nonetheless knows that she, like bears, produces her fair share of waste. Certainly, this revelation about bears undermines the idea that the nonhuman is inherently neater, cleaner, and more sanitary than the human or vice versa.

Bagese's role as a pollutive element in the sense that Certeau describes is evident in the fact that she lives in the city but does not follow the rules of the city. She even leads others to see the city as a wild space of boundless possibility and tremendous freedom. She teaches Laundry to become a wild animal, to refigure the city through his relationships to the nonhuman as well as the human. Indeed, she not only positively pollutes and subverts what it is to be a human in a city, but she also does so with stereotypes, another panoptic device, of what it means to be an Indian, within the city or without. Laundry notes, "She would never be considered traditional, or even an urban pretender who treasured the romantic revisions of the tribal past. She was closer to stones, trickster stories, and tribal chance, than the tragedies of a vanishing race" (6). This last phrase, "the tragedies of a vanishing race," represents the worst stereotype of American Indians, that they are no more, encapsulated in an ever-receding past. Instead, Vizenor insists on his narratives being ones of survivance, another of his neologisms, which combines survival and resistance. Vizenor believes that "survivance . . . is more obvious in my stories. So maybe upsetting binaries and resistance are the same as survivance" (*Postindian Conversations* 79).

Bagese becomes a deconstructor, polluter, penetrant, and permeator of borders, showing the connections between the human and the non-human, the inside and the outside, and the spiritual and the everyday human. She comments, "We struggled to hear the flowers over the trash, but even then we were at the trash of the natural world. . . . The more we held to flowers and leaves, the less cultural trash we noticed near the lake" (40). Again, the trash in this narrative is not only the product of human cultures—though there are some forms of specifically cultural trash. If trees and plants create trash (by dropping unneeded flowers and leaves), then we cannot ignore our trash as some part of our existence outside our very natures, or as outside nature itself. Moreover, we suspect "cultural trash" might represent something more than—though not necessarily excluding—our physical waste. Our cultural trash may be those elements of human cultures that encourage us to distinguish ourselves from the rest of the world.

Bagese's apartment serves as a site for collecting, for carrying objects back and forth between inside and outside and between human and natural. She also carries objects that serve to show the connection between the human and the spiritual. The narrator informs us that Bagese "carried the sacred stones and the miigis [shells] of creation" (11). Within the version of the Anishinaabe creation narrative retold within *Dead Voices*, the world comes from stones. A young girl gives birth to the three "first crossblood tricksters on the earth" after being impregnated by a west wind sent by the sun. The first is Naanabozho, the second appeared somewhat human, and the third was a stone. Naanabozho, who wants to wander, tries to kill his brother Stone, because he was ordered to never leave Stone's side. Naanabozho tries to kill Stone with an ax but only succeeds, as one might expect, in destroying a perfectly good ax. Stone tells Naanabozho how to destroy him, instructing Naanabozho to place him in a fire and wait until he is red-hot. Once he is, he tells

Naanabozho to pour water over him, and he shatters into thousands of pieces. These pieces fly around the world, and now, no matter where Naanabozho goes, he can never be far from his brother. Stone is the source of all the rocks in the world. The fact that Bagese carries the sacred stones of creation shows her importance. In a manner of speaking, she carries the source of all things, a relic of the first family. We also note that stones are not dead objects but living beings. Within this narrative, "Stone created the world of nature and the wanaki cards, and taught the tribes how to meditate. He created three sets of seven cards," and "The third set of wanaki cards has been used to teach the tribes to remember stories" (28). The players create their own cards, but the seven must picture the seven animals that appear on Stone's cards. Bagese shows the failure of the boundaries that have been imagined and mandated to separate humans from all else; she reminds the reader of the liquidity of identity. A. Robert Lee notes that Vizenor engages in "assaults on . . . essentialist templates" (5). As we have seen in his inclusion of interactions between animal, plant, mineral, human, and spiritual communities, his assaults also take particular aim at essential images of the Indian, in all their forms.

Ultimately, community within this novel comes in the form of relationships between humans and plants and animals and the interactions between creatures in the city. While, as many authors have noted, the city enables a diversity of interactions with other humans, Vizenor shows the depth of interspecies "contact" (to make use of a phrase from Samuel Delaney) that is possible even in urban settings. Delaney, borrowing from Jane Jacobs, calls contact "a fundamentally urban phenomenon" in which chance encounters, rather than planned networking, arise out of simply bumping into strangers (123–26). Of course, if we extend this idea of contact to nonhuman communities, we see that this is not a fundamentally urban experience at all but one which can take place absolutely anywhere. In Dead Voices Oakland serves as an emblem of such an interspecies community. It also serves metonymically to represent all cities, especially those centers of American Indian relocation.[10]

Within Dead Voices Bagese continues to reflect Certeau's theories about urban spaces, particularly in terms of the experience of the flaneur, the chance meetings that occur in city spaces, and the positively pollutive acts that those who live in cities engage in. As I discuss in my introduction, Certeau asserts that place "excludes the possibility of two things being in the same location (*place*). The law of the 'proper' rules in the place. . . . A *space* exists when one take into consideration vectors of direction, velocities, and time variables. Thus space is composed of intersections of mobile elements" (117). In the concept of space, we see the liquid movements and interpenetrations of lived reality. Similarly, Bagese teaches Laundry the importance of mobility and flux. Vizenor notes, "The trickster is eternal motion and transformation in the stories" (*Summer in the Spring* 13). And the narrator of *Dead Voices* describes Bagese as "a wild bear who . . . enchanted me with her trickster stories" (5). As Chris LaLonde writes of this novel, "Liminality is the space and time of transition for individuals and cultures as they confront themselves. Vizenor makes clear that is also the transformational time and space for healing" (29). For Certeau as well as for Vizenor, the healing that comes from shared stories happens in the flux, in the spaces that are in-between. Vizenor comments elsewhere, "Native American Indian stories are told and heard in motion, imagined and read over and over on a landscape that is never seen at once; words are heard in winter rivers, crows are written on poplars, last words are never the end" (*Narrative Chance* xiii).

We learn still more that Bagese serves as a boundary-crossing figure (or a figure who shows those boundaries to be false) through Laundry's discussion of her history, especially her birth. He notes, "Bagese was born without a last name near a town on the crossroads at the border of the Leech Lake Reservation in Minnesota" (8). Everything in this statement seems to speak of liminality. To be born without a last name is to be born outside the administrative U.S. power structure, which marks and codes individuals based on patrilineal surname. One could read this as a statement that she was born without a father, but needn't necessarily. The narrator notes, "Bagese Bear assumed a surname when she moved from the treeline to Oakland, California" (11). This ability to assume a name further speaks to liquid identities, the construction of names, nicknames (a tribal tradition), and family connection beyond what is passed on either genetically or governmentally (a parallel to the neonyms of *Tropic of Orange* as well as a contrast to the heteronormative procreative continuations of *The Rag Doll Plagues*). Second, the location of her birth is marked always by being near places, but no place in and of itself. It is "near a town," "on the crossroads," "at the border." All of this marks proximity (as space) without location (as place).

NATIVE OAKLAND, RELOCATION, AND RE-PLACING

Within the opening lines of this text, we encounter a number of traits within this narrative that counter stereotypes of Native fiction. The novel begins, "Shadows: February 1982. Bagese, as you must have heard by now, became a bear last year in the city. She is the same tribal woman who was haunted by stones and mirrors, and she wanted me never to publish these stories or reveal the location of her apartment" (5). First, we note this will be an urban narrative. Vizenor creates this narrative of Indian urbanity not only as an artistic project but as a material concern that grows out of the fact that "more than two-thirds of the total American Indian population of 2.1 million lives in urban areas" (Fixico, foreword ix). Accordingly, the Native American literary canon abounds with urban novels, poetry, and short stories from many of its most celebrated authors: Leslie Marmon Silko, Sherman Alexie, Adrian Louis, Joy Harjo, Louise Erdrich, and Gerald Vizenor, to name a few. Nonetheless, a number of critics and scholars have noted the difficulty in discussing urban Indian issues with those who imagine Native people to be exclusively reservation bound. And while many scholars have studied urban Indian histories and conditions, readers often continue to think of Native literature as consisting exclusively of stories about reservations or homing plots.[11] We lack a firm base of critical work examining urban Indian narratives within the ever-growing field of Native literary studies. One part of Vizenor's project is creating a space for urban narratives within tribal discourse. Moreover, we recognize this to be a contemporary tale, set not even in the recent past but in our time.

Native-authored literature is not generally associated with positive urban narratives like that of *Dead Voices*. Instead, the city is often imagined as a place to be fled. And while Oakland, California, can itself be seen as a wilderness within contemporary discourse, Vizenor's text challenges this image. Perhaps the most famous (and misunderstood) quip about

Oakland is Gertrude Stein's "there is no there there." This quote, from *Everybody's Autobiography* (1937), has been used to describe "the other city by the bay" as a sleepy suburb, an industrial wasteland, or, in more recent years, an urban wilderness. Yet what Stein means is that since her family is no longer in Oakland, since she has not lived there for so long and it has changed so much that she does not recognize it and cannot find her way around, it no longer feels like home. She writes, "Anyway what was the use of my having come from Oakland it was not natural to have come from there yes write about it if I like or anything if I like but not there, there is no there there" (251). What makes it unnatural to have come from Oakland is the fact that she has no connections to the space or place. This lack of connection makes her unable to write about it as a place, as a "there," only as an "it." Nonetheless, perhaps more interesting than the quote itself is how people have used it since. And the story of the evolution of Oakland and its shifting reception by the surrounding areas (especially San Francisco) is critical for understanding *Dead Voices*.

Oakland was founded in 1852 and was a small, rural town for about fifteen years. However, in 1869, with the completion of the transcontinental railroad, Oakland began to have a boom in growth. Oakland's Seventh Street depot was chosen as the great railroad's terminus, and the city grew from a population of 1,543 in 1860 to 34,555 in 1880 (Cooper). Oakland experienced another spike in population as residents of San Francisco moved to the East Bay after the earthquake and fires of 1906. In the first half of the twentieth century, Oakland's economy was dominated by canning and shipbuilding, with a brief period in automotive manufacturing. In the 1950s and 1960s Oakland retained this industrial base and supported and housed the labor of those industries. It remains the terminus for three transcontinental railroads, emphasizing the cargo-loading capacities of the city's docks (Oakland Convention and Visitors Bureau). Oakland was and is perceived as an industrial city—lacking the beauty and romance of San Francisco—as well as an inner-city ghetto, as advertised by hip-hop artist Tupac Shakur, among others. The largest ethnic group in Oakland is African American, and European Americans comprise 31 percent of the total population, of which roughly 20 percent live at or below poverty levels; the national poverty average according to the 2000 U.S. census is 11.3 percent. All these factors add up to Oakland being seen, within the psyche of the Bay Area, as a place to be avoided by those who feel they can afford to do so.

As an industrial city, Oakland became a center of the Bureau of Indian Affairs Relocation Program, which began in the 1950s and lasted until 1973, in which Native people were encouraged, coerced, or forced to move away from ancestral land and reservations to cities to learn industrial trades. Thousands of Indian people settled in and around Oakland in the 1950s and 1960s. Moreover, the Intertribal Friendship House in Oakland and "the Chicago Indian Center, both established in the 1950s . . . are the oldest still-operating Indian organizations in the country" and have served as loci of pan-Indian communities for over fifty years (Lobo xix).[12] Oakland, with its Native community and support structure, is an urban space reclaimed by a diverse Native population, not only historically locally situated tribes such as Ohlone, Miwok, and Pomo but also Anishinaabe, Diné, D/L/Nakota, Pima, Creek, and many others. Indeed, of the over 625,000 Native people in California (the most of any state) (U.S. Census Bureau 4), only about 12 percent are from Native Californian nations (Moisa 21). Bradley Monsma shows how, within Vizenor's work, "imagination can begin to reclaim the world's most desecrated spaces. Vizenor's writing reminds readers that forced flight or migration does not always mean complete cultural loss for tribal peoples" (66). Oakland, within the dominant hegemonic psyche of the Bay Area, is a desecrated and abject space. This city, then, serves as a space of reclamation whose transformations have always marked it as an Othered space, an industrial wasteland, a suburban nonplace, or an urban ghetto. Such inner-city, predominantly "minority" enclaves (much like Santa Ana within *The Rag Doll Plagues* and Los Angeles in the parable novels) serve as the contemporary wilderness, the places that respectable people don't ever go, where sin (either in the form of depravity or supposedly self-imposed poverty and sloth) pervades. They are places of senseless violence and horror. For Vizenor to claim this space as a location for the re-creation of the world and the retelling of the Anishinaabe earthdiver narrative (as we will see) serves to recognize the cultural toxins of these urban flight narratives and the importance and centrality of the city. We must differentiate Vizenor's approach from that undertaken by Erdrich as well. Hers seeks to reclaim a regionally defined and ethnically Ojibwa space for her Ojibwa characters. Vizenor's, on the other hand, seeks to claim a distant locale within an Anishinaabe (though not exclusively so) religious context. Both, however, focus on cities that served as centers of the Bureau of Indian Affairs Relocation Program.

LaLonde notes, "Because of these intimate interrelationships [between Native people and the landscapes and creatures with whom they live], relocation was an assault upon Native culture, identity, and personhood" (29). But within the narrative of Bagese and Laundry, relocation becomes a possibly less dehumanizing venture. Instead of serving to displace the characters, this movement serves as the impetus for re-placing. They form new relationships with the physical landscape and the animals therein, a kind of mobile indigeneity. In so doing, Vizenor's characters show the possibility of liquid identifications with spaces, rather than the limiting static identification with only one place. Not only are the people liberated from the "dead voices" on reservations (themselves originally containment locations—if not outright prisons—for Indian people), but also, as Laundry notes, "Stones, animals, and birds were liberated at last in the city" (6). In theory, people can reform and re-place in any place they find themselves. Relocation ceases to sound a death knell for Native people (or for any community) but instead creates new worlds of possibility and can rekindle relationships and revitalize the stories of creation.

CHIVAREE, AURALITY, AND COMMUNITY

Rather than privileging the reservation or traditional ancestral lands while vilifying the city, the characters within this novel complicate such simplistic binaries. The city is held, as we have seen, in high regard as a place of regeneration, while the reservation is seen as a space in which survivance is paired with corruption and which is sometimes consumed with the cultural toxin of purity discourse. These complications of reservations, cultural traditionalism, and purity are leveled by an unnamed narrator in the story about Chivaree, the creator of "Touch the Earth paper cups" from the "Tricksters" chapter.[13] I read this section somewhat ambivalently, since I am uncertain how much Chivaree's point of view can be trusted. She certainly raises valid points about individual greed, but she also embodies that greed, refusing to share either her stories or her wealth with the community.

Chivaree "discovered a birch that wanted to be paper, a birch that heard stories and would become the word in the stories, in this case paper cups, from slabs and sawdust. [She] was the only one who knew the trickster stories that would inspire the birch to breed paper products. When the birch heard these stories their remains became paper cups and multiplied on their own, a wild parthenogenesis in the birch" (118). Chivaree has the power to get the trees to produce paper cups that yield no waste and actually decompose so rapidly that they help their ecosystems by assisting in composting and regeneration. However, Chivaree will not tell anyone, Native or otherwise, how she gets the trees to do this marvelous thing. The narrator explains, "You can understand why she refused to reveal the birch stories to timber companies, but her protection of the birch stories invited severe criticism on the reservation. Some people were convinced that she was no longer tribal, because if she were, she would teach others the stories that would make them rich. So, down on the harmonies of the tribe, she moved her stories and best birch breeders to the city" (118–119). Vizenor is having some fun with tribal identity here, showing that some people are primarily interested in the wealth that Chivaree's stories can provide and not in the stories that inspire the trees toward their magic. By the same token, instead of recognizing a communal responsibility, Chivaree relocates to the city to create a new life for herself. The fact that she can move the birches to the city reinforces the interspecies community we see throughout the novel as well as the potential for nonhuman life within urban spaces.

Chivaree goes on to critique reservation culture more overtly: "You know they just want the money, but the tribe pretends like the stories are some sacred power that would be wasted on me [because she is a cross-blood]. That's the trouble, they pretend to be traditional, dance and speak the language some, but no one remembers the stories of the trees, and no wonder they don't hear the trees anymore because the tribal politicians sold every tree they got their hands on in the past century" (122). That some tribal politicians have been corrupt and sold land, timber, and mineral rights out from under tribes and nations across North America should by now be news to no one. Chivaree focuses on what is wrong with some members and citizens of reservations, including their greed and alienation from the nonhuman. I would not go so far as to claim that Vizenor rejects the reservation outright, however. Indeed, throughout much of his work, Vizenor maintains some critique of reservation traditionalists, though he also portrays reservations (especially those newly formed and intertribal ones) as potentially extremely positive and empowering locations. We must not forget that Bagese, Laundry's teacher and mentor, comes from (near) the Leech Lake Reservation. Moreover, the ties to stories of creation reach back to ancestral lands. The focus of this novel is simply the ways that urban Indians can maintain culture and aboriginal connections. To that end, and to counter the dominant messages of the exclusivity of reservation spaces to Native health, this text foregrounds the city.[14]

Chivaree's critiques of the reservation are somewhat less surprising given the fact that she serves as a participant in a trickster tradition. The narrator explains, "Chivaree was the only one who knew the trickster stories that would inspire the birch to breed paper products" (118). It is the trickster stories that carry the power to transform, to allow a tree to change into a living producer of paper, rather than a cut down, dead, never-to-be-again producer of paper. We can relate this emphasis on a living entity producing to Vizenor's notion of survivance, which argues for survival and resistance, an ability to adapt (or evolve), grow, and continue. Again, the stories seem to carry tangible results and consequences, but it's really the other way around. As the narrator notes, "The real came from the stories." That is, the stories exist before the tree, before the people, long before the paper cups. The stories are what create reality; the words carry all that we perceive.

Bonds to ancestral homelands and storytelling are reinforced as Chivaree learns to tell these stories by listening to her grandmother. Furthermore, the exact method of the transfer of these stories is important. First, we must note that Chivaree's "grandmother had the power of stories"; "she could start fires with stories and change the direction of the wind and . . . heal people of the reservation" (120). These stories have powerful material consequences, wielding fire, healing people. The portrayal of such a power is what Vizenor calls "mythic verism," a term that better describes what others have called magic or magical realism in Native texts (*Postindian Conversations* 129). Chivaree is not motivated to learn these stories in order to wield that kind of power, however. She does not even set out to study her grandmother's words; she does not write them down or take notes. Chivaree does not learn the stories as Laundry might at the university. *Dead Voices* emphasizes oral teaching and learning but not rote memorization. Chivaree explains, "Nobody taught me anything. . . . I just listened, and in my head practiced the exact sound, the rise and fall of the voice, the way my grandmother spoke to the birch" (121). Chivaree learns these stories, this culture, by observing her grandmother, not with the anthropologist's eye, but with the child's ear; Vizenor again favors the aural and oral over the visual and written. Her grandmother is a living woman from whom she learns, not a textbook and certainly not a dead, static, historical account—not a dead voice. Chivaree, in fact, *absorbs* these stories; they permeate and seep into her because of her proximity to her grandmother. For Chadwick Allen, this narrative tradition, passed between generations, represents the liquid image of "stories in the blood."

In discussing a story within N. Scott Momaday's memoir *The Names*, Allen explains blood memory, which works through storytelling. We are told stories; we retell them; and through this telling, participating, and living in and with the stories, they imbed themselves in our blood, in our lives. We connect, reconnect, and reaffirm our connections to family across generations and to a people and community. The positive side of this concept of blood memory is that it "boldly converts the supposedly objective arithmetic of measuring American Indian blood into an obviously subjective system of recognizing narratives—memories—of Indian indigeneity" (111). Allen continues, "American Indian writers call upon the imaginative power of blood memory to defy attempts by legislators and others to quantify contemporary indigenous identities for their own ends, to inscribe indigenous identities as a number always *less than* that of the generations that came safely before, as a number moving inevitably toward zero" (111, emphasis original). Blood memory places the power of defining Native identity within the cultural frameworks of the nations and tribes rather than within the blood quantum of the federal government.

Just as these stories in the blood that Chivaree absorbs extend from an oral and aural tradition, Bagese stresses that "tribal stories must be told not recorded, told to listeners but not readers, and she insisted that stories be heard through the ear not the eye" (6). She continues, "Our voices died in the cold hands of the wordies, the missionaries and anthropologists" (136). Laundry learns that the stories are to be kept in a *shared* discursive community. This emphasis on the communal nature of the story, this oral/aural participation relates directly to the *we* of the wanaki game. The *we* in this situation represents the shared experience of the narrator, the author, the audience, and the interspecies communities of each of them. Each of us shapes the narratives we tell, of course, but also the narratives we hear and read. And if we take those narratives and pass them on, emit and absorb them, we continue to foster this community, as by a feedback loop, which extends to and permeates everyone who interacts with anyone within the narrative community.

Moreover, communal storytelling is interactive, as the audience positively pollutes, engages with, and participates in the narrative. If we do not participate in this shared discourse, we run the risk of winding up like Laundry at the beginning of the novel. Bagese says, "He got lost in his own wilderness of words" (32). Rather than the separation of humans from nature coming in a physical setting called the *wilderness* or the *city*, that separation comes from a toxic psychology that privileges written words over spoken ones. The wilderness lies in dead voices, in trusting the culturally toxic linear, static narratives, histories, and stories. Bagese concludes that this oral tradition is important not only so language and stories remain alive, vibrant, and liquid but also because "silence and isolation were learned with the eyes not the ears" (10). Not only does the aural necessitate community; the visual eliminates it.

STORIES OF TOXICITY AND WASTE

Within *Dead Voices* the reader encounters three other stories that deal directly with issues relating to waste and toxicity: the stories that narrate the rebellion of the fleas ("Fleas"), the landfill meditation ("Tricksters"), and the reimagined Anishinaabe earthdiver story ("Beavers"). In each of these threads, we note a great concern with poison, garbage, and toxicity but also a clear move away from the image of American Indian people as inherently closer to the earth. Murray explains that Vizenor sets out "to mount an attack on notions of purity and geopiety, in which the earth and Nature are used as sources of spiritual value uniquely accessible to Indians" (31). Or as Russell Means more generally notes, "Indians have been stereotyped far too long by the environmental movement as those with the mystical, ancient wisdom that alone can save the planet" (xvi). Those who support this stereotype, of course, almost never want to hear about the environment from the actual Indians they tout as ecological saviors, but rather employ a notion of Indianness that is mediated and distanced from the speakers, preferably by both time and space (or falsified like the supposed speeches of Chief Seattle). Moreover, while indigenous ties to land might be idealized by many, as Craig Womack notes, Native claims and rights to land are not.

In "Fleas," we see an indigenized examination of toxicity and positive pollution. This chapter begins, "Our apartment had been taken over by fleas, not just the fleas in the game, but hordes of other fleas, hundreds of generations of fleas" (45). An exterminator is called in about whom Bagese says, "He recited the diseases that fleas could cause, such as typhus and bubonic plague, but the fear of fleas he spread became the survival of the exterminator in a chemical civilization. His poison was worse than our bite or the diseases he blamed on the fleas" (45). Within this narrative, the main toxic agent that the exterminator spreads around the world is not insecticide but the fear of fleas, the stories about how polluting the fleas are (we can think of the rhetoric of disease wielded in *Talents* in chapter 1). We can extend the image of the fleas to represent the indigenous peoples of the Americas, who have been associated with disease or contamination and have been deemed unclean, especially by those who have set out to exterminate them. Similarly, the fleas note, "There were demons on the block who would fasten collars to the garden statues, houses, power poles, bird feeders, even the birds, and the world" (55). Flea collars here, like the lies and poison the exterminator spreads and like Laundry's soap, are toxic and sterilizing; the attempt to rid the world of fleas is hateful and shortsighted.

Bagese decides that "the exterminator was not allowed to poison our apartment" (45) and instead spreads eucalyptus leaves and seed crowns around the apartment to repel the fleas, which works. Meanwhile, the fleas begin to plan their rebellion against the exterminator. Market, one of the fleas, "learned from the cockroaches that a little bit of poison is the best defense in the chemical world . . . the right to mount, ride, and such on bird and beast is aboriginal" (47). He concludes, "We must attack the exterminator at dawn with his own poison" (47). It is at this point in the narrative that the connection between these fleas and American Indian people becomes most clear. The fleas narrate their emergence story, the way they were carried into this world on a giant cat who escaped a massive fire. The narrator creates a connection between the fleas and the cat similar to the connections between American Indian nations and emergence locations, noting, "Our families were wise enough never to bite the cat that carried them" (51). This flea and cat relationship seems at first to be an environmentalist statement, one that likens Indian cultures to environmental stewards. However, as Jace Weaver points out, "Native peoples must be very careful in the use of guardianship language, smacking as it does of the guardian/ward relationship that has for so long oppressed Native peoples" (16). The fleas do not see the cat as a thing to be protected but one with agency and that can become rather dangerous. That is, the fleas do not avoid biting the cat completely out of respect for having saved them but because the cat would eat the fleas that bit her.

The fleas, after much debate about the merits of war (the fleas who ride on hawks want to fight; the ones who ride on doves do not), decide to attack in the morning. In another move to connect the fleas to Native nations of North America, the narrator notes that the fleas band together despite the fact that they "had never shared their political or chemical enemies in the past, and there was no reason to believe that an exterminator in one building would obligate other fleas to a war" (48). Still, they attacked his crotch and sucked his blood until he screamed, while "birds [upon whom the fleas rode] shit on his face and shoulders" and crows "pecked at his ears, and pulled his hair" (56–57). Next, "Three fleas burrowed into his ass and the exterminator fainted with pain, and came close to death" (57).[15] This scatological story imagines the creatures of the world fighting back against "chemical civilization," which attempts to poison every bit of life that does not fit within its domesticated sphere.

Hawk, the war leader of the fleas, leaves a message on the exterminator's windshield for when he awakens: "The fleas that sucked your blood were chemical mutants, the dead voices of your poison now run in your blood, and the vengeance of the fleas is only the beginning of the war with chemical civilization" (58). This final note connects poisoners to their poisons, of course, but it does more than that. First, it shows the permeability of the exterminator, who thinks himself far removed from the fleas and their world. Second, it shows the connection between species that we see throughout *Positive Pollutions and Cultural Toxins*, as the fleas, birds, cat, and exterminator all share the same blood; and as one is poisoned, all are poisoned. As he learns that he has perhaps led to his own demise, the exterminator comes to grips with the first law of ecology: "Everything is connected to everything else." With the emphasis on the stories in the blood that we see in this novel, our cultural connections become further extolled.

The human connections to land, and especially idealized stereotypes of Indian people as environmental stewards, in this novel are most richly investigated in Vizenor's treatment of Martin Bear Charme, who "established the Landfill Meditation Reservation on San Francisco Bay" (132). The narrator explains, "He made a fortune hauling and filling wetlands with urban swill and solid waste" (132). Certainly, Bear Charme, as a character, offends the sensibilities of those environmentalists who would embrace Native people as closer to the earth. He becomes rich by toxifying the ecology of the bay. Not only is he actively participating in land reclamation; he is filling in the wetlands with "urban swill and solid waste." The diction here is important. The phrase "urban swill" reaffirms the aforementioned ideas that the city is portrayed in this novel as a place of trash. At the same time, the word "swill" connotes that this waste is just a little more disgusting than normal trash. Swill is a liquid combination of waste and water, and this combination further ensures that the trash that Bear Charme is dumping will seep and leech into other parts of the bay.

The reservation that Bear Charme founds is based on the idea "that the wordies should turn their minds and hearts back to the earth, to meditate on trash, imagine the earth once more and connect the refusers with their refuse" (133). Bear Charme's pun here, connecting refuse

with refusers, requires attention. Jennifer Gillan notes, "By re-establish-
ing a connection between people and their wastes, refuse meditation
makes them confront the results of their actions, forcing them to take
responsibility for their lives. It shows the drive toward cleanliness to be
merely a desire to push aside the complexities of identity. To maintain
a separation from trash is a refusal of contact and responsibility" (249).
Gillan shows that our refuse, that which we cast off, is our responsibility
and that cleanliness is simply a code for an overly simplistic concept of
identity and purity in which we are separate from the people and things
we cast off. Beyond that, Gillan states of the landfill meditators what I
have elsewhere noted of literary *pepenadores*: "Refuse Meditation is part
of what Eve Sedgwick has called 'reoccupying the site of injury.' By accepting the negative appellations imposed by others and transforming
them into signs of survivance, the landfill meditators, scavenging among
fragments of cultures, learn to accept the indeterminate nature of their
lives" (249). Indeed, this analysis can be taken one step further, as the
Landfill Meditation Reservation is not only the site of injury. This is not
a place turned into a pile of garbage exclusively by the dominant governments of the cities surrounding the San Francisco Bay. While he argues
that "the wordies lost their connections with the earth. . . . Wordies have
forgotten how to hear and when to surrender to nature and their stories"
and that "the cultures that poison rivers are cultures of evil, and the
demons of the chemical underworld must be outwitted to hear our stories on the river" (132), Bear Charme himself creates this landfill made
of swill and waste. This is very much a site of the abject, not only in
terms of the people society has cast off, but of the real material waste we
produce. We see it and recognize that it is *of* us but not that it *is* us. But
if we are what we produce, we are also what we discard. If a society, a
nation, an individual attempts to argue that it can be evaluated by what
it produces consciously, purposely—be it art, economy, money, music,
law—then that society must also be judged by the garbage, the waste, the
shit, the blood that it produces and throws away. It is not so much that
we produce this trash but that we *are* this trash. We are this shit. And we
see this connection between humans and their fecal detritus bolstered in
Vizenor's revisiting of the earthdiver tale within *Dead Voices*.

In this section in "Beavers," the narrator meets up with an old woman who introduces herself as Naanabozho, the shape-shifting trickster who figures centrally within the Anishinaabe earthdiver tale during which a great flood covers the land. Naanabozho seeks higher ground and eventually climbs a tree to escape the ever-rising waters.[16] The water reaches his mouth, and suddenly he feels the urgent need to defecate. His feces floats up and rests at the waterline, just around his mouth. Finding this rather intolerable, Naanabozho begins to ask the animals in the water (usually swimming rodents—beaver, muskrat—and otter, but also sometimes ducks, herons, kingfisher, and loons) to dive down and retrieve some earth from beneath the floodwaters. Muskrat succeeds in retrieving some sand, which he gives to Naanabozho, who casts the sand across the water and creates an island. From this island grow the lands on which the animals live. This comic story serves to explain the emergence of tribal lands as well as to unify human existence with that of various sacred animal species.

In *Dead Voices*, Vizenor also offers another creation story, one clearly based on this Anishinaabe earthdiver narrative and which describes the creation of anthropologists. The story describes "a crossblood blonde with webbed toes who could swim faster than anyone in the world[;] on her way to school one morning she heard that seductive purr and distant thunder deep down in the sewer and vanished in the manhole" (110). The trickster claims to have made the blonde "out of shit to tease the teachers" (110). Cats are enlisted first to go save her, but they won't do it. In order to retrieve her, "the trickster created an anthropologist out of shit, named him Shicer, a doctor in the new school of tribal care and rescue, and sent him deep down into the sewer" (110). The anthropologist is proud to be accepted and enthusiastic about his task. Lest there be any doubt, Bagese notes how similar this story is to the earthdiver story, reflecting, "Naanabozho asked the beaver to do the same thing after the great flood" (111). In this version, however, when Shicer finds the blonde, she "held him so close that their bodies melted one into the other, and no one could figure out how to pull that shit apart" (111). One cat eventually pulls the two apart and brings most of them back to the surface, but their heads stay stuck together and become "a mutant in their heat, a sewer creature in the city" (112) who creates sewer gas lights and holograms and produces an especially bad stench that "could wound tribal children at night" (115). Bagese avoids manhole covers from this point on.[17]

That Vizenor offers an imagined anthropologist made by the trickster out of shit is not surprising considering his disdain for anthropology. His name, Shicer, plays both on the German *scheisse* (shit) and shyster (which has the same German root). In *Postindian Conversations*, Vizenor discusses the dead voices of social sciences (137) and states, "I have not been fierce enough about anthropology. There are no measures of fierceness that could be reparations for the theft of native irony, humor, and original stories. There's not enough time to be critical of the academic enterprise of cultural anthropology" (90).[18] Anthropology leads, ultimately, to what Baudrillard calls "extermination by museumification," the disappearance that comes from being categorized and studied as objects (10). Vizenor's portrayal of this anthropologist made of shit is comical; all the feces is supposed to be funny. In case the reader missed that, Naanabozho states, "You must remember me as a trickster, because who else can do things with shit that make people laugh so much" (108). The need for such a statement comes from the frequent misreading of earthdiver narratives and Native stories that feature feces as being representations of the tragic rather than the comic. Vizenor contends, "Theorists [of tricksters] burdened with coprophilia would have done better to construe shit as a universal comic sign than to bind the literal malodor in social science monologues" (203).

The image of the anthropologist qua shit is also an imaginative empowerment. Anthropologists have done much to define Indian identities for Native American people and the U.S. federal government; they have categorized and described as static Indian traditions that were never static before; they have had tremendous influence on externally and, ultimately, internally deeming what is and is not "Indian." As such, to claim that anthropologists come from Naanabozho places them within an Anishinaabe creation. Beyond that, though, it also places anthropologists within the same refuse trope that Vizenor employs throughout so much of this novel. Anthropologists may be cultural waste, but that waste is part of us and needs reclaiming and reuse like all the trash on the Landfill Meditation Reservation. Vizenor's text argues that Native people have to recognize the *we* of the anthropologist. We can read this imperative in at least two senses. First, anthropologists are products of a society, a community, in which Natives live as well. To simply discount anthropologists as Other is to replicate the same *refusal* that has already led to so many problems and cultural castoffs. Second, anthropologists have had a hand in creating the often internalized images and definitions about what being Indian means. And despite the fact that Vizenor clearly argues that we must move beyond these definitions, indeed overcome them as we progress toward postindian identities, he nonetheless recognizes the current power of those definitions and images.[19] We cannot pretend they do not exist and cast them away to some landfill to be forgotten. We must remember them, even, or perhaps especially, if that remembering is for the purpose of moving on and away from them. Finally, we must note that this reimagination of anthropologists as an Anishinaabe creation is only possible in the sewers of the city, the site of relocation. A new emergence takes place, and Indian identities become bound to the city. This is an important part of Vizenor's project, to make space for urban narratives within tribal discourse.

Louis Owens wrote that "Vizenor's art is nearly always difficult, disturbing, disorienting, and disquieting, but it is never dishonest" (introduction 1). The end of this novel is no exception, as the penultimate section of the book takes a somber tone. It opens, "We must go on, but there is nothing more to be done with our voices in the cities. The tribes are dead, our voices are traced, published, and buried, our voices are dead in the eye of the missionaries" (135).[20] And despite the fact that the name of the wanaki game means "place of peace" and that the goal of the game is to find such a place, the narrator states, "There is no peace, and our best stories must be heard in a trickster war, in the shadows, in a world of chance. Peace is a tragic end, we are lost in peace" (135). He continues, "The stories we remember would never survive the peace on federal reservations" (136). The choice that Vizenor offers is between the liquid chance of tricksters, the mobility they offer, and the "drone of cultural pride on reservations" (136) by those who wear "plastic chokers, beaded buckles, and imported leathers" (137). Put more concisely, Vizenor's narrator claims, "The past, not death, is our silence" (138). The past adheres only to ancestral lands and cannot adapt to present realities of movement from and between such places and urban centers or accept changes in which Native people learn to live, survive, and thrive in the cities. Peace becomes another emblem of the tragic—one that disallows change in favor of agreeability.

Vizenor seeks to move beyond mere traditionalism and beyond isolationism to get to a point at which the cities can become sanctuaries and Native people can be closer to the natural world in their stories. He writes, "At last the bear in the cities was heard in sacred tribal histories." This is the point. Native people can still be who they are, even in the city. Being tricksters will allow postindians to survive. And this survival is Vizenor's ultimate goal. Not just the survival of the traditions and old ways, not just the survival of ancestral lands, not even the survival of the tribes and nations, but the tactical survival of the people and species who make up and are made up of all those traditions and places. In a moment of welcome succinctness, Vizenor closes with a simple sentence: "We must go on."

EPILOGUE

I can't see why you want to talk to me
When your vision of America is crystalline and clean.
COUNTING CROWS, "When I Dream of Michelangelo"

In an interview conducted immediately prior to his acceptance of the Nobel Prize, Al Gore said, "It's hard to celebrate recognition of an effort that has thus far failed." While it is undeniable that his work—and particularly his film, PowerPoint presentation, and lecture *An Inconvenient Truth*—has increased awareness of global climate change, the solutions to that and a host of other ecologically unsound practices lag far behind. Gore continued, "I'm not finished, but thus far, I have failed. We have all failed." Environmentalism, as a movement, has simply not done enough. Even in our successes, we see how much more remains.

Part of this failure comes from environmentalism's inability to effect change in corporate models. We have made changes at the individual level and must continue to do so; but without a change in a culture that values financial gain over ecological community or an easy status quo over any form of sacrifice, hope is hard to come by. As Peet and Watts illustrate, "An examination of the GATT/WTO ideological apparatus reveals a fundamental commitment to trade-induced growth that most basically denies its environmental consequences" (xv). So long as we see the environment, or nature, as a commodity, that which is not us, or that which is Other, we will continue to struggle to effect positive changes.

Another of environmentalism's failures comes in the perception that it is a movement of, by, and for the white middle class, a perception that is fostered both within and without the movement. As such, working-class and poor communities are unlikely to rally around environmentalism; members of communities of color often do not feel welcome, often because they are not. Similarly, environmentalism must work to overcome its paternalistic undertones if it wishes to combat right-wing propaganda that labels it the purview of effete leftist intellectuals.[1]

This book is an attempt to offer methods by which we can recognize the inherently intertwined issues of social and environmental justice. It offers a methodology by which these issues can be addressed and a vocabulary by which to counter purity discourse and the socially toxic rhetoric of isolation or containment. I hope to show that environmentalism need not be locked into the overly simplistic molds into which it has been cast (and has cast itself) over the past forty years. We need not accept the nature/humanity binary. Indeed, we must constantly work to overturn it, illustrating, arguing, and teaching the fact that we are not and cannot be differentiated from the other life and lives of the planet.

The rhetoric of pollution and the rhetoric of pure wilderness spaces to be preserved from human contamination add to the perception of environmentalism as a movement of exclusivity. It invites accusations that environmentalists are simply tree huggers who have no interest in social justice or equality unless the victims or the marginalized are nonhuman species. It invites accusations of NIMBYism, paternalism, and condescension. And those charges hurt our cause. A discourse that moves away from pollution to toxicity will help to some degree. Environmentalists must show that our concern is the health of our ecosystems rather than preservationism. We must insist on the inclusion of the people within that equation because people *are* part of the equation. Deming and Savoy wonder how "mainstream environmentalism and nature writing" change if "one's primary experience of land and place is indigenous or urban or indentured or exiled or degraded or toxic" (8). *Positive Pollutions and Cultural Toxins* seeks to address that question. Similarly, ecocriticism must continue to move beyond a nostalgic attachment to nature writing to take a hard look at the ecosystemic representations in urban literature and literature by authors of color if it hopes to survive as something more than a field reserved for white, middle-class environmentalists.

In American studies we talk a great deal about American exceptionalism, a term credited to Alexis de Tocqueville that refers to some quality or qualities that mark the United States as inherently different from other nations. The concept is often associated with notions of American superiority; it justifies actions that the United States and its people would find unacceptable (or at least objectionable) from other nations. The most obvious example of this internal American exceptionalism is the federal border expansion that took place under Manifest Destiny. In this instance, U.S. federal and state lawmakers and their agents considered U.S. expansionism their divine right. But Deborah L. Madsen argues that American exceptionalism "permeates every period of American history and is the single most powerful agent in a series of arguments that have been fought down the centuries concerning the identity of America and Americans" (1). *Positive Pollutions and Cultural Toxins* is not meant to overturn U.S. exceptionalism; it is meant to challenge *human exceptionalism*, the idea that human beings are intrinsically distinct (either superior to, inferior to, or capable of being rightly understood as separate from other species), the idea that we are not a part of nature, the idea that we are not natural.

This book also hopes to continue recent work in comparative- and mixed-ethnicity scholarship. In an increasingly multiethnic era, such work is fundamental. I have no intention to eliminate ethnic studies or any single-ethnicity field therein. I only encourage even greater comparative and collaborative work. As I discuss in my introduction, mine is hardly the only text to advocate such an approach. But comparative approaches make particular sense in an ecologically minded literary study. Just as humanity (or any species) cannot be accurately understood in isolation to other species—ethnic, racialized, and indigenous communities are most completely comprehended in relation to others. We are always defined aporiatically by what we are not. But more than that, we must realize that we can never be defined without (by which I mean both sans and outside) those other communities. They interact and intersect with our communities (whatever they are) and as such become part of what we are. This text means to combat exceptionalism broadly speaking, whether that exceptionalism rests its focus on national, ethnic, racial, or species segregation, isolation, or containment. Such exceptionalism represents the cultural toxin of purity discourse and contrasts the positive pollutions advocated by the texts studied here.

Finally, this book means to reclaim cities and urban dwellers within an ecocritical framework, directly opposing the favoring of rural and wilderness landscapes by this discipline. Similarly, it means to show the value in reclaimed waste objects and cast-off communities. If ecocriticism is to grow as a field, it must recognize the centrality of urban and social issues as they intersect with ecological and environmentalist ones. If it does not, it will remain on the fringes, having failed to gain the allies that it could so easily have reached.

NOTES

INTRODUCTION

1. Although it is not my intention to establish a division between humanity and nonhumanity in any conceptualization of nature, nor do I use "pollution" in a pejorative sense, my usage of these terms throughout this work is necessary for challenging these ubiquitous but problematic constructs.
2. In another groundbreaking examination of the gendered history of the natural, Donna Haraway calls for a move away from naturalizing metaphors in favor of new, technologically based ones, calling the cyborg a "creature in a post-gender world" with tremendous liberatory potential (150). I will revisit Haraway's work in chapter 2.
3. Meanwhile, in his article, "Is Nature Necessary?" Dana Phillips builds on McKibbin in order to mark a postmodern conception of the natural. He avers, "nature is now man-made," a commodity branded for human consumption from which we inevitably become alienated (216). Phillips's answer to his own titular question seems pretty clearly to be "yes, nature is necessary," because if we eliminate the difference and the mystery of nature, we will inevitably destroy it.
4. His other three laws as laid out in *The Closing Circle* are: everything must go somewhere; nature knows best; and there is no such thing as a free lunch.
5. Obviously, calling these nonhuman cells ours is problematic. Our bodies are as much theirs.
6. William Cronon addresses some of these issues pertaining to human exceptionalism or distinctions between humans and other elements and species of the earth. In *Uncommon Ground*, he asserts, "The time has come to rethink wilderness," specifically because wilderness, rather than being an a priori setting, is, in fact, "quite profoundly a human creation" (69). Wilderness, as the opposite of civilization, is as problematic a node of binary construction as those of nature and culture. These binaries *create* a distinction between humans and the rest of the world; they do not illustrate or underline a distinction that really exists. A number of material problems arise because of these constructions. The first is that, when

we construct such binaries, we per usual imply a hierarchical structure to them. In this instance, the hierarchy can cut both ways. If humans are seen as the superior part of the dyad, then ecological toxification can be easily dismissed as a part of our birthright at the top of the food chain (itself a confused assumption that consumption is hierarchical; most, if not all, species are eaten, ultimately, by invertebrate and bacterial life). On the other hand, in constructions in which nature or wilderness is seen as preferable to that which humans have made or had a hand in making (and one would be hard-pressed to find spaces in which we have not), human presence is disallowed, seen as inherently destructive. Moreover, Boyce, Narain, and Stanton demonstrate, "Reclaiming nature as our home means seeing humans as a part of nature, not apart from nature. It means rejecting the notion that human beings are like a cancer on the face of the planet, a malignant growth that threatens to destroy its host, and instead recognizing that we can improve our home or degrade it" (3). This ideology distinguishing the human from the natural has a number of other effects as well. Cronon points out, for example, that "the romantic ideology of wilderness leaves precisely nowhere for human beings actually to make their living from the land" and that, within this construction, "our very presence in nature represents its fall" (80–81). This leaves rural people rather out of the equation, as they defile the land with their very presence. Meanwhile, the obverse denigrates the people who actually live in or, heaven forbid, enjoy cities as people who have lost touch with nature, people who are, in terms of this central, controlling metaphor of U.S. identity, corrupt. See also John Beck on wilderness as a trope and space created for the purposes of exclusion.

7. Throughout this book, I similarly attempt to privilege the term "ecosystem" over "environment" and "ecocriticism" over "environmental" or "green" criticism, following a path charted by Cheryll Glotfelty and Tom Lynch among others. Glotfelty, in her introduction to *The Ecocriticism Reader*—to which all ecocritics are deeply indebted—demonstrates that "in its connotations, *enviro-* is anthropocentric and dualistic, implying that we humans are at the center, surrounded by everything that is not us, the environment. *Eco-*, in contrast, implies interdependent communities, integrated systems, and strong connections among constituent parts" (xx). Lynch expands on Glotfelty's reasoning: "As I interpret the word *ecocriticism*, the *eco* prefix has three distinct, albeit related, references: the scientific, the political, and the emplaced" (14). Ecocriticism encompasses interdisciplinarity, in part because it recognizes connections between disciplines, the social, political, humanity, all species, and all spaces. Finally, Lynch's work, like Scott Slovic's collection *Getting Over the Color Green*, emphasizes the dangers of using "green" to mean "ecologically concerned." Both texts focus on spaces

not dominated by greenness, particularly the arid southwestern corner of the United States.

8. This is not, of course, to say that Thoreau and Muir were not concerned with marginalized human communities as well.

9. Many will note a correlation between the threats to ecological communities within the novels studied here and what Ulrich Beck has dubbed "risk society," a globalized world in which certain byproducts of modernization represent unbounded ecological toxins. Beck explains, "By risks I mean above all radioactivity, which completely evades human perceptive abilities, but also toxins and pollutants in the air, the water and foodstuffs, together with the accompanying short- and long-term effects on plants, animals and people" (22). More specifically Beck correlates toxic risks and economic modernization. He further asserts, "risks produce *new international inequalities*, firstly between the Third World and the industrial states, secondly among the industrial states themselves" (23). Similarly, Watts and Peet aver that contemporary environmental thinking embodies an "enhanced knowledge of, and sensitivity to, trans-border and global forms of environmental harm (ozone depletion, global climate change, toxic dumping), and the extent to which green issues are legislated through inter-state agreements . . . and multilateral (inter-governmental) organizations" (4). Ecological toxins in the contemporary moment (which itself can no longer be understood as temporally isolated) cannot be understood as temporally or geographically isolated.

10. Pellow describes such toxic threats as "hazards [that] directly and indirectly contribute to high rates of human (and nonhuman) morbidity and mortality and to ecosystem damage on every continent and ocean system" (3).

11. For more on toxicity see David Naguib Pellow's *Resisting Global Toxics*, Jennifer Clapp's *Toxic Exports*, and Phil Brown's *Toxic Exposures*.

12. Phil Brown refers to the ailments disputed under such circumstances as "contested illnesses" (xiv).

13. Sohn's quote comes from an e-mail to the author dated January 28, 2010.

14. One might also note a correlation between the terms I use, particularly "liquidity" and "waste," and the work of Zygmunt Bauman. Bauman writes of what he terms "liquid modernity" in a number of venues. As he describes them, "'Liquid life' and 'liquid modernity' are intimately connected. 'Liquid life' is a kind of life that tends to be lived in a liquid modern society. 'Liquid modern' is a society in which the conditions under which its members act change faster than it takes the ways of acting to consolidate into habits and routines. . . . Liquid life, just like liquid modern society, cannot keep its shape or stay on course for long" (*Liquid Life* 1). While such liquidity could represent positive possibilities for subversion (as seen in Certeau, Hayles, and Haraway), Bauman marks it as negative and destructive. He

writes, "Life in a liquid society cannot stand still. It must modernize (read: go on stripping itself daily of attributes that are past their sell-by dates and go on dismantling/shedding the identities currently assembled/put on)—or perish . . . . The need here is to run with all one's strength just to stay in the same place and away from the rubbish bin where the hindmost are doomed to land" (*Liquid Life* 3). Contemporary existence in the world of neoliberal globalization entails a constant race in which there is no room for rest or reflection. Bauman's tone can tend to sound wistful for an earlier time when people had such time to reflect, a moment in which the world was not constantly on the move. However, Bauman's work is not so simple. In fact, for Bauman, the difference between "our form of modernity" that makes it "novel and different" lies in the "gradual collapse and swift decline of early modern *illusion* . . . that there is an end to the road [of societal progress], along which we proceed" (*Liquid Modernity* 29, emphasis mine). Note that Bauman marks the belief that progress ended was an illusion not a reality. The universe is in flux and always has been, though reading the procession of time as progress is itself deeply flawed (as Bauman likewise asserts).

Bauman connects liquid modernity to waste in particular. I find much of Bauman's description deeply useful: "The production of 'human waste,' or more correctly wasted humans (the 'excessive' and 'redundant,' that is the population of those who either could not or were not wished to be recognized or allowed to stay), is an inevitable outcome of modernization, and an inseparable accompaniment of modernity" (*Wasted* 5). He continues, "For the resulting population pressures, the old familiar colonialist pressures but reversed in direction, there are no readily available outlets— either for 'recycling' or for safe 'disposal.' Hence the alarms about the overpopulation of the globe; hence also the new centrality of 'immigrant' and 'asylum seeker' problems to the contemporary political agenda and the rising role played by vague and diffuse 'security fears' in the emergent global strategies and the logic of power struggles" (*Wasted* 7). However, while Bauman asserts these fears and political strategies of fear are unique to the modern and especially contemporary moment, we recognize that they are ancient and common methodologies of nationalism as well as basic xenophobia and separatism. These cultural toxins have been circulating for centuries across empires, nation-states, towns, cities, and villages. Moreover, although Bauman claims that globalization has led either to a lack of safe disposal sites or to an anxiety about the closeness of those sites to the productive members of societies, I put forth that these anxieties have always been central to processes of distinction of "us" from "them." There is nothing new in any of this, and perhaps Bauman's prevailing assertions that everything is getting worse and worse might be somewhat nostalgic for a past that never actually existed.

15. This is not to say that all discourses share this rather negative view of urbanity. Sarah Casteel notes that there are those who identify cities as ideal spaces of postnational liberation: "The denationalization of the city, which these theorists celebrate, may also be understood as limiting the possibilities for emplacement among diasporic and minority populations. The modern metropolis as we have conventionally imagined it is the theater in which new forms of belonging are worked out. For many, however, the city would appear to disallow an extensive experience of belonging insofar as it remains deeply bound up with modernist tropes of alienation and exile" (4–5).

16. But, of course, human spaces have interacted, overlapped, and interpenetrated all terrestrial space for millennia. We know, for example, that the Americas, far from being the virgin spaces prior to contact with Europeans that settler colonists have claimed them to be, have been profoundly shaped by human hands for ages. In *Virgin Land: The American West as Symbol and Myth*, Henry Nash Smith points to the inherent irony of the fact that "one of the most persistent generalizations concerning American life and character is the notion that our society has been shaped by the pull of a vacant continent drawing population westward" (3). Simultaneously echoing and complicating Turner's frontier hypothesis, Smith notes how many central political, cultural, and artistic leaders craft a need for untrammeled and unconquered lands *and* the need to trammel and conquer them. Similarly, in her foundational *The Lay of the Land*, Annette Kolodny describes enduring images of the Americas as an ambivalently constructed and maintained virgin/whore dichotomy, a land simultaneously meant to be claimed as unspoiled and lamented for having been despoiled. Cultural geographer Edward Soja calls quests for such pure places "desperate and nostalgic searches for origins, authenticity, and comforting continuities" (3). These nostalgic searches offer settler colonial U.S. culture an origin story and a legitimized claim to the virgin and unclaimed *terra nulia* of the Americas. The cities that are placed atop that virgin land, within its own rhetoric, serve, nonetheless, to simultaneously civilize and despoil it, particularly in terms of racialized, ethnicized, classed, and ultimately ecological contaminants.

17. Throughout this piece, I use the terms "Native American," "Native," "Native person/people," and "Indian" interchangeably. All these terms serve as placeholders for shifting groups of people who trace their ancestry to the indigenous peoples of the Americas.

18. Along these lines, Mike Davis asserts that "the urge to strike out and destroy, to wipe out an entire city and untold thousands of its inhabitants—is rooted in racial anxiety . . . , white fear of the dark races lies at the heart of such visions" (281). I am indebted to Gina Valentino for the term

"academic white flight." Valentino uses this term to describe another area of literary and cultural studies. Nor do I think it is mere coincidence that ecocriticism's rise to academic acceptance corresponds to the rise to prominence of ethnic studies.

19. For more on these events in particular, see Elizabeth D. Blum's *Love Canal Revisited* and Eileen McGurty's *Transforming Environmentalism*. Other environmental justice texts beyond those I have already named include J. Timmons Roberts and Melissa M. Toffolon-Weiss's *Chronicles from the Environmental Justice Frontline*, Edwardo Lao Rhodes's *Environmental Justice in America*, Richard Peet and Michael Watts's *Liberation Ecologies*, J. D. Wulfhorst and Anne K. Haugestad's *Building Sustainable Communities*, and Daniel Faber's *The Struggle for Ecological Democracy*.

20. See Kuletz, *The Tainted Desert*, and Shrader-Frechette, *Environmental Justice*.

21. Of course, ecocriticism is not alone in problematizing a distinct human self. N. Katherine Hayles offers her concept of the posthuman to demonstrate the fallacy of that self. Instead, Hayles contends, "the idea of the feedback loop implies that the boundaries of the autonomous subject are up for grabs, since feedback loops can flow not only *within* the subject but also *between* the subject and the environment" (*How We Became Posthuman* 2). Any attempt to distinguish the single human self from the elements around it, be they other-than-human or human-made technology, cannot stand. However, rather than coding this complication of the human as something negative and anticipating such a misinterpretation of her work, Hayles contends, "the posthuman does not really mean the end of humanity. It signals instead the end of a certain conception of the human, a conception that may have applied, at best, to that fraction of humanity who had the wealth, power, and leisure to conceptualize themselves as autonomous beings exercising their will through individual agency and choice. What is lethal is not the posthuman as such but the grafting of the posthuman onto a liberal humanist view of the self" (286–87). This humanist view of the self that continues to uphold the idea of the self as distinct from the rest of the world, independent and sovereign, has always been false. We are composed and comprised of infinite forces that intersect with our subjectivities. While her work is often read exclusively as relevant within the contemporary moment of technological mediation in our lives, Hayles concludes by reminding the reader, "we have always been posthuman" (291). More to the point, we have never been the humans that humanism thought—and continues to think—we are.

Hayles argues, in effect, that the dissolution of the distinction between humans and technology renders the latter natural *because* it is intertwined with our biological and material processes and embodiment. We are technological, so technology is natural. But more to the point, for Hayles, the notion of the liberal humanist self—the autonomous, bounded self comprised mainly by a mind that is coincidentally attached to a body (its biology)—is obviously flawed. We can use this reconception of the European ideal of the human to accept our technologies as literal parts of our very selves. *Positive Pollutions and Cultural Toxins* strives to make a similar claim about the rest of the natural world (of which we have *always* been a part). We can read cyborg and posthuman figures as extensions of the human that indicate and emphasize our permeable boundaries and selfhoods. We cannot be distinguished from the technological. This argument seems to stretch us toward our technological advancements, our progress. But this progressivist, linear humanist view flies in the face of posthumanism, which seeks to move beyond the conceptions of liberal humanist philosophies that are merely rendered more obviously false (to some) by our interfaces with artificial life and artificial intelligence. I am not arguing toward a nostalgic, atavistic, or retrograde return to our animal past but rather a recognition or understanding that we are animal—far less different from other life than we often think. We represent not a progress away from other life; we are merely alive, immersed in the sea of all life.

22. For more on mobile space see Doreen Massey's *Space, Place, and Gender* and James Clifford's *Routes*. We can further these emphases on movement and relationality with environmental studies scholar Mitchell Thomashow's concept of place-based transience. Specifically, Thomashow hopes to foster an educational practice by which people can confront the earth's burgeoning sixth megaextinction and global climate change by applying connections to local place and intersecting, enveloping global ecologies. Thomashow argues that such approaches are possible, even necessary, amid transnational and global migrations and diasporas. He likewise asserts that there "is no room for place-based environmental learning unless it deals with the movement of people *and* species" (169). Ursula K. Heise, on the other hand, while lauding Thomashow's emphasis on the possibilities of an ecologically grounded consciousness in the face of transnationalism and diaspora, challenges Thomashow's rooting of that consciousness in place. Heise argues, "the environmentalist emphasis on restoring individuals' sense of place, while it might function as one useful tool among others for environmentally oriented arguments, becomes a visionary dead end if it is understood as a founding ideological principle or a principal didactic means of guiding individuals and communities back to nature" (*Sense of Place and Sense of Planet* 21). Heise, building on Deleuze and Guattari among others, offers her idea of deteritorialization and eco-cosmopolitanism as antidotes to excessively place-based identities that are common in environmentalist and ecocritical discourses. She posits, "In the

context of rapidly increasing connections around the globe, what is crucial for ecological awareness and environmental ethics is arguably not so much a sense of place as a sense of planet" (55). The texts I study here move from a grounded and somewhat static sense of place to a notion of global community that is always in flux and in process, and in which characters are capable of ranging movements without a loss of that sense of community and responsibility. For more on transnational environmental justice, see Andonova, *Transnational Politics of the Environment*; Compston and Bailey, *Turning Down the Heat*; Boyce, Narain, and Stanton, *Reclaiming Nature*; McGranahan et al., *The Citizens at Risk*; Carruthers, *Environmental Justice in Latin America*; and Curtin, *Environmental Ethics for a Postcolonial World*; as well as the aforementioned works from Pellow and Brown.

23. This is not to say that Certeau is alone in this line of thinking. Henri Lefebvre, for example, argues that the modern state "promotes and imposes itself as the stable centre" and attempts to enforce "a logic that puts an end to conflict and contradictions" (23). Lefebvre insists, "there are, however, other forces on the boil, because the rationality of the state, of its techniques, plans and programmes, provokes opposition" (23).

24. Joseph Meeker's ecologically engaged concept of comic survival bears similarities to Certeau's subversive poaching. Meeker avers, "the tragic hero suffers or dies for his ideals, the comic hero survives without them. At the end of his tale he manages to . . . slip by the oppressive authorities, avoid drastic punishment, and to stay alive. His victories are small, but he lives in a world where only small victories are possible" (159).

25. The fact that I am consciously laying an ecocritical framework on top of Certeau's work in this instance does not mean he ignores the connections between the human and nonhuman on the count of tactical movement. In fact, he demonstrates an awareness of a space-based knowledge system integral to many nature writers and critics of rural spaces, going so far as to correspond this type of knowledge to evolutionary methods for survival. Certeau describes urban tactics as "microbe-like," comparing urban human movements to uncontrollable and unpredictable aspects of the biological world. Urban people, within this worldview, are no less natural than any other element or entity. Microbes adapt, though these changes often go unnoticed by people who nonetheless might come to recognize their effects in time. He continues with this theme, describing "operational logic whose models may go as far back as the age-old ruses of fishes and insects that disguise or transform themselves in order to survive" (xi). Human beings maintain shared traits of camouflage, subterfuge, and mobility even in what might seem like the most tamed, domesticated, and nonnatural of spaces: the city. Finally, he shows the interrelational aspects of human life, noting, "Analysis shows that a relation (always social) determines its terms,

and not the reverse, and that each individual is a locus in which an inco-
herent (and often contradictory) plurality of such relational determinations
interact" (xi). Identities here are liquid, defined by process and motion. In
emphasizing relationality, Certeau nods toward ecology's focus on interrelationality.

26. For more on environmental justice and urban spaces, see Bullard, *Growing
Smarter*; Bullard and Wright, *Race, Place, and Environmental Justice after
Hurricane Katrina*; and McGranahan et al., *The Citizens at Risk*.

27. But these postwar antiurban narratives certainly had their predecessors.
Richard Jefferies's *After London; or, Wild England*, published in 1885, portrayed London sinking beneath a toxic swamp, which he imagines growing out of the city's own waste. One hundred and seventy years before,
Jonathan Swift chastised London for its gutters and open sewers in "A
Description of a City Shower." And later, as Cynthia Deitering points out,
the 1980s saw a number of critically acclaimed novels that she sees as rising out of a new "toxic consciousness," in which we see "a shift from a culture defined by its production to a culture defined by its waste" (196). The
1990s saw a continuation of this trend with the publication of a remark-
able number of texts dealing especially with issues of waste and toxicity:
David Foster Wallace's *Infinite Jest*, Don DeLillo's *Underworld*, Evan Dara's
The Lost Scrapbook, Leslie Marmon Silko's *Almanac of the Dead*, as well as
the novels I examine in this project, all carry on this tradition. Moreover,
during this period, we saw a wave of filmic portrayals of environmental destruction. Blockbuster movies like *Twister*, *Volcano*, *Outbreak*, *Armageddon*,
and *Deep Impact* (and to some degree *The Perfect Storm*, *Jurassic Park*, and
12 Monkeys) all portray nature getting a little out of hand with fatal results
for humans or humanity, either in specific locales and regions or more
globally. Similarly, *Medicine Man* puts an anthropocentric spin on the de-
forestation of the Amazon basin by showing a cure for cancer lost to bulldozers and chainsaws. We are also reminded of the trend of disaster movies during the 1970s. See Keane, *Disaster Movies*; and Newman, *Apocalypse
Movies*.

28. Gus diZerega explains, "The common interest of an ecological community
is the well-being of the species comprising it" (72).

29. A pepenador is a person who searches the trash (or debris) for items of use
or value.

1. "FAILING ECONOMIES AND TORTURED ECOLOGIES"

1. Henceforth *Sower* and *Talents*, respectively. The abbreviation sf is em-
ployed to denote both "speculative fiction" and "science fiction" (or to
ambiguate the two). Butler's novels could easily be labeled with either of

these terms. Some scholars and writers move away from the term "science fiction" for any number of reasons, including its second-class standing in certain publishing, literary, academic, and artistic circles as well as its perceived tendency to reinforce privileged (and modernist) worldviews and positionalities.

Butler's mode is apropos, particularly because, as Eric Avila points out, science fiction's "portrait of aliens invading and annihilating Los Angeles alludes to the racialized 'imagination of disaster' that informed popular perceptions of urban life during the postwar period" (8). However, Butler's novels could, without a tremendous stretch, be classified as what Gene Andrew Jarrett calls "racial realism," which "pertains to a long history in which authors have sought to re-create a lived or living world according to prevailing ideologies of race or racial difference" (8). It may be sheer coincidence that Butler names one of the characters in her novel Andrew Jarrett.

2. Many critics note the activism involved in Butler's fictional diversity. For example, Jim Miller argues, "Butler is . . . far more class-conscious than many other utopian feminist science-fiction writers. Thus, her largely dystopian fictions challenge not only patriarchal myths, but also capitalist myths, racist myths, and feminist-utopian myths" (337). Zaki illustrates, Butler's "works chiefly differ from those of her Anglo sisters in that they embody an indirect critique of the liberal feminist imagination and politics expressed in contemporary feminist SF" (239). Ellen Peel describes the parable diptych as representing a "pragmatic utopia." And, Ramirez asserts, *Sower* critiques "fixed concepts of race, gender, sexuality and humanity, and subsequently, 'fictions' of identity and community" (375).

3. The family is comprised of her unnamed father; her stepmother, Corazon; and her brothers, Keith, Marcus, and Gregory, from oldest to youngest. Similarly, Lauren notes of Acorn, "We're you name it: Black, White, Latino, Asian, and any mixture at all—the kind of thing you'd expect to find in a city" (43).

4. Lauren explains, "I've never felt that I was making any of this up—not the name, Earthseed, not any of it. I mean, I've never felt that it was anything other than real: discovery rather than invention, exploration rather than creation" (*Sower* 69). As Mathias Nilges notes, "Change is the functional norm of the world Butler describes" (1335).

5. Lauren is born on July 20, like her mother and her mother's father. The Christian Crusaders seem in many ways to be a dystopic version of the Promise Keepers, an evangelical Christian consortium that emphasized paternalism and masculinity as the path toward personal and cultural salvation. The Promise Keepers were particularly active in the period contemporaneous to the publication of these novels. The Crusaders' penchant

for burning things (and occasionally witches) while wearing white tunics is certainly meant to illicit images of the Ku Klux Klan. Olamina also notes similarities with Nazi Germany, the Spanish Inquisition, and obviously the Crusades of the Middle Ages (21).

6. Most notably, in describing Bankole, Lauren asserts, "He shook his shaggy head, his hair, beard, and serious expression making him look more than a little like an old picture I used to have of Frederick Douglass" (*Sower* 295). As in flights from slavery and as during the great migration, the characters of these novels follow what Henry Louis Gates Jr. calls "the vertical 'ascent' from South to North" (xxv). Critics make further connections. Ramirez asserts, for example, "Like Harriet Tubman, Lauren disguises herself as a man as she travels" (387).

7. *Narrative of the Life of Frederick Douglass, an American Slave* (1845) and Harriet Jacob's *Incidents in the Life of a Slave Girl* (1861) are perhaps the two most widely known autobiographical slave narratives. Neo–slave narratives, contemporary historiographic works examining U.S. chattel slavery, include Morrison's *Beloved*, Johnson's *Middle Passage*, Butler's *Kindred*, Jones's *Corregidora*, and Williams's *Dessa Rose*. Many texts study neo–slave narratives, including Rushdy's *Neo–Slave Narratives*, Beaulieu's *Black Women Writers and the American Neo–Slave Narrative*, and Spaulding's *Re-forming the Past*.

8. See Paul Baepler's *White Slaves, African Masters*.

9. The HOLC was part of FDR's New Deal and served to refinance home loans in order to prevent foreclosures and to bail out the banks that held non-farm–real estate loans.

10. Similarly, Zygmunt Bauman describes, "Heavily armoured trenches and bunkers intended to separate out strangers, keep them away and bar their entry are fast becoming one of the most visible aspects of contemporary cities[,] 'normalizing' the state of emergency in which the safety-addicted urban residents dwell" (*Liquid Life* 73).

11. Other critics who reference Davis include Agusti, Hampton, Miller, and Stillman.

12. J. Martin Favor makes a similarly focused examination of pastoralism in *Authentic Blackness: The Folk in the New Negro Renaissance*.

13. Perhaps most strikingly, Lauren, a piece of California trash, is also a savior figure, one who is conflated with Jesus in a number of ways. Many examples exist, such as the fact that Lauren travels with twelve disciples as well as the titles of the novels themselves. Lauren even tells her close comrade, Allie, "Watch with me. . . . Stay awake and watch with me," echoing Jesus's similar request of Peter and the two sons of Zebedee (*Sower* 227, Matt. 26:38). Stillman notes, "Like Jesus fishing for men, Olamina as she walks gathers about her a small group of twelve other homeless wanderers—

men, women, and children" (7). Melzer adds, "Butler speaks to a historical pattern of strong spiritual leaders in the African American community—most of whom were/are men, and offers an alternative to contemporary U.S. society" (41).

14. At one point Lauren feels a dog's death (40).

15. This allusion to Native Californians is furthered (albeit troublingly relegated to the past tense) as Lauren recommends a book to a friend in Robledo "about California Indians, the plants they used, and how they used them" (52).

16. We should also note the similarity of rebuking parental deities that commence *Sower* and *Talents*, with (as we will see) Larkin's, "They'll make a God of her."

17. The parable from which the title of the second novel comes includes images of planting—or at least burying—as well.

18. We note a similarity to Gabriel's planting of nonendemic and difficult to maintain plants in his Mazatlán garden in *Tropic of Orange*.

19. *Sequoia sempervirens* comprise the only species of this genus.

20. In "Tactical Mobility as Survivance: *Bone Game* and *Dark River* by Louis Owens," I make use of the term "situational ethics" to signify the ways in which marginalized groups (reservation-based American Indians, in particular) seize opportunities based on fleeting moments of access out of necessity and on a recognition that deems it acceptable to operate outside or under the radar of corrupt and exclusionary systems (of government, law, economy, and education) (Gamber 225).

21. My use of the term "shiftiness" is meant to play off Johnson Jones Hooper's oft-quoted line in *The Adventures of Captain Simon Suggs*: "it is good to be shifty in a new country."

22. Of course, Gates's is far from being the sole text on the role of tricksters in African American literature. See also Luczak, "'Brer Rabbit Takes a Walk.'" For more on the Uncle Remus stories, see Brasch, *Brer Rabbit, Uncle Remus, and the 'Cornfield Journalist.'* Nor is Gates's account accepted at face value. For example, Sandra Adell's "The Crisis in Black American Literary Criticism and the Postmodern Cures of Houston A. Baker, Jr., and Henry Louis Gates, Jr." challenges the coherence of Gates's argument. At least one collection examines the correlations between African American and Native American trickster stories: Jonathan Brennan's *When Brer Rabbit Meets Coyote*.

23. I allude of course to Joseph Meeker's foundational text of literary ecology and ecocriticism, "The Comic Mode," in which he states, "comedy grows from the biological circumstances of life" and works to overturn the idea that "the metaphysical morality that encourages man to rise above his natural environment and his animal origins is mankind's best hope for the future" (158).

24. See for example Cynthia Kadohata's *In the Heart of the Valley of Love* and Yamashita's *Tropic of Orange.*

25. Yamashita chooses this passage as her second epigraph for *Tropic of Orange.*

26. We see another image of the people as a geologic feature, paralleling Davis's naturalized image above.

27. See also Lisa McGirr's *Suburban Warriors: The Origins of the New American Right.* We will revisit the Reagan era in terms of his environmental record shortly.

28. Stillman argues, the "dystopia of eviscerated and impotent government [in *Sower*] reflects the realization and intensification of the dreams of the Republican right in the Reagan years, dreams that were proclaimed again, in strident and apocalyptic terms, by Speaker of the House Newt Gingrich in his 1994 'Contract with America,' which promised lower taxes, less governmental regulation and other 'interference' with the market, lower levels of aid to the poor, and a general reliance on the market to reward and penalize." We note another connection with *Tropic of Orange* with its representation of El Contrato Con America (1).

29. As well as a five-and-a-half-year stint from Joseph Bonaparte, Napolean's brother, from 1808 until the restoration of the Bourbons in 1813.

30. It might also be near Pasadena, itself an idealized suburban enclave as well as Butler's longtime home.

31. However, this is not to say that the Valley is or has been as homogenously European American as it has been thought, in popular imagination, to be. As Josh Sides notes, "Farther away from South Central, blacks found homes in previously restricted San Fernando Valley communities such as Northridge and Sylmar and in the distant suburb of Pomona, at the far eastern edge of Los Angeles County" (193). Nor are communities of color in the Valley (as in the southland in general) homogenous. Avila explains, "The San Fernando Valley now shelters a heterogeneous mix of Mexicans, Salvadorans, Guatemalans, Armenians, and African Americans. . . . The landscape of today's Valley . . . reveals a striking record of the demographic changes that have ensued over the past thirty years" (235).

32. Marlene D. Allen describes this as "Butler's lesson for how to avoid the boomerang of history" (1362).

2. TOXIC METROPOLIS

1. I use these multiple terms to indicate Morales's text's movements between Mexican and Chicana/o points of view. Because many of these figures dwell in the shifting spaces of national boundaries between Spain, Mexico, and the United States (and beyond), they are difficult to broadly categorize

with a single term. The terms Chicano and Chicana refer especially to U.S. Americans of Mexican ancestry, and likely derive from a Hispanicization of the Nahuatl pronunciation of Mexicano.

2. For more on Mexico–U.S. border studies and history, see Ramón Saldivar, Gloria Anzaldúa, and Rodolfo Acuña.

3. *Mexica* is the name adopted by the group commonly referred to as the Aztecs or Aztecas in their move toward what became the Valley of Mexico.

4. Three articles to date relate somewhat closely to my work in this chapter, those of María Herrera-Sobek, Miguel López Lozano, and Marc Priewe. In her 1996 article "Epidemics, Epistemophilia, and Racism: Ecological Literary Criticism and *The Rag Doll Plagues*," Herrera-Sobek centers her "attention on Morales's epistemological and ecological concerns and posit[s] that he is the first Chicano novelist to systematically sustain an ecological perspective throughout his novel *The Rag Doll Plagues*. [She] further underscore[s] the interrelationship between ecological concerns and social and racial injustice found in the novel" (100). Herrera-Sobek also states that *The Rag Doll Plagues* "is one of the first and possibly the only Chicano novel to seriously address the issue of environmental responsibility without neglecting the social issues of racism and social injustice" (108). Certainly, a number of classic Chicano texts deal heavily with the human community and its relationships with the landscape and animals with whom we live. Novels like *The Squatter and the Don*, *Bless Me Ultima*, *George Washington Gómez*, and more recently *y no se lo tragó la tierra*, *So Far from God* and *Under the Feet of Jesus* are but a few examples. But this novel's emphasis on responsibility and ecological conscientiousness sets it apart.

Similarly, in his 2003 article "The Politics of Blood: Miscegenation and Phobias of Contagion in Alejandro Morales's *The Rag Doll Plagues*," Miguel López Lozano examines the role of contagion in this novel. And while our approaches may appear similar at first, our conclusions differ in critical ways. First, I focus more on the roles of contamination and pollution as wide-reaching, interspecies metaphors and material realities. My approach is not anthropocentric and is open to cyclicality, whereas his centers on human beings and human culture. Second, López Lozano focuses on transculturation and contagion as metaphor and not a real bodily concern, while I examine the material ecological destruction and degradation portrayed and imagined in this text. Priewe's 2004 essay "Bio-Politics and the ContamiNation of the Body in Alejandro Morales's *The Rag Doll Plagues*" is similarly anthropocentric, focusing on the challenges to the purity of the nation-state in this novel.

5. DF stands for "Distrito Federal," the name of Mexico City. There is some confusion as to the temporal setting of book 2 in particular. Franco, for example, states that it takes place "during the early Reagan era" (375–76).

This period makes sense in terms of the book's focus on HIV/AIDS and the social ostracism associated with that disease. However, because the narrator of book 2 describes the fall of Saigon (April 30, 1975) and the death of Francisco Franco (November 20, 1975), I lean toward a slightly earlier period.

6. These childlike representations are more classically putti. Indeed, as cherubs are angels (of the second order) who guard the eastern border of the Garden of Eden (Gen. 3:24), this contrast separates these savage humans even more from the sacred. That cherubs' gift to the world is knowledge may serve to contrast the science and Christianity of the Europeans to the imagined ignorance and bestial identities of the indigenous population. Moreover, as cherubs are also (and technically accurately) portrayed as winged entities with four faces, those of a man, lion, ox, and eagle, we can further assert that while some mixtures might be sacred and sanctioned by God, Gregorio cannot recognize any such sanctioning in the racial blending of the people of Mexico.

7. This is another textual positive pollution akin to the talking book discussed in my analysis of Butler's novels.

8. This coincidentality begins in one of Gregorio's dreams, in which he sees two men, the narrators of the later books, and "noticed that there were strange wires overhead running from pole to pole. A large blue and white carriage parked beyond a fence moved without horses" (23). This passage begins with a description of a time like our own, one in which telephone and power cables still hang from poles and with two-tone government cars. Gregorio sees into the future just as the repetition of his name foreshadows the next two books and their narrators. Morales reinforces his message: these Spaniards, Mexicans, and Mexican Americans are united across time and space and serve to destroy the perceived boundaries (geographic, cultural, linguistic, and temporal) that seem to separate them.

9. Papá Damián, like Gregorio Revueltas, also appears in Morales's prior historiographic novel, *The Brick People*, which examines the lives of the people who worked the Simons Brickyard, which also appears in *The Rag Doll Plagues*. This blending, melting, and meeting between figures occurs not only between time periods but between Morales's texts as well.

10. Quetzalcoatl and Tezcatlipoca are the children of Ometeotl, the god of duality, who is also expressed with the names Tonacatecuhtli and Tonacacihuatl, the lord and lady of sustenance, the supreme god of creation. These two siblings embody the same dualism, with Quetzalcoatl representing balance, harmony, and life, while Tezcatlipoca represents conflict and change (Taube 31–32).

11. See chapters 3 and 4 of her foundational *Borderlands/La frontera: The New Mestiza*.

12. That Gregorio pairs sex with this disease of colonialism is not surprising, especially when read in terms of Robert Young's addressing of the fear of contact between colonizer and colonized as primarily sexual, or at least sexualized. Young notes, "the races and their intermixture circulate around an ambivalent axis of desire and aversion: a structure of attraction where people and cultures intermix and merge, transforming themselves as a result, and a structure of repulsion, where the different elements remain distinct and are set against each other dialogically" (19).

13. The debates surrounding the origins of syphilis bear some import in this context. It has historically been regarded as a disease brought to Europe by personnel returning from the Americas in the 1490s; however, recent scholarship has challenged this, suggesting that syphilis existed in Europe prior to this era. Still others assert that different strains of syphilis were exchanged at contact.

14. For more on indigenous bodies as "rapable" within colonial discourse, see Andrea Smith's Conquest.

15. Llorente (1756–1823) was a historian and ardent opponent of the inquisition.

16. We note striking similarities between this passage and Bankole's discussion of the causes of the Pox in chapter 1.

17. This tree may well be, then, a Leyland cypress, otherwise known as 'Naylor's Blue' (Cupressusocyparis lylandii), which is especially recognized for its blue-green foliage. The image of this tree proves effective especially because this species is a hybrid, a cross between the Alaska yellow cedar (Chamaecyparis nootkatensis) and the Monterey cypress, and a product of postcontact horticulture (human-plant interaction).

18. Measurements for Santa Ana, California.

19. We should note that, despite his emphasis on connection, Morales seems to contrast human industry to "natural life."

20. However, Orange County has, in recent decades, also served as a site of large waves of immigration, especially from Latin America and East and Southeast Asia, and can no longer be understood as a lily-white suburban enclave.

21. Although, an analysis of rhizomes, both biologically and in terms of Deleuze and Guattari's metaphorical use of them, could complicate this rootedness.

22. HIV remains lethal in the worldview and temporality of this novel, though this is certainly not the case today.

23. We can parallel this microorganism evolution to the microbial adaptation Certeau advocates as well as to marginalized populations' often administratively unobserved transformations for survival.

24. See Allison Byerly's "The Picturesque Aesthetic and the National Park System."

25. We must not overlook that there are Mexican attitudes toward death at work here as well. The most obvious are traditions surrounding el Día de los Muertos in which the dead are celebrated by the living and welcomed into their homes and that likely trace their roots in part to celebrations honoring Mictecacihuatl, the Mexica goddess associated with death as well as the harvest. Such traditions emphasize the connections and permeability between life and death and the living and the dead.

26. William Cronon examines the nature of Orange County as überplanned and somewhat soulless, as well (41).

27. "El plan espiritual de Aztlán," a manifesto adopted by the First National Chicano Liberation Conference in 1969, lays the groundwork for Chicano nationalism. It begins, "In the spirit of a new people that is conscious not only of its proud historical heritage but also of the brutal 'gringo' invasion of our territories, we, the Chicano inhabitants and civilizers of the northern land of Aztlán from whence came our forefathers, reclaiming the land of their birth and consecrating the determination of our people of the sun, *declare* that the call of our blood is our power, our responsibility, and our inevitable destiny."

28. Of course, this image of uncontrollable flow has been applied to female bodies for centuries.

29. In this sense, Morales's novel invokes Oscar Zeta Acosta's foundational Chicano novel *The Revolt of the Cockroach People* (1972). We must recognize this reclamation as reminiscent of the Landfill Meditation Reservation we will examine in chapter 5, as well as the salvage and compost heaps in *Talents* and the homeless in *Tropic of Orange*.

30. MacMARCKS refers to myristoylated alanine-rich protein kinase C substrate.

31. Franco connects the amputations of book 1 to the removal of Gabi's arm for the computerized prosthetic (380). While Sohn notes in an August 17, 2010, e-mail to the author, "Gabi's experience is placed in direct contrast to the MCMS, or the Mexico City Mexicans who achieve a new and hallowed place within LAMEX, a positioning that subverts a long historical lineage that casts the Chicano/a subject as the sacrificial laboring body for the state's modernizing imperatives."

32. Sohn's quote comes from an e-mail to the author dated August 17, 2010.

33. These notions of cyborg play and irony are also reminiscent of those of the genderless trickster in Vizenor's work.

34. López Lozano discusses the role of compulsory heterosexuality in the colonial project described in book 1 but not in book 3.

35. Morales goes so far as to cite a specific form of pollution as the cause of this new strain of la mona: Plutonium oxide. Plutonium oxide (PuO), which represents a small percentage of nuclear waste, is a naturally occur-

ring form of plutonium that is very stable and difficult to dissolve in water. Pure plutonium reacts spontaneously with oxygen to form plutonium oxide. However, other oxides have been found to form in this process, and these new plutonium oxides are much less stable and dissolve easily in water. In these more soluble forms, plutonium can easily move through groundwater, contaminating aquifers (Wu). The main threat to human beings, however, comes in the form of inhalation, and inhalation relates this toxic agent to the fact that these plagues are ultimately respiratory ("Plutonium").

36. However, to show that Mexico City's in not the exact plight of all major cities in his vision of the future, Morales writes the following sentence, giving it its own paragraph: "Mexico City was the most contaminated city of the Triple Alliance" (163).

3. RIDDING THE WORLD OF WASTE

1. I use the term "Ojibwa" rather than "Ojibwe," "Chippewa," or "Anishinaabe" in this chapter simply because Erdrich uses it primarily, though not exclusively, throughout *The Antelope Wife*. For further discussion of these terms see Gerald Vizenor's *The People Named the Chippewa* (13–21).

2. We suspect, however, that this novel will treat such issues from the acknowledgement, in which Erdrich refers to her "brother, Louis, [who] has kept a strict eye on environmental engineering at several reservations" (n. pag.).

3. See, for example, LeAnne Howe's *Shell Shaker* for a discussion of these elements. Gerald Vizenor also discusses the need for greater communal and global responsibility from Indian gaming (*Manifest Manners* 147, *Postindian Conversations* 46).

4. Contemporary Indian gaming began in 1979 when the Seminole Tribe of Florida began operating a high-stakes bingo hall on the Hollywood Reservation. The sovereign rights of Native nations to operate gaming ventures were reinforced in 1987 with the U.S. Supreme Court's decision in *California v. Cabazon Band of Mission Indians*, which states that Native tribes may operate such businesses in states where gambling (including state-run lotteries) is not expressly prohibited. For more on gambling in Native traditions, see Pasquaretta's *Gambling and Survival in Native North America*. For more on Indian gaming, see Jessica Cattelino's *High Stakes*, Steven Andrew Light and Kathyryn R. L. Rand's *Indian Gaming and Tribal Sovereignty*, and W. Dale Mason's *Indian Gaming*.

5. Erdrich's focus on connection is represented in her examination of family, tradition, and continuity. Rozin speaks of her children and the expansion

of her sense of self that came with their births. She says, "I love them more than I thought was possible—my boundary stretched. . . . I was solid, before my children. Now I'm subject to earthquakes" (39). Rozin describes the ways that love, commitment, and responsibility shake the foundations of the self and expand an individual person into a community. Similarly, Julie Barak points out, "The Shawanos and the Roys and the Whiteheart Beads are really one family, so blended by time and marriage that they can't be sorted out any more" (19).

6. Such charges have been levied, for example, at a number of California tribes including the Pechanga Band of Luiseño Indians and the Redding Rancheria. These processes, of course, vary from nation to nation and are seen by most as the sovereign rights of specific tribal governments. Some nations have provisions that speak to when an individual can be disen-rolled, cases such as fraudulent enrollment.

7. We note Erdrich's play with names here, as Frank becomes overly frank. Richard, likewise, is overly concerned with riches (and is kind of a dick).

8. On their first anniversary, both Frank and Rozin prepare surprises for one another. Frank invites all their friends to his house for a party, while Rozin "cover[s], or rather decorate[s], herself strategically with stick on bows" (234–35). As she comes down the stairs to present herself to him, all their friends leap out and yell "surprise." Rather than running away or shuddering with embarrassment, everyone involved bursts into laughter.

9. Gerald Vizenor has reproached Erdrich (as well as her former husband Michael Dorris), as have other critics, for reinforcing such stereotypes of the firewater myth (*Postindian Conversations* 170, *Manifest Manners* 30). Sherman Alexie discusses similar critiques of his work in the introduction to the reissued *The Lone Ranger and Tonto Fistfight in Heaven*.

10. *Midewiwin* refers to the Ojibwa Great Medicine Society or medicine lodge.

11. We will see this correlation between marginalized people and garbage bags in the next chapter as well.

12. I am reminded here of Rozin's comparison (above) of her own life (and Richard's presence in it) to a body of water that she hopes not to have to poison.

13. But this casting of fish as a parallel to waste and humanity must also be contextualized within an Ojibwa framework. The casual reader might consider the fish to be an odd choice considering the fact that the fish's environment is quite alien to humans. But such a human/fish distinction is not universal. Members of the Anishinaabe fish clan, Gi-goon', for example, are revered as intellectuals and moderators. The fish clan is also associated with the Ojibwa earthdiver story, which we visit in more detail in chapter 5. Turtle (on whose back Naanabozho casts sand to form the earth in some versions of the earthdiver story) is the leader of the clan

(Benton-Benai 75). The move of associating an urban Indian story with a fish-out-of-water tale is not too great. Certainly, as we will see, this novel oscillates in a sphere of ambivalence in terms of Native urbanity. At any rate, within this ichthyologic metaphor, we note a definite hierarchy with bottom-feeders seen as lesser creatures. Such a statement does not reflect the underpinnings of ecology, of course. Bottom feeders, critical contributors to ecosystems, should be valued. Their role, just like that of Richard and Klaus (ideally), is in preventing the habitat from becoming toxic; it is in processing and stabilizing the waste of the community.

14. We should note that these processed foods also relate to the Native slang term *twinkie*—a person, usually of European descent, who deals in a co-opted, new-agey, Native spirituality. The term derives from the Hostess snack cake, as both are full of an appealing, mainly inoffensive, mass-produced consumability with almost no substance or sustaining ingredients. That is, these are not truly holy people, not those interested in or concerned with an honest pursuit of spirituality or connection. Twinkies are also known to argue vehemently for their own entitlement to Native spirituality, but not because of being either members or citizens of any Native nations or communities (though they are likely to claim to have been taught their craft by some old medicine man or another). It should be noted that this term is not meant to denote any spiritual person, Indian or otherwise, only those out-group members who appropriate Native spirituality, particularly for profit.

15. Laura Furlan also points out that the role of commodities is fundamental in understanding Gakahbekong as a trading village; objects have always been important here.

16. *Magizha* means "maybe."

17. Minneapolis became a center of the Bureau of Indian Affairs Relocation Program of the 1950s–1970s. For more on relocation, see Donald L. Fixico's chapter in *The Urban Indian Experience* (8–25). This is not to say that cities have ever been foreign concepts to Native people. But the recent trend toward urbanity in Native communities began in earnest around World War II (Carol Miller 29).

18. We are reminded of the rivulet and the cypress tree in book 2 of *The Rag Doll Plagues*, the highway as river in *Sower*, and the freeway as circulatory system in *Tropic of Orange*.

19. Bevis discusses the homing plot in "Native American Novels: Homing In." He contrasts the "American white" bildungsroman tradition, in which the protagonist leaves home to find himself, to the Native tradition of protagonists' "coming home, staying put," and reconnecting with tribal traditions (582).

20. It should be noted here that proprietorship of the land on which Minne-

apolis now sits was a source of conflict long before contact. The Ojibwa and Mdewakanton Dakota especially both claimed this region. The city's name derives from the Dakota word for water, "mni," being combined with the Greek suffix, "-polis"—a naming that does not come from a Native syncretism but a settler colonial appropriation.

21. See, for example, "The Urban Tradition among Native Americans." As Laura Furlan notes, "The boundary between city and 'rez' becomes blurred in this novel as characters move across that 'border' frequently. In fact the dichotomy between city and rez becomes obsolete when Minneapolis gets remapped as Indian land" (55).

22. These shells, themselves, represent images of Ojibwa motion from the eastern sea to the northern lakes.

23. The Twin Cities (along with Fresno, California) have a particularly large concentration of Hmong Americans.

24. I relate Klaus's statement to one made later by Almost Soup, who notes, "There is a little of a coyote in me" and "I don't mind saying to you that I'm not a full-blood Ojibwa reservation dog" (75). Again, Erdrich draws a positive and playful parallel between humans and dogs.

25. My allusion to James Brooks's *Confounding the Color Line: The Indian-Black Experience in North America* here is intentional. Brooks's text collects essays on the subject of the interaction of Indian and black communities and the resulting intermarriages and intercultural exchanges.

4. "AN EERIE LIQUID ELASTICITY"

1. The Department of Water and Power, as we will see, is referenced in Yamashita's novel (57).

2. Manzanar reflects on his time spent in the internment camp for which he is named, recalling particularly the landscape: "For a moment, he saw his childhood in the desert between Lone Pine and Independence, the stubble of Manzanita and the snow-covered Sierras against the azure skies" (170).

3. Rody avers that *Tropic of Orange*'s characters "are barely connected to ethnic families" and instead emerge "as participants in a heteroglossic metropolis and region, who, through their discourse, their relationships, their work, and increasingly, as the novel progresses, the interlacing of their stories, exceed ethnic and national definitions" (136). Similarly, Wallace explains, "*Tropic of Orange* puts the issues of border-crossing in a much larger geopolitical context of transnational flows" (151).

4. The novel's three one-named characters continue Yamashita's play with names and naming. Emi's name puns on both Emmy, the award for television programming, and M-E, or me, as she comes across as the most self-indulgent figure of the novel (we learn that Emi's mother's surname is

Sakai, and we suspect that her father's might be Murikami). Emi is a fairly common name as well, of course. It may be derived from terms meaning "beauty," "look," or "reflection." Emi's focus on visuality and on-screen representations relates in some ways to these translations. Arcangel transforms into El Gran Mojado (the Great Wetback), becoming a representative figure of all (but certainly primarily undocumented) Latin Americans in the United States. Buzzworm's name combines buzz—a term that often refers both to insects, bees especially, and to electronics—with worm, which refers to nonarthropod invertebrate animals (these come from hundreds of thousands of species that live on and in land and water). As such, his name combines technical mediation with references to the nonhuman, particularly the seemingly small and insignificant species that nonetheless affect their ecosystems tremendously. Names throughout this novel are tied to the interrelated conception of time and space as well as to place.

5. I skip over the second epigraph because it comes from a passage from *Parable of the Sower*, which I examine in chapter 1.

6. Bobby's cousin has travelled by ship from China.

7. Or like the garbage that forms the Matacão in *Through the Arc of the Rain Forest*.

8. Emi's correlation between riots and wind is, however, a bit unclear.

9. Los Angeles as a place is difficult to define even in a legal sense, as it refers both to a city and county; but the city does not make up the entirety of that county (as opposed, for example, to the city and county New York—in which case the city's five boroughs are larger than the county, which comprises only, tellingly, Manhattan).

10. We see one of these waterways in the aqueduct from the Owens Valley.

11. Bénézet reminds us of the novel's employment of a "more insidious type of violence . . . related to the issues of employment, ethnicity and poverty" (171).

12. "El Contrato con America" puns on the Newt Gingrich–driven Contract with America and also on contraction in a more general sense, as the land and the earth are *contracting*.

13. Cancer, or malignant neoplasm, stems from uncontrolled cellular growth, be it from contact with carcinogens or from inherited DNA (or more likely a combination of several of these). We can relate this uncontrolled growth to both Southern California, which is seen as a site of ungoverned sprawl, and to the U.S. economy and its transnational reach.

14. Sadowski-Smith explains that Rafaela, who has assumed the shape of a snake, "ends up devouring Hernando, who is meant to invoke Spanish conquistador Hernán Cortés" (101–02). She also identifies references throughout the text to La Malinche (102). For more on the Jaguar, see chapter 2, detailing *The Rag Doll Plagues*.

15. Florence Hsiao-ching Li is one of a few critics to note that crabs are the animal associated with Cancer (152).

16. However, Gabriel's metaphor includes the net fraying and holes expanding. Because nets and webs are porous, defined as much by their negative space as by their positive space, they are incapable of capturing either the too large or too small.

5. "OUTCASTS AND DREAMERS IN THE CITIES"

1. For more on Gerald Vizenor's life and work see Kimberly M. Blaeser's *Gerald Vizenor*, SAIL 9.1 (1997) special issue on Vizenor, A. Robert Lee's *Loosening the Seams*, and Vizenor and Lee's *Postindian Conversations*.

2. Carol Miller notes that in "almost every . . . fictive intersection of Indianness and Euro-American urbanity—town and city spaces are, for Indian people, places of risk, separation, disillusion, and dissolution" (31). However, she also points to texts like Brokers's *Night Flying Woman* and Sarris's *Grand Avenue*, which subvert such negative portrayals of urban Indian life (40–45).

3. Jace Weaver notes, "The 'dead voices' of the title are those heard by non-Natives. Divorced from nature, they have lost the stories that liberate the mind and hold the world together. Now they are only 'wordies'" (*That the People Might Live* 143).

4. We can relate this to Hayles's assertion: "Each person who thinks this way begins to envision herself or himself as a posthuman collectivity, an 'I' transformed into the 'we' of autonomous agents operating together to make a self" (*How We Became Posthuman* 6).

5. Vizenor clarifies that Naanabozho's name appears in written form as Wenebojo, "manibozho, nanibozhu, wanibozhu, manabozho, nanabozho, nanabush, and other variations from the oral tradition" (*Earthdivers* xii).

6. Anishinaabemowin is the Anishinaabe language. It should be noted that this story does not appear in most collections of Anishinaabe tales.

7. Paul Pasquaretta also studies the role of gambling in "Sacred Chance: Gambling and the Contemporary Native American Indian Novel." He makes clear the importance of narratives about gambling as more than merely metaphorical but rather as foundational to "the primacy of creation and the dominance of life giving forces" (24). Thus, games of chance and the very forces of life become aligned.

8. Victor Shklovsky coins the term "defamiliarization," of which he notes, "The technique of art is to make objects 'unfamiliar,' to make forms difficult, to increase the difficulty and length of perception because the process of perception is an aesthetic end in itself and must be prolonged" (720). While Shklovsky emphasizes shifting the viewer's perceptions in art,

Bagese's lessons (though imagined and artistic) have more to do with daily experience in the physical world.

9. We can compare the animalistic emphasis on the sense of smell to the role of odor in *The Rag Doll Plagues*.

10. Sites of relocation are also relevant to my examination of *The Antelope Wife* in chapter 3.

11. For more on urban Indian studies, see Donald L. Fixico's *The Urban Indian Experience in America*, Susan Lobo and Kurt Peters's *American Indians and the Urban Experience*, Deborah Davis Jackson's *Our Elders Lived It*, and Bonita Lawrence's *"Real" Indians and Others*.

12. See Susan Lobo's *Urban Voices: The Bay Area American Indian Community*. One cannot overlook the fact that the reclamation and occupation of Alcatraz Island from 1967–1971 was also carried out by a pan-tribal Bay Area–based coalition, though the occupational strategies of this action are different from those in *Dead Voices*.

13. A chivaree is a mock serenade sung to newlyweds to disturb them (in a friendly, joking way). Vizenor shows Chivaree as a teasing mockery of tribal traditionalism as well as a somewhat unreliable narrator.

14. Nor is this to say that Vizenor excludes the city from his critiques. Indeed, he generally reserves his most scathing eviscerations for the American Indian Movement (AIM) activists whom he sees as "urban pretenders." Kimberly M. Blaeser's text discusses Vizenor's stand on these AIM factions (57–63). For other sources on AIM, see Paul Chaat Smith and Robert Allen Warrior's *Like a Hurricane*, Joane Nagel's *American Indian Ethnic Renewal*, and Dennis Banks's *Ojibwa Warrior*. Vizenor also discusses certain members in *Manifest Manners* (43).

15. Some of these images, of course, remind the reader of Orwell's *Animal Farm*.

16. Sometimes instead of fleeing on foot, Naanabozho builds a raft or floats on a log. Vizenor relates this story in *The People Named the Chippewa* and *Earthdivers* and cites Victor Barnouw's *Wisconsin Chippewa Myths and Tales and Their Relation to Chippewa Life* as one source. For more on Anishinaabe stories and history, see Basil Johnston's *The Manitous* and Edward Benton-Banai's *The Mishomis Book*.

17. I argue that the reclamation of sewers in this novel is much like that of sewage in general in *The Rag Doll Plagues* and the homeless community by the LA River in *Tropic of Orange*.

18. Vizenor is hardly alone in his critique of anthropology. Vine Deloria's send-up of the field in "Anthropologists and Other Friends" in *Custer Died for Your Sins* inspired Biolsi and Zimmerman's *Indians and Anthropologists*. Sherman Alexie similarly lampoons anthropologists in "Dear John Wayne."

19. In order to more directly overturn these less-than-helpful conceptualiza-
    tions of American Indians, Vizenor offers the "postindian." Vizenor states,
    "The *indian* is a simulation, the absence of natives; the *indian* transposes
    the real, and the simulation of the real has no referent, memory, or na-
    tive stories. The *postindian* must waver over the aesthetic ruins of *indian*
    simulations" (*Postindian Conversations* 1). The term "Indian" reflects all the
    cultural baggage of stereotypes of Native people. If the term itself reflects
    a static past that does not allow for contemporary Native identities to be
    formed or recognized, then perhaps we must reimagine this term and
    these images.
20. Vizenor's repetition of the phrase "we must go on," throughout this sec-
    tion, echoes Samuel Beckett's *The Unnamable*, which Vizenor excerpts as
    an epigraph to this novel.

EPILOGUE

1. It is always critical to remember that members of marginalized communities are often so embroiled in a day-by-day struggle to survive that long-
   term planning becomes an unaffordable luxury.

WORKS CITED

Acuña, Rodolfo. *Occupied America: A History of Chicanos*. New York: Pearson, Longman, 2004.

Adams, Rachel. "The Ends of America, the Ends of Postmodernism." *Twentieth-Century Literature* 53.3 (2007): 248–72.

Adamson, Joni. *American Indian Literature, Environmental Justice, and Ecocriticism: The Middle Place*. Tucson: University of Arizona Press, 2001.

Adamson, Joni, Mei Mei Evans, and Rachel Stein, eds. *The Environmental Justice Reader: Politics, Poetics, and Pedagogy*. Tucson: University of Arizona Press, 2002.

Adell, Sandra. "The Crisis in Black American Literary Criticism and the Postmodern Cures of Houston A. Baker, Jr., and Henry Louis Gates, Jr." *Double-Consciousness/Double Bind: Theoretical Issues in Twentieth-Century Black Literature*. Champaign: University of Illinois Press, 1994.

Agusti, Clara Escoda. "The Relationship between Community and Subjectivity in Octavia E. Butler's *Parable of the Sower*." *Extrapolation* 46.3 (Fall 2005): 351–60.

Aldama, Arturo J. *Disrupting Savagism: Intersecting Chicana/o, Mexican Immigrant, and Native American Struggles for Self-Representation*. Durham: Duke University Press, 2001.

Alexie, Sherman. "Dear John Wayne." *The Toughest Indian in the World*. New York: Atlantic Monthly, 2000. 189–208.

———. "How to Write the Great American Indian Novel." *The Summer of Black Widows*. New York: Hanging Loose, 1996. 94–95.

Alfred, Taiaiake. *Peace, Power, Righteousness: An Indigenous Manifesto*. Oxford: Oxford University Press, 1999.

Allen, Chadwick. "Blood (and) Memory." *American Literature* 71.1 (1999): 93–116.

Allen, Marlene D. "Octavia Butler's *Parable* Novels and the 'Boomerang' of African American History." *Callaloo* 32.4 (2009): 1353–65.

Allen, Paula Gunn. *Grandmothers of the Light: A Medicine Woman's Sourcebook*. Boston: Beacon, 1991.

Andonova, Liliana B. *Transnational Politics of the Environment: The European*

Union and Environmental Policy in Central and Eastern Europe. Cambridge: MIT Press, 2004.

Anzaldúa, Gloria. *Borderlands/La Frontera: The New Mestiza*. San Francisco: Aunt Lute Books, 1987.

Arnold, Linda. *Bureaucracy and Bureaucrats in Mexico City, 1742–1835*. Tucson: University of Arizona Press, 1988.

Augé, Marc. *Non-places: Introduction to an Anthropology of Supermodernity*. Trans. John Howe. London: Verso, 1999.

Austin, Mary. *Stories from the Country of Lost Borders*. Ed. Marjorie Pryse. New Brunswick: Rutgers University Press, 1987.

Avila, Eric. *Popular Culture in the Age of White Flight: Fear and Fantasy in Suburban Los Angeles*. Berkeley: University of California Press, 2004.

Baarschers, William H. *Eco-facts and Eco-fiction: Understanding the Environmental Debate*. New York: Routledge, 1996.

Babcock, Barbara. "'A Tolerated Margin of Mess': The Trickster and His Tales Reconsidered." *Critical Essays on Native American Literature*. Ed. Andrew Wiget. Boston: G. K. Hall, 1985. 153–85.

Baepler, Paul, ed. *White Slaves, African Masters: An Anthology of American Barbary Captivity Narratives*. Chicago: University of Chicago Press, 1999.

Banks, Dennis, and Richard Erdoes. *Ojibwa Warrior: Dennis Banks and the Rise of the American Indian Movement*. Norman: University of Oklahoma Press, 2005.

Barak, Julie. "Un-Becoming White: Identity Transformation in Louise Erdrich's *The Antelope Wife*." *SAIL* 13.4 (2001): 1–23.

Barnouw, Victor. *Wisconsin Chippewa Myth and Tales and Their Relation to Chippewa Life*. Madison: University of Wisconsin Press, 1993.

Barton, Gay. "Family as Character in Erdrich's Novels." *Approaches to Teaching the Works of Louise Erdrich*. Ed. Greg Sarris, Connie A. Jacobs, and James R. Giles. New York: Modern Language Association, 2004. 77–82.

Baudrillard, Jean. *Simulacra and Simulation*. Trans. Sheila Faria Glaser. Ann Arbor: University of Michigan Press, 1994.

Bauman, Zygmunt. *Liquid Life*. Cambridge: Polity, 2005.

———. *Liquid Modernity*. Cambridge: Polity, 2000.

———. *Modernity and Ambivalence*. Cambridge: Polity, 1991.

———. *Wasted Lives: Modernity and Its Outcasts*. Cambridge: Polity, 2004.

Beaulieu, Elizabeth Ann. *Black Women Writers and the American Neo-slave Narrative: Femininity Unfettered*. Westport CT: Greenwood, 1999.

Beck, John. *Dirty Wars: Landscape, Power, and Waste in Western American Literature*. Lincoln: University of Nebraska Press, 2009.

Beck, Ulrich. *Risk Society: Towards a New Modernism*. London: Sage, 1992.

Beidler, Peter G., and Gay Barton. *A Readers Guide to the Novels of Louise Erdrich*. Columbia: University of Missouri Press, 1999.

Beil, Susan Crawford. "The Diaper Dilemma: The Environmental Cost of Diapers." *All Natural Mamas* 2004. Accessed 3 Jan. 2012. http://www .punkinbutt.com/pdfs/dd-envr%20costs.pdf.

Bénézet, Delphine. "Beyond Blank Fiction, Palimpsestic *Flânerie* and Converging Imaginaries in Karen Tei Yamashita's *Tropic of Orange*." *The Idea of the City: Early-Modern, Modern and Post-Modern Locations and Communities*. Ed. Joan Fitzpatrick. Newcastle upon Tyne: Cambridge Scholars, 2009. 169–79.

Bennett, Michael, and David W. Teague, eds. *The Nature of Cities: Ecocriticism and Urban Environments*. Tucson: University of Arizona Press, 1999.

Benton-Banai, Edward. *The Mishomis Book: The Voice of the Ojibway*. Hayward WI: Indian Country Communications, 1988.

Bevis, William. "Native American Novels: Homing In." *Recovering the Word: Essays on Native American Literature*. Ed. Brian Swann and Arnold Krupat. Berkeley: University of California Press, 1987. 580–620.

The Bible: Authorized King James Version. Ed. Robert Carroll. Oxford: Oxford University Press, 1997.

Biolsi, Thomas, and Larry J. Zimmerman, eds. *Indians and Anthropologists: Vine Deloria, Jr., and the Critique of Anthropology*. Tucson: University of Arizona Press, 1997.

Blaeser, Kimberly M. *Gerald Vizenor: Writing in the Oral Tradition*. Norman: University of Oklahoma Press, 1996.

Blum, Elizabeth D. *Love Canal Revisited: Race, Class, and Gender in Environmental Activism*. Lawrence: University of Kansas Press, 2008.

Bolton, Herbert Eugene. *Fray Juan Crespi: Missionary Explorer on the Pacific Coast 1769–1774*. Berkeley: University of California Press, 1927.

Botanica's Trees and Shrubs. San Diego: Laurel Glen Press, 1999.

Boyce, James K., Sunita Narain, and Elizabeth A. Stanton, eds. *Reclaiming Nature: Environmental Justice and Ecological Restoration*. London: Anthem, 2007.

Brasch, Walter M. *Brer Rabbit, Uncle Remus, and the 'Cornfield Journalist': The Tale of Joel Chandler Harris*. Macon GA: Mercer University Press, 2000.

Brennan, Jonathan. *When Brer Rabbit Meets Coyote: African-Native American Literature*. Champaign: University of Illinois Press, 2003.

Brooks, James F, ed. *Confounding the Color Line: The Indian-Black Experience in North America*. Lincoln: University of Nebraska Press, 2002.

Brown, Alanna Kathleen. "'Patterns and Waves Generation to Generation': *The Antelope Wife*." *Approaches to Teaching the Works of Louise Erdrich*. Ed. Greg Sarris, Connie A. Jacobs, and James R. Giles. New York: Modern Language Association, 2004. 88–94.

Brown, Phil. *Toxic Exposures: Contested Illnesses and the Environmental Health Movement*. New York: Columbia University Press, 2007.

Buell, Lawrence. *Writing for an Endangered World: Literature, Culture, and Environment in the U.S. and Beyond.* Cambridge: Harvard University Press, 2001.

Bullard, Robert D., ed. *Growing Smarter: Achieving Livable Communities, Environmental Justice, and Regional Equity.* Cambridge: MIT Press, 2007.

Bullard, Robert D., and Beverly Wright, eds. *Race, Place, and Environmental Justice after Hurricane Katrina.* Boulder CO: Westview Press, 2009.

Butler, Octavia E. *Kindred.* Boston: Beacon, 2004.

———. *Parable of the Sower.* New York: Warner, 1993.

———. *Parable of the Talents.* New York: Warner, 1998.

Byerly, Allison. "The Picturesque Aesthetic and the National Park System." Glotfelty and Fromm 52–68.

Carrasco, Davíd. *Religions of Mesoamerica: Cosmovision and Ceremonial Centers.* San Francisco: Harper and Row, 1990.

Carruthers, David V., ed. *Environmental Justice in Latin America: Problems, Promise, and Practice.* Cambridge: MIT Press, 2008.

Carson, Rachel. *Silent Spring.* Greenwich CT: Crest, 1964.

Casteel, Sarah Phillips. *Second Arrivals: Landscape and Belonging in the Contemporary Writing of the Americas.* Charlottesville: University of Virginia Press, 2007.

Castor, Laura. "Ecological Politics and Comic Redemption in Louise Erdrich's *The Antelope Wife.*" *Nordlit* 15 (2004): 121–34.

Cattelino, Jessica. *High Stakes: Florida Seminole Gaming and Sovereignty.* Durham: Duke University Press, 2008.

Certeau, Michel de. *The Practice of Everyday Life.* Trans. Steven Rendall. Berkeley: University of California Press, 1984.

Champagne, Duane, ed. *Contemporary Native American Cultural Issues.* Walnut Creek CA: Alta Mira, 1999.

Chavis, Benjamin. Foreword. *Confronting Environmental Racism: Voices from the Grassroots.* Ed. Robert D. Bullard. Boston: South End Press, 1993. 3–5.

Cheung, King-Kok, ed. *Words Matter: Conversations with Asian American Writers.* Honolulu: University of Hawai'i Press, 2000.

Chick, Nancy L. "Does Power Travel in the Bloodlines? A Genealogical Red Herring." *Approaches to Teaching the Works of Louise Erdrich.* Ed. Greg Sarris, Connie A. Jacobs, and James R. Giles. New York: Modern Language Association, 2004. 83–87.

Chuh, Kandice. "Of Hemispheres and Other Spheres: Navigating Karen Tei Yamashita's Literary World." *American Literary History* 18.3 (2006): 618–37.

Clapp, Jennifer. *Toxic Exports: The Transfer of Hazardous Wastes from Rich to Poor Countries.* Ithaca: Cornell University Press, 2001.

Clifford, James. *Routes: Travel and Translation in the Late Twentieth Century.* Cambridge: Harvard University Press, 1997.

Commoner, Barry. *The Closing Circle: Nature, Man, and Technology*. New York: Bantam, 1971.

Compston, Hugh, and Ian Bailey, eds. *Turning Down the Heat: The Politics of Climate Policy in Affluent Democracies*. London: Palgrave, 2008.

Cook-Lynn, Elizabeth. "The American Indian Fiction Writers: Cosmopolitanism, Nationalism, the Third World, and First Nation Sovereignty." *Nothing but the Truth: An Anthology of Native American Literature*. Ed. John L. Purdy and James Ruppert. Upper Saddle River NJ: Prentice Hall, 2001. 23–38.

———. *Anti-Indianism in Modern America: A Voice from Tatekeya's Earth*. Urbana: University of Illinois Press, 2001.

Cooney, Kevin. "Metafictional Geographies: Los Angeles in Karen Tei Yamashita's *Tropic of Orange* and Salvador Plascencia's *People of Paper*." *On and Off the Page: Mapping Place in Text and Culture*. Ed. M. B. Hackler. Newcastle upon Tyne: Cambridge Scholars Press, 2009. 189–218.

Cooper, Deborah. "The Transcontinental Railroad Comes to Town." *Walk along the Water*. Oakland Museum of California. Accessed 16 Feb. 2012. http://www.waterfrontaction.org/history/44.htm.

Cronon, William, ed. *Uncommon Ground: Rethinking the Human Place in Nature*. New York: Norton, 1995.

Curtin, Deane. *Environmental Ethics for a Postcolonial World*. Lanham MD: Rowman and Littlefield, 2005.

Dara, Evan. *The Lost Scrapbook*. Normal IL: Fiction Collective Two, 1995.

Davis, Angela Y., and Dylan Rodriguez. "The Challenge of Prison Abolition: A Conversation." History Is a Weapon. Accessed 3 Jan. 2012. http://www.historyisaweapon.com/defcon1/davisinterview.html.

Davis, Mike. *City of Quartz: Excavating the Future in Los Angeles*. London: Verso, 1990.

———. *Ecology of Fear: Los Angeles and the Imagination of Disaster*. New York: Vintage, 1998.

Deitering, Cynthia. "The Postnatural Novel: Toxic Consciousness in Fiction of the 1980s." Glotfelty and Fromm 196–203.

Delaney, Samuel R. *Times Square Red, Times Square Blue*. New York: New York University Press, 1999.

DeLillo, Don. *Underworld*. New York: Scribner, 1997.

Deloria, Vine, Jr. *Custer Died for Your Sins: An Indian Manifesto*. Norman: University of Oklahoma Press, 1988.

———. "Indian Humor." *Nothing but the Truth: An Anthology of Native American Literature*. Ed. John L. Purdy and James Ruppert. Upper Saddle River NJ: Prentice Hall, 2001. 39–53.

Deming, Alison H., and Lauret E. Savoy, eds. *The Colors of Nature: Culture, Identity, and the Natural World*. Minneapolis: Milkweed, 2002.

Dethlefsen, Les, et al. "Assembly of the Human Intestinal Microbiota. *Trends in Ecology and Evolution* 21.9 (2006): 517–23.

De Vos, George A. "The Dangers of Pure Theory in Social Anthropology." *Ethos* 3.1 (1975): 77–91.

Diaz, David R. *Barrio Urbanism: Chicanos, Planning, and American Cities.* New York: Routledge, 2005.

Dix, Douglas, et al. "Textual Interstices: Mirrored Shadows in Gerald Vizenor's *Dead Voices.*" A. Robert Lee 178–91.

Dixon, Terrell F., ed. *City Wilds: Essays and Stories about Urban Nature.* Athens: University of Georgia Press, 2002.

DiZerega, Gus. "Empathy, Society, Nature, and the Relational Self: Deep Ecology and Liberal Modernity." Gottlieb 56–81.

Douglas, Mary. *Purity and Danger: An Analysis of the Concepts of Pollution and Taboo.* London: Routledge, 1966.

Douglass, Frederick. *Narrative of the Life of Frederick Douglass, an American Slave.* New York: Barnes and Noble Classics, 2005.

Dreese, Donelle N. *Ecocriticism: Creating Self and Place in Environmental and American Indian Literatures.* New York: Peter Lang, 2002.

Dubey, Madhu. "Folk and Urban Communities in African-American Women's Fiction: Octavia Butler's *Parable of the Sower.*" *Studies in American Fiction* 27.1 (1999): 103–28.

Ehrlich, Paul. *The Population Bomb.* New York: Ballantine, 1968.

Erdrich, Louise. *The Antelope Wife.* New York: Harper, 1998.

Faber, Daniel, ed. *The Struggle for Ecological Democracy: Environmental Justice Movements in the United States.* New York: Guilford, 1998.

Favor, J. Martin. *Authentic Blackness: The Folk in the New Negro Renaissance.* Durham: Duke University Press, 1999.

Finseth, Ian Frederick. *Shades of Green: Visions of Nature in the Literature of American Slavery, 1770–1860.* Athens: University of Georgia Press, 2009.

Fixico, Donald L. Foreword. Lobo and Peters ix–x.

———. *The Urban Indian Experience in America.* Albuquerque: University of New Mexico Press, 2000.

Forbes, Jack D. "Blood Quantum: A Relic of Racism and Termination." *Native Intelligence* 27 Nov. 2000. University of California, Davis. Accessed 3 Jan. 2012. http://nas.ucdavis.edu/jack-d-forbes/2000/11/27/blood-quantum-a -relic-of-racism-and-termination/.

———. "The Urban Tradition among Native Americans." Lobo and Peters 5–25.

Franco, Dean. "Working through the Archive: Trauma and History in Alejandro Morales's *The Rag Doll Plagues.*" PMLA 120.2 (2005): 375–87.

Furlan, Laura. "Remapping Indian Country in Louise Erdrich's *Antelope Wife.*" SAIL 19.4 (2007): 54–76.

Gamber, John. "Tactical Mobility as Survivance: *Bone Game* and *Dark River* by Louis Owens." *Survivance: Narratives of Native Presence.* Ed. Gerald Vizenor. Lincoln: University of Nebraska Press, 2008. 221–46.

Garber, Marjorie. Foreword. *Lieutenant Nun: Memoir of a Basque Transvestite in the New World.* By Catalina de Erauso. Trans. Michele Stepto and Gabriel Stepto. Boston: Beacon, 1996. vii–xxiv.

Garrard, David. *Ecocriticism.* London: Rutledge, 2004.

Garroutte, Eva Marie. *Real Indians: Identity and Survival of Native America.* Berkeley: University of California Press, 2003.

Gates, Henry Louis, Jr. *The Signifying Monkey: A Theory of African-American Literary Criticism.* Oxford: Oxford University Press, 1988.

Gillan, Jennifer. "Restoring the Flow: Comic Circulation in Gerald Vizenor's Fiction." *North Dakota Quarterly* 67.3–4 (2000): 242–55.

Glotfelty, Cheryll, and Harold Fromm, eds. *The Ecocriticism Reader: Landmarks in Literary Ecology.* Athens: University of Georgia Press, 1996.

Gottlieb, Roger S., ed. *Ecological Community: Environmental Challenges for Philosophy, Politics, and Morality.* New York: Routledge, 1997.

Hampton, Gregory. "Migration and Capital of the Body: Octavia Butler's *Parable of the Sower.*" CLA *Journal* 49.1 (2005): 56–73.

Haraway, Donna J. *Simians, Cyborgs, and Women: The Reinvention of Nature.* New York: Routledge, 1991.

Harris, Trudier. *Saints, Sinners, and Saviors: Strong, Black Women in African American Literature.* New York: Palgrave Macmillan, 2001.

Hayles, N. Katherine. *How We Became Posthuman: Virtual Bodies in Cybernetics, Literature, and Informatics.* Chicago: University of Chicago Press, 1999.

———. "Searching for Common Ground." *Reinventing Nature? Responses to Postmodern Deconstruction.* Ed. Michael E. Soulé and Gary Lease. Washington DC: Island Press, 1995.

Heise, Ursula K. "Local Rock and Global Plastic: World Ecology and the Experience of Place." *Comparative Literature Studies* 41.1 (2004): 126–52.

———. *Sense of Place and Sense of Planet: The Environmental Imagination of the Global.* Oxford: Oxford University Press, 2008.

Herrera-Sobek, María. "Epidemics, Epistemophilia, and Racism: Ecological Literary Criticism and *The Rag Doll Plagues.*" *Alejandro Morales and His Work.* Ed. José Antonio Gurpegui. Tempe: Bilingual Review Press, 1996: 99–108.

hooks, bell. "Touching the Earth." *At Home on the Earth: Becoming Nature to Our Place; A Multicultural Anthology.* Ed. David Landis Barnhill. Berkeley: University of California Press, 1999. 51–56.

Howe, LeAnne. *Shell Shaker.* San Francisco: Aunt Lute, 2001.

Hsu, Ruth Y. "The Cartography of Justice and Truthful Refractions in Karen Tei Yamashita's *Tropic of Orange.*" *Transnational Asian American Literature: Sites and Transits*. Ed. Shirley Geok-lin Lim, et al. Philadelphia: Temple University Press, 2006. 75–99.

Jackson, Deborah Davis. *Our Elders Lived It: American Indian Identity in the City*. Dekalb: Northern Illinois University Press, 2002.

Jacobs, Harriet. *Incidents in the Life of a Slave Girl*. New York: Dover, 2001.

Jahner, Elaine A. "Trickster Discourse and Postmodern Strategies." A. Robert Lee 38–58.

Jarrett, Gene Andrew. *Deans and Truants: Race and Realism in African American Literature*. Philadelphia: University of Pennsylvania Press, 2007.

Jefferies, Richard. *After London; or, Wild England*. Oxford: Oxford World Classics, 1980.

Johnson, Charles. *Middle Passage*. New York: Scribner, 1998.

Johnston, Basil. *The Manitous: The Spiritual World of the Ojibway*. New York: Harper Collins, 1995.

Jones, Gayl. *Corregidora*. London: Serpent's Tail, 2000.

Kadohata, Cynthia. *In the Heart of the Valley of Love*. Berkeley: University of California Press, 1997.

Kaplan, Caren. *Questions of Travel: Postmodern Discourses of Displacement*. Durham: Duke University Press, 1996.

Kase, Yasuko. "Remapping L.A.: Spatio-Temporal Rupture in *Tropic of Orange*." *AALA Journal* 11.11 (2005): 142–52.

Katz, Eric. "Imperialism and Environmentalism." Gottlieb 163–74.

Keane, Stephen. *Disaster Movies: Cinema of Catastrophe*. London: Wallflower, 2006.

Kim, Elaine H. *Asian American Literature: An Introduction to the Writings and Their Social Context*. Philadelphia: Temple University Press, 1982.

Kleiner, Elaine, and Angela Vlaicus. "Revisioning Woman in America: A Study of Louise Erdrich's Novel *The Antelope Wife*." *Femspec* 2.2 (2001): 56–65.

Knight, Alan. *Mexico: The Colonial Era*. Cambridge: Cambridge University Press, 2002.

Kolodny, Annette. *The Lay of the Land: Metaphor as Experience and History in American Life and Letters*. Chapel Hill: University of North Carolina Press, 1975.

Kosek, Jake. "Purity and Pollution: Racial Degradation and Environmental Anxieties." Peet and Watts 125–65.

Kuletz, Valerie L. *The Tainted Desert: Environmental and Social Ruin in the American West*. New York: Routledge, 1998.

Kunin, Seth Daniel. *The Logic of Incest: A Structuralist Analysis of Hebrew Mythology*. Sheffield: Sheffield Academic Press, 1995.

LaLonde, Chris. "The Ceded Landscape of Gerald Vizenor's Fiction." *SAIL* 9.1 (1997): 16–32.

Lang, Leslie H. "Study: Air Pollution Causes Lung Disease in School-Age Children." *News* 26 Nov. 2001. University of North Carolina School of Medicine. Accessed 17 Feb. 2012. http://www.unc.edu/news/archives/nov01/airpol112801.htm.

Latour, Bruno. *We Have Never Been Modern*. Trans. Catherine Porter. Cambridge: Harvard University Press, 1993.

Lawrence, Bonita. *"Real" Indians and Others: Mixed-Blood Urban Native Peoples and Indigenous Nationhood*. Lincoln: University of Nebraska Press, 2004.

Lee, A. Robert, ed. *Loosening the Seams: Interpretations of Gerald Vizenor*. Bowling Green OH: Bowling Green State University Popular Press, 2000.

Lee, James Kyung-Jin. *Urban Triage: Race and the Fictions of Multiculturalism*. Minneapolis: University of Minnesota Press, 2004.

Lee, Rachel. "Asian American Cultural Production in Asian-Pacific Perspective." *boundary 2* 26.2 (1999): 231–54.

Lee, Sue-Im. "'We Are Not the World': Global Village, Universalism, and Karen Tei Yamashita's *Tropic of Orange*." *Modern Fiction Studies* 52.3 (2007): 501–27.

Lefebvre, Henri. *The Production of Space*. Trans. Donald Nicholson-Smith. Malden MA: Blackwell, 1991.

Leopold, Aldo. *Sand County Almanac*. New York: Ballantine, 1970.

Li, Florence Hsiao-ching. "Imagining the Mother/Motherland: Karen Tei Yamashita's *Tropic of Orange* and Theresa Hak Kyung Cha's *Dictee*." *Concentric: Literary and Cultural Studies* 30.1 (2004): 149–67.

Light, Andrew. "Boyz in the Woods: Urban Wilderness in American Cinema." Bennet and Teague 137–68.

Light, Steven Andrew, and Kathyryn R. L. Rand. *Indian Gaming and Tribal Sovereignty: The Casino Compromise*. Lawrence: University of Kansas Press, 2005.

Lincoln, Kenneth. *Indi'n Humor: Bicultural Play in Native America*. Oxford: Oxford University Press, 1993.

Lischke, Ute. "'Blitzkuchen': An Exploration of Story-Telling in Louise Erdrich's *The Antelope Wife*." *Interdisciplinary and Cross-Cultural Narratives in North America*. Ed. Mark Cronlund Anderson and Irene Maria F. Blayer. New York: Peter Lang, 2005. 61–72.

Little, Jonathan. "Beading the Multicultural World: Louise Erdrich's *The Antelope Wife* and the Sacred Metaphysic." *Contemporary Literature* 41.3 (2000): 495–524.

Lobo, Susan, ed. *Urban Voices: The Bay Area Indian Community*. Tucson: University of Arizona Press, 2002.

Lobo, Susan, and Kurt Peters, eds. *American Indians and the Urban Experience*. Walnut Creek CA: Alta Mira, 2001.

López Lozano, Miguel. "The Politics of Blood: Miscegenation and Phobias of

Contagion in Alejandro Morales's *The Rag Doll Plagues.*" *Aztlán* 28.1 (Spring 2003): 39–73.

Lowe, John. "Monkey Kings and Mojo: Postmodern Ethnic Humor in Kingston, Reed, and Vizenor." MELUS 21.4 (1996): 103–26.

Luczak, Ewa. "'Brer Rabbit Takes a Walk': The Trickster in Afro-American Folklore and Fiction." *Animal Magic: Essays on Animals in the American Imagination.* Ed. Jopi Nyman and Carol R. Smith. Joensuu, Finland: Faculty of Humanities, University of Joensuu, 2004. 137–50.

Lugones, Maria. "Purity, Impurity, and Separation." *Signs* 19.2 (1994): 458–97.

Lynch, Tom. *Xerophilia: Ecocritical Explorations in Southwestern Literature.* Lubbock: Texas Tech University Press, 2008.

Madsen, Deborah L. *American Exceptionalism.* Jackson: University Press of Mississippi, 1998.

Márquez, Antonio C. "The Use and Abuse of History in Alejandro Morales's *The Brick People* and *The Rag Doll Plagues.*" *Alejandro Morales and His Work.* Ed. José Antonio Gurpegui. Tempe: Bilingual Review Press, 1996. 76–85.

Martín-Rodríguez, Manuel M. "The Global Border: Transnationalism and Cultural Hybridism in Alejandro Morales's *The Rag Doll Plagues.*" *Alejandro Morales and His Work.* Ed. José Antonio Gurpegui. Tempe: Bilingual Review Press, 1996. 86–98.

Marx, Karl. *Capital.* Ed. David McLellan. Oxford: Oxford University Press, 1999.

Marx, Leo. *The Pilot and the Passenger: Essays on Literature, Technology, and Culture in the United States.* Oxford: Oxford University Press, 1988.

Mason, W. Dale. *Indian Gaming: Tribal Sovereignty and American Politics.* Norman: University of Oklahoma Press, 2000.

Massey, Doreen. *Space, Place, and Gender.* Minneapolis: University of Minnesota Press, 1994.

Matchie, Thomas. "*The Antelope Wife*: Louise Erdrich's 'Cloud Chamber.'" *North Dakota Quarterly* 67.2 (2000): 26–37.

May, Philip A. "The Epidemiology of Alcohol Abuse among Native Americans: The Mythical and Real Properties." Champagne 227–44.

Mayer, Sylvia. "Genre and Environmentalism: Octavia Butler's *Parable of the Sower*, Speculative Fiction, and the African American Slave Narrative." Mayer, *Restoring the Connection to the Natural World* 175–96.

———, ed. *Restoring the Connection to the Natural World: Essays on the African American Environmental Imagination.* London: Lit Verlag, 2003.

McGirr, Lisa. *Suburban Warriors: The Origins of the New American Right.* Princeton: Princeton University Press, 2001.

McGranahan, Gordon, et al. *The Citizens at Risk: From Urban Sanitation to Sustainable Cities.* London: Earthscan, 2001.

McGurty, Eileen. *Transforming Environmentalism: Warren County, PCBS, and the Origins of Environmental Justice*. New Brunswick: Rutgers University Press, 2007.

McKibbin, Bill. *The End of Nature*. New York: Random House, 2006.

Means, Russell. Foreword. Weaver, *Defending Mother Earth* xi–xiv.

Meeker, Joseph. "The Comic Mode." Glotfelty and Fromm 155–69.

Melzer, Patricia. "All That You Touch You Change: Utopian Desire and the Concept of Change in Octavia Butler's *Parable of the Sower* and *Parable of the Talents*." *Femspec* 3.2 (2002): 31–52.

Merchant, Carolyn. *The Death of Nature: Women, Ecology and the Scientific Revolution*. San Francisco: Harper, 1990.

Mihesuah, Devon A. "American Indian Identities: Issues of Individual Choice and Development." Champagne 13–38.

Miller, Carol. "Telling the Indian Urban: Representations in American Indian Fiction." Lobo and Peters 29–45.

Miller, Jim. "Post-Apocalyptic Hoping: Octavia Butler's Dystopian/Utopian Vision." *Science-Fiction Studies* 25.2 (1998): 336–60.

Mogen, David. "Tribal Images of the 'New World': Apocalyptic Transformation in *Almanac of the Dead* and Gerald Vizenor's Fiction." A. Robert Lee 192–202.

Moisa, Ray. "Relocation: The Promise and the Lie." Lobo 21–28.

Momaday, N. Scott. *House Made of Dawn*. New York: Harper and Row, 1968.

Monsma, Bradley John. "Liminal Landscapes: Motion, Perspective, and Place in Gerald Vizenor's Fiction." *SAIL* 9.1 (1997): 60–72.

Morace, Robert A. "From Sacred Hoops to Bingo Palaces: Louise Erdrich's Carnivalesque Fiction." *The Chippewa Landscape of Louise Erdrich*. Ed. Allan Chavkin. Tuscaloosa: University of Alabama Press, 1999. 36–66.

Morales, Alejandro. "Dynamic Identities in Heterotopia." *Alejandro Morales and His Work*. Ed. José Antonio Gurpegui. Tempe: Bilingual Review Press, 1996. 14–27.

———. *The Rag Doll Plagues*. Houston: Arte Público Press, 1992.

Morrison, Toni. *Beloved*. New York: Vintage, 2004.

Murray, David. "Crossblood Strategies in the Writings of Gerald Vizenor." A. Robert Lee 20–37.

Myers, Jeffrey. *Converging Stories: Race, Ecology, and Environmental Justice in American Literature*. Athens: University of Georgia Press, 2005.

Nagel, Joane. *American Indian Ethnic Renewal: Red Power and the Resurgence of Identity and Culture*. Oxford: Oxford University Press, 1996.

Napier, Winston. *African American Literary Theory: A Reader*. New York: New York University Press, 2000.

Newman, Kim. *Apocalypse Movies: End of the World Cinema*. New York: St. Martin's Griffin, 2000.

Nietzsche, Friedrich. *On the Genealogy of Morals*. Trans. Walter Kaufmann and R. J. Hollingdale. Ed. Walter Kaufmann. New York: Vintage, 1989.

Nilges, Mathias. "'We Need the Stars': Change, Community, and the Absent Father in Octavia Butler's *Parable of the Sower* and *Parable of the Talents.*" *Callalloo* 32.4 (2009): 1332–52.

Oakland Convention and Visitors Bureau website. <www.oaklandcvb.com>.

O'Connell, Barry. "Gerald Vizenor's 'Delicious Dancing with Time': Tricking History from Ideology." A. Robert Lee 59–84.

Outka, Paul. *Race and Nature from Transcendentalism to the Harlem Renaissance*. New York: Palgrave Macmillan, 2008.

Owens, Louis. Introduction. *SAIL* 9.1 (1997): 1–2.

——. *Mixedblood Messages: Literature, Film, Family, and Place*. Norman: University of Oklahoma Press, 1998.

——. *Other Destinies: Understanding the American Indian Novel*. Norman: University of Oklahoma Press, 1992.

Pasquaretta, Paul. *Gambling and Survival in Native North America*. Tucson: University of Arizona Press, 2003.

——. "Sacred Chance: Gambling and the Contemporary Native American Indian Novel." *MELUS* 21.2 (1996): 21–33.

Peel, Ellen. "'God Is Change': Persuasion and Pragmatic Utopianism in Octavia E. Butler's Earthseed Novels." *Afro-Future Females: Future Females: Black Writers Chart Science Fiction's Newest New-Wave Trajectory*. Ed. Marleen S. Barr. Columbus: Ohio State University Press, 2008. 53–74.

Peet, Richard, and Michael Watts, eds. *Liberation Ecologies: Environment, Development, Social Movements*. London: Routledge, 2004.

Pellow, David Naguib. *Resisting Global Toxics: Transnational Movements for Environmental Justice*. Cambridge: MIT Press, 2007.

Phillips, Dana. "Is Nature Necessary?" Glotfelty and Fromm 204–22.

Phillips, Jerry. "The Intuition of the Future: Utopia and Catastrophe in Octavia Butler's *Parable of the Sower.*" *Novel* (2002): 299–311.

"Plan Espiritual de Aztlán." 20 May 1997. University of Texas–Pan American. Accessed 17 Feb. 2012. http://www.utpa.edu/orgs/mecha/aztlan.html.

"Plutonium: Nuclear Issues Briefing Paper 18." *Albawaba* 9 Jan. 2001. Uranium Information Centre. Accessed 17 Feb. 2012. http://www.albawaba.com/business/plutonium-nuclear-issues-briefing-paper-18-%E2%80%93-part-one.

Potts, Stephen W. "'We Keep Playing the Same Record': A Conversation with Octavia E. Butler." *Science-Fiction Studies* 23 (1996): 331–38.

Priewe, Marc. "Bio-Politics and the ContamiNation of the Body in Alejandro Morales's *The Rag Doll Plagues.*" *MELUS* 29.3–4 (2004): 397–412.

Purdy, John. "Against All Odds: Games of Chance in the Novels of Louise

Erdrich." *The Chippewa Landscape of Louise Erdrich.* Ed. Allan Chavkin. Tuscaloosa: University of Alabama Press, 1999. 8–35.

Quintana, Alvia E. "Performing Tricksters: Karen Tei Yamashita and Guillermo Gómez-Peña." *Amerasia Journal* 28.2 (2002): 217–25.

Rainwater, Catherine. "Ethnic Signs in Erdrich's *Tracks* and *The Bingo Palace.*" *The Chippewa Landscape of Louise Erdrich.* Ed. Allan Chavkin. Tuscaloosa: University of Alabama Press, 1999. 144–60.

Ramirez, Catherine S. "Cyborg Feminism: The Science Fiction of Octavia E. Butler and Gloria Anzaldúa." *Reload: Rethinking Women and Cyberculture.* Ed. Mary Flanagan and Austin Booth. Cambridge: MIT Press, 2002. 374–402.

Rhodes, Edwardo Lao. *Environmental Justice in America: A New Paradigm.* Bloomington: University of Indiana Press, 2003.

Roberts, J. Timmons, and Melissa M. Toffolon-Weiss. *Chronicles from the Environmental Justice Frontline.* Cambridge: Cambridge University Press, 2001.

Rody, Caroline. "The Transnational Imagination: Karen Tei Yamashita's *Tropic of Orange.*" *Asian North American Identities: Beyond the Hyphen.* Ed. Eleanor Rose Ty and Donald C. Goellnicht. Bloomington: University of Indian Press, 2004. 130–48.

Ruffin, Kimberly J. "Parable of a 21st Century Religion: Octavia Butler's Bridge between Science and Religion." *Obsidian: Literature in the African Diaspora* 6.2–7.1 (2006): 87–104.

Ruoff, A. LaVonne Brown. Afterword. *The Chippewa Landscape of Louise Erdrich.* Ed. Allan Chavkin. Tuscaloosa: University of Alabama Press, 1999. 182–88.

Rushdy, Ashraf H. A. *Neo–Slave Narratives: Studies in the Social Logic of a Literary Form.* Oxford: Oxford University Press, 1999.

Sackman, Douglas Cazaux. *Orange Empire: California and the Fruits of Eden.* Berkeley: University of California Press, 2005.

Sadowski-Smith, Claudia. "The U.S.-Mexico Borderlands Write Back: Cross-Cultural Transnationalism in Contemporary U.S. Women of Color Fiction." *Arizona Quarterly* 57.1 (2001): 91–112.

Saldivar, Ramón. *The Borderlands of Culture: Américo Paredes and the Transnational Imaginary.* Durham: Duke University Press, 2006.

Sarve-Gorham, Kristan. "Games of Chance: Gambling and Land Tenure in *Tracks, Love Medicine,* and *The Bingo Palace.*" *Western American Literature* 34.3 (Fall 1999): 277–300.

Schein, Richard H., ed. *Landscape and Race in the United States.* London: Routledge, 2006.

Schweninger, Lee. *Listening to the Land: Native American Literary Responses to the Landscape.* Athens: University of Georgia Press, 2008.

Science and Environmental Health Network. "Precautionary Principle."
    Accessed 14 Feb. 2012. http://sehn.org/precaution.html.
Shakur, Tupac. "Never B Peace." *Better Dayz.* Interscope, 2007.
Shklovsky, Victor. "Art as Technique." *The Critical Tradition: Classic Texts and
    Contemporary Trends.* Ed. David H. Richter. 717–26.
Shrader-Frechette, Kristin. *Environmental Justice: Creating Equality, Reclaiming
    Democracy.* Oxford: Oxford University Press, 2002.
Sides, Josh. *L.A. City Limits: African American Los Angeles from the Great
    Depression to the Present.* Berkeley: University of California Press, 2003.
Silko, Leslie Marmon. *Almanac of the Dead.* New York: Penguin, 1991.
Smith, Andrea. *Conquest: Sexual Violence and American Indian Genocide.*
    Cambridge MA: South End Press, 2005.
Smith, Carlton. *Coyote Kills John Wayne: Postmodernism and Contemporary
    Fictions of the Transcultural Frontier.* Hanover: University Press of New
    England, 2000.
Smith, Henry Nash. *Virgin Land: The American West as Symbol and Myth.*
    Cambridge: Harvard University Press, 1978.
Smith, Lindsey Claire. *Indians, Environment, and Identity on the Borders of
    American Literature: From Faulkner and Morrison to Walker and Silko.* New
    York: Palgrave Macmillan, 2008.
Smith, Paul Chaat, and Robert Allen Warrior. *Like a Hurricane: The Indian
    Movement from Alcatraz to Wounded Knee.* New York: New Press, 1997.
Snyder, Gary. "The Etiquette of Freedom." *The Practice of the Wild.* New York:
    North Point Press, 1990. 3–24.
Sohn, Stephen Hong. Message to the author. 28 Jan. 2010. E-mail.
———. Message to the author. 17 Aug. 2010. E-mail.
Soja, Edward. *Postmodern Geographies: The Reassertion of Space within Critical
    Social Theory.* New York: Verso, 1989.
Spaulding, A. Timothy. *Re-forming the Past: History, the Fantastic, and the
    Postmodern Slave Narrative.* Columbus: Ohio State University Press, 2005.
Stepto, Michelle. Introduction. *Lieutenant Nun: Memoir of a Basque Transvestite
    in the New World.* By Catalina de Erauso. Trans. Michele Stepto and Gabriel
    Stepto. Boston: Beacon, 1996. xxv–xlii.
Stillman, Peter G. "Dystopian Critiques, Utopian Possibilities, and Human
    Purposes in Octavia Butler's Parables." *Utopian Studies* 14.1 (2003): 15–27.
Stokes, Karah. "What about the Sweetheart? The 'Different Shape' of
    Anishinabe Two Sisters Stories in Louise Erdrich's *Love Medicine* and *Tales of
    Burning Love.*" *MELUS* 24.2 (1999): 89–105.
Swift, Jonathan. "A Description of a City Shower." *Norton Anthology of English
    Literature.* Ed. M. H. Abrams, et al. 6th ed. Vol. 1. New York: Norton, 1993.
    2009–10.
Szanto, Laura Furlan. "An Annotated Secondary Bibliography of Louise

Erdrich's Recent Fiction: *The Bingo Palace, Tales of Burning Love,* and *The Antelope Wife*." *SAIL* 1.2 (2000): 61–90.

Sze, Julie. "'Not by Politics Alone': Gender and Environmental Justice in Karen Tei Yamashita's *Tropic of Orange*." *Bucknell Review* 44.1 (2000): 29–42.

Taube, Karl. *Aztec and Maya Myths: The Legendary Past.* Austin: University of Texas Press, 1993.

Tharp, Julie. "Windigo Ways: Eating and Excess in Louise Erdrich's *The Antelope Wife*." *American Indian Culture and Research Journal* 27.4 (2003): 117–31.

Thoreau, Henry David. *Walden and Other Writings.* Ed. Joseph Wood Krutch. New York: Bantam, 1981.

Townsend, Richard F. *The Aztecs.* Rev. ed. London: Thames and Hudson, 2000.

Trafzer, Clifford. *American Indian Identity: Today's Changing Perspectives.* Sacramento: Sierra Oaks Press, 1989.

Treuer, David. "Reading Culture." *SAIL* 14.1 (2002): 51–64.

Turner, Frederick. "Cultivating the American Garden." Glotfelty and Fromm 40–51.

U.S. Census Bureau. "The American Indian and Alaskan Native Population 2000." *United States Census* Feb. 2002. Accessed 6 Jan. 2012. <www.census .gov/prob/2002pubs/c2kbr01-15.pdf>.

Velie, Alan R. "Gerald Vizenor's Indian Gothic." *MELUS* 17.1 (1992): 75–85.

———. "The Trickster Novel." Vizenor, *Narrative Chance* 121–39.

Villa, Raúl Homero. *Barrio-Logos: Space and Place in Urban Chicano Literature and Culture.* Austin: University of Texas Press, 2000.

Villalobos, José Pablo. "Border Read, Border Metaphor: Altering Boundaries in Miguel Méndez and Alejandro Morales." *Arizona Journal of Hispanic Cultural Studies* 4 (2000): 131–40.

Vizenor, Gerald. *Dead Voices: Natural Agonies in the New World.* Norman: University of Oklahoma Press, 1992.

———. *Earthdivers: Tribal Narratives on Mixed Descent.* Minneapolis: University of Minnesota Press, 1981.

———. *The Heirs of Columbus.* New York: Fire Keepers, 1991.

———. *Manifest Manners: Narratives on Postindian Survivance.* Lincoln: University of Nebraska Press, 1994.

———, ed. *Narrative Chance: Postmodern Discourse on Native American Indian Literatures.* Norman: University of Oklahoma Press, 1989.

———. *The People Named the Chippewa: Narrative Histories.* Minneapolis: University of Minnesota Press, 1984.

———. "The Ruins of Representation: Shadow Survivance and the Literature of Dominance." *American Indian Quarterly* 17.1 (1993): 7–30.

———, ed. *Summer in the Spring: Anishinaabe Lyric Poems and Stories.* New ed. Norman: University of Oklahoma Press, 1993.

———. "Trickster Discourse: Comic Holotropes and Language Games."
Vizenor, *Narrative Chance* 187–211.

Vizenor, Gerald, and A. Robert Lee, eds. *Postindian Conversations*. Lincoln:
University of Nebraska Press, 1999.

Wallace, David Foster. *Infinite Jest*. Boston: Little, Brown, and Co., 1996.

Wallace, Molly. "Tropics of Globalization: Reading the New North America."
Symploke 9.1–2 (2001): 146–60.

Waller, David. "Friendly Fire: When Environmentalists Dehumanize American
Indians." Champagne 277–92.

Warfield, Angela. "Reassessing the Utopian Novel: Octavia Butler, Jacques
Derrida, and the Impossible Future of Utopia." *Obsidian: Literature of the
African Diaspora* 6.2–7.1 (2006): 61–71.

Warrior, Robert Allen. *Tribal Secrets: Recovering American Indian Intellectual
Traditions*. Minneapolis: University of Minnesota Press, 1995.

Weaver, Jace. "Introduction: Notes from a Miner's Canary." *Defending Mother
Earth: Native American Perspectives on Environmental Justice*. Ed. Jace Weaver.
Maryknoll NY: Orbis, 1996.

———. *That the People Might Live: Native American Literatures and Native
American Community*. Oxford: Oxford University Press, 1997.

Wenz, Peter S. "Environmentalism and Human Oppression." Gottlieb 3–21.

Williams, Raymond. *The Country and the City*. London: Hogarth, 1986.

Williams, Sherley Anne. *Dessa Rose*. New York: Harper, 1999.

Wolfe, Cary. *Animal Rites: American Culture, the Discourse of Species, and
Posthuman Theory*. Chicago: University of Chicago Press, 2003.

Womack, Craig S. *Red on Red: Native American Literary Separatism*.
Minneapolis: University of Minnesota Press, 1999.

World Health Organization and the United Nations Environment Programme.
Urban Air Pollution in Megacities of the World. Oxford: Blackwell, 1992.

Wu, C. "Oxidized Plutonium Reaches a Higher State." *Science News* 15 Jan.
2000.

WorldClimate.com. "Santa Ana Fire Stn, Orange County, California USA:
Average Maximum Temperature." Accessed 8 Jan. 2012. http://www.world
climate.com/cgi-bin/data.pl?ref=N33W117+1300+047888C.

Wulfhorst, J. D., and Anne K. Haugestad, eds. *Building Sustainable
Communities: Environmental Justice and Global Citizenship*. Amsterdam:
Rodopi, 2006.

X, Malcolm. *Malcolm X Speaks: Selected Speeches and Statements*. Ed. George
Breitman. New York: Grove, 1990.

Yamashita, Karen Tei. *Tropic of Orange*. Minneapolis: Coffee House, 1997.

Young, Robert J. C. *Colonial Desire: Hybridity in Theory, Culture and Race*. New
York: Routledge, 1995.

Zaki, Hoda M. "Utopia, Dystopia, and Ideology in the Science Fiction of Octavia Butler." *Science Fiction Studies* 17 (1990): 239–51.

Zepeda, Alexis. "The Lieutenant Nun: Construction of Masculinity in Colonial Latin America." *Entrecaminos 2000: New Ideas for a New Millennium: Latin America in the XXI Century.* http://www7.georgetown.edu/sfs/programs/clas/entre2000.html.

INDEX

IN THE POSTWESTERN HORIZONS SERIES

To order or obtain more information on these or other University of Nebraska Press titles, visit www.nebraskapress.unl.edu.